Research Methods

for Studying Legal Issues in Education

Steve Permuth &
Ralph D. Mawdsley

EDUCATION LAW ASSOCIATION
DAYTON, OHIO

Education Law Association®

Disclaimer

The Education Law Association (ELA) is a private, nonadvocacy, nonprofit, international member association. The opinions expressed in this publication are those of the authors and do not represent official views of the Association.

300 College Park - 0528 / Dayton, OH 45469
(937) 229-3589
www.educationlaw.org

Printed in the United States of America
ISBN 1-56534-122-8

About the Author

Co-editors and Authors:

Steve Permuth is Professor of Educational Leadership and Policy Studies at the University of South Florida. His primary interest lies in the area of educational policy and law with emphasis on the nature of the applied research practitioner, who uses information to influence how the parameters of law impact administration, faculty and students in the operation of the schools. He has authored/co-authored five texts, including *Legal Issues of Private and Religious Schools*, *The Law, The Student and Catholic Schools*, and *The Principal, School Law, and Student Discipline* in addition to this text. He has also published some fifty articles on a variety of topics from negligence and copyright to freedom of speech and religious freedom in periodicals including *West's Education Law Reporter*, the *International Journal of Education Reform*, *St. Mary's Law Journal,* National Association of Secondary School Principal (NASSP) publications including the *Bulletin, Principal Leadership* and a number of *Legal Memorandums*. He has also served as Scholar-In-Residence for NASSP. Dr. Permuth also serves as editor of the *International Journal of Education Reform* and on the editorial board of the *Journal of Urban Education*. Steve can be contacted at permuth@tempest.coedu.usf.edu.

Ralph D. Mawdsley is Professor of Educational Administration at Cleveland State University. He holds a J.D. degree from the University of Illinois and a Ph.D. from the University of Minnesota. In 2005 as a Fulbright Scholar he spent 6 months in South Africa at the University of Pretoria as Visiting Fulbright Professor of Law and Education where he researched and published a number of comparative articles on South African and American law. Dr. Mawdsley teaches courses in, and publishes in the areas of, school law, sports law, and special education law and has been awarded Cleveland State University's highest awards for teaching, the Distinguished Faculty Teaching Award and the Dr. Jennie S. Hwang Award for Faculty Excellence. In 2001 he was President of the Education Law Association and in 2004 was awarded the organization's Marion McGhehey Award for Outstanding Service in the Field of Education Law. Dr. Mawdsley is a regular speaker at education law conferences in the United States, South Africa, Australia, and various venues in Europe and is a member of publication boards for a number of the leading education law journals throughout the world.

About the Author *(continued)*

Authors (in alphabetical order):

Louise Adler, Ph.D., Claremont Graduate University. Dr. Adler is chair of the Educational Leadership Department and Coordinator of the Ed.D. at California State University, Fullerton. She teaches classes in education law, ethical and legal dimensions of instructional leadership, human resources, and organizational theory. She has published articles and book chapters related to curriculum challenges, participation of principals in local economic development planning, and school linked social services. Recent research explores the use of classified managers to assist principals at school sites.

Grover H. Baldwin is a former Professor and Chair of Educational Leadership at the University of Toledo. He has taught school law and dealt with issues related to collective bargaining, labor relations, and governance of public schools. Dr. Baldwin taught research methodology at the doctoral level and school finance. He is currently concluding research on equity and access issues pertinent to urban and rural poor school districts in Ohio. Dr. Baldwin holds an Ed.D. and a M.Ed. in Educational Administration and Supervision from Lehigh University, a Bachelor of Arts in History and Economics from Wittenberg University, and was a 1995 Fellow at the Management Development Program at Harvard University. Dr. Baldwin is now retired and living in Kansas. He continues to deal with the vagaries of the constitution of Kansas and Kansas school finance for the constitutionality of projected changes in school funding.

Dennis W. Van Berkum is a professor and program coordinator for educational leadership at Minnesota State University Moorhead. In addition, he serves as a co-chairperson of the Tri-College University educational leadership program. His programs lead efforts to deliver courses and programs to distant areas through interactive and online instruction. He has authored and co-authored more than 40 publications and co-edited *The School Safety Handbook: Taking Action for Student and Staff Protection*. He serves on the technology committee and the publications committee for the Educational Law Association. With his involvement in the IDEA partnership, he has assisted in developing courses and related materials for special education and administrator programs. He serves as a director for one of the National Association of Secondary School Principal's Lead Assessment Center projects and as a trainer for several of the support modules. He serves as a folio reviewer for the Educational Leadership Constituent Council and remains active in the development of the knowledge and skill base for entry level school leaders. He has been a high school principal, K-12 athletic director and coordinator for curriculum development, special education, and vocational education programs. Dr. Van Berkum earned a B.A. Degree from Northwestern College, Orange City, IA, a M.S. degree from South Dakota State University and an Ed.D. from the University of South Dakota.

Kermit G. Buckner is a professor in and former Chair of the Department of Educational Leadership at East Carolina University. He has also served as Director of Professional Development for the National Association of Secondary Schools Principals (NASSP). At NASSP, he participated in the creation of professional development and assessment programs for individuals interested in school leadership. He was a member of the consortium that developed the Interstate School Leaders Licensure Standards, the first national standards for school leadership and served as a reviewer for *Breaking Ranks II*. He has also served as Director of the North Carolina Assessment and Development Center, a principal, an assistant principal, and a teacher. He is a member of the National Council for Accreditation of Teacher Education (NCATE) Board of Examiners and a reviewer for the Educational Leadership Constitute Council (ELCC). As a member of the first NASSP Task Force on Principal Preparation, he served as its chair. His primary teaching responsibilities and research interests are education law and leadership. He has published over twenty books, book chapters, and articles and has made over forty presentations at national conventions. His undergraduate and Master's degrees are from the University of North Carolina at Chapel Hill and his Doctorate is from the University of North Carolina at Greensboro.

John M. Ferron is a Professor of Educational Measurement and Research at the University of South Florida. He teaches methods for analyzing quantitative research data, including ANOVA, regression, factor analysis, structural equation modeling, interrupted time series analysis, and multilevel modeling. His research interests include the development and understanding of methods used to analyze educational data, and methods of teaching educational data analysis. This methodological work has been published in the *Encyclopedia of Statistics in Behavioral Science*, *Journal of Educational and Behavioral Statistics*, *Multivariate Behavioral Research*, *The Journal of Experimental Education*, *Psychometrika*, and *Educational and Psychological Measurement*, among others. He earned his Ph.D. at the University of North Carolina.

Patricia F. First, J.D., Ed.D. is Professor of Educational Leadership at the University of Arizona. Her research and teaching are focused on the legal and policy issues of the educational system, particularly those issues intersecting with ethical leadership, the role of school boards and the financing of education. She is the author of *Educational Policy for School Administrators*, and co-editor, with Herbert Walberg, of *School Boards: Changing Local Control*. She has also written legal monographs, books for practitioners, numerous chapters and articles and was a founding co-editor, with Joan Curcio, of *The Journal for a Just and Caring Education*. Dr. First has served as Dean of the School of Education at the University of Dayton and Chairperson of the faculties of Educational Leadership at the University of Arizona, Western Michigan University and Northern Illinois University. She has also been a teacher and administrator in K-12 education, a policy analyst with both state and federal government and a National Education Policy Fellow. She earned the Ed.D. and M.S. at Illinois State University, the B.S. at the University of Massachusetts, and the J.D. at the University of Dayton School of Law. Dr. First sits on editorial and advisory boards and is the Legislation Editor for the *Journal of Law and Education*. Dr. First may be contacted at: First@u.arizona.edu

David H. Goldenberg is Dean of Hillyer College and Professor of Education Law at the University of Hartford in Connecticut. His work in education law dates back to the 1970's during which time he arbitrated cases in the K-12 system serving as an assistant to the Commissioner of Education in New York State. While there he co-authored *Guidelines for Students Rights and Responsibilities* as well as *Recycling Resources: Models for Shared Learning*. Later, at Bradley University, he co-authored *The Principal, The Law and Student Discipline* for the Illinois Principals Association. He is author of numerous articles and chapters on matters pertaining to higher education. He has been the recipient of numerous national awards and recognition for his work in academic advising and retention of undergraduate students, including the ACT/NACADA award for the Outstanding Institutional Advising in the nation. He has degrees in math, business and education from the University of Hartford where he was selected as Distinguished Alumnus. His doctorate is from Illinois State University where he was also selected for alumni recognition. He has post doctoral studies in labor studies /labor law at Cornell University in the Institute for Labor Relations.

Kristine Y. Hogarty is the Director of Assessment for the College of Education at the University of South Florida. Her experiences include instrument development, research design and data analysis in Education, Criminology, Business and Industry. Her primary research interests are applied statistics and data analysis. Her work has been published in *Behavior Research Methods, Instruments, & Computers*, *Educational and Psychological Measurement, Journal of College Teaching & Learning, Journal of Police and Criminal Psychology, Journal of Research on Computing in Education, Journal of Research in Education, Multiple Linear Regression Viewpoints*, and *Psychometrika.*

Jeffrey D. Kromrey is Professor and Chair in the Department of Educational Measurement and Research at the University of South Florida. His research interests have focused primarily on methodological issues in the analysis of quantitative data. He teaches doctoral courses in statistical analysis, applied research design and General Systems Theory. Dr. Kromrey's previous funded research includes grants from the National Science Foundation, Fund for Improvement of Post-Secondary Education, American Association of Medical Colleges, Educational Testing Services, Department of Defense and the Florida Department of Education. Reports of his research have won four distinguished paper awards at research conferences and he was awarded the Researcher of the Year in 1997 by the Florida Educational Research Association and the President's Award for Faculty Excellence in 2003. He is a former editor of *Review of Educational Research* and currently serves as editor of *Florida Journal of Educational Research* and executive editor of *Journal of Experimental Education*. Reports of his research have been published in *Educational and Psychological Measurement*, *Psychometrika*, *Multivariate Behavioral Research*, *Educational Researcher*, *Communications in Statistics*, *Applied Psychological Measurement* and *Journal of Educational Measurement.*

Kenneth E. Lane, Ed.D. is a Professor of Educational Administration at California State University, San Bernardino, where he teaches legal aspects of education for aspiring K-12 school administrators. He makes extensive use of the Internet in the teaching of this classes and in research on legal issues. Currently, he is the Director of the National Center for Excellence in Distance Learning which works with the US. Navy to develop skill content for its civilian employees for delivery via the Internet and to develop simulations to teach leadership skills in critical thinking and decision making to officers and enlisted personnel. Additionally, Dr. Lane is a member of the Board of Directors for the Education Law Association and Executive Director of the International Academy of Educational Leaders.

Joyce Lee, Ed.D., is an Associate Professor in the Educational Leadership Department in the College of Education at California State University, Fullerton. Dr. Lee has been a teacher and administrator in both K-12 and higher education. She currently teaches graduate courses in educational leadership and qualitative research methods classes at the doctoral level. She is the author of numerous articles in educational journals and co-author of *Collaborative Inquiry in Practice: Action, Reflection, and Making Meaning* which was published by Sage in 2000. She earned her Ed.D. at Teachers College, Columbia University in Adult and Organizational Learning. Dr. Lee may be contacted at: joycelee@fullerton.edu

Anthony J. Onwuegbuzie (Ph.D., University of South Carolina) is associate professor in the Department of Educational Measurement and Research at the University of South Florida. He teaches courses in qualitative research, quantitative research, and mixed methods. His research topics primarily involve disadvantaged and under-served populations such as minorities, children living in war zones, students with special needs, and juvenile delinquents. He also writes extensively on methodological topics. He has secured 154 publications in refereed journals and has made more than 300 presentations and keynote addresses at regional, national, and international conferences. Dr. Onwuegbuzie recently published a book entitled: *Library anxiety: Theory, research, and applications* (Scarecrow Press). He has also received several outstanding paper awards, including the Literati Club Award for Excellence 2003, an International Award. Dr. Onwuegbuzie is co-editor of *Research in the Schools* and is an editorial board member of *Educational and Psychological Measurement, American Educational*

Research Journal, and several other journals. He has reviewed articles for 18 journals. Recently, he received the 2005 Outstanding Reviewer Award for reviewing articles submitted to the *American Educational Research Journal.* He is passionate about mixed methods research, writing several book chapters, encyclopedia chapters, and articles on this topic across several disciplines.

Charles J. Russo, J.D., Ed. D., is the Joseph Panzer Chair in Education in the School of Education and Allied Professions and Adjunct Professor in the School of Law at the University of Dayton. The 1998-99 President of the Education Law Association, and winner of its 2002 McGhehey Award, he has authored or co-authored more than 150 articles in peer-reviewed journals, authored, co-authored, edited, or co-edited twenty books, and has in excess of 500 publications. Dr. Russo also speaks extensively on issues in Education Law in the United States and overseas has also formally served as a Visiting Professor in Australia, Bosnia, Macedonia, and South Africa. In May 2004 he received a Ph.D. Honoris Causa from Potchefstroom University, now the Potchefstroom Campus of Northwest University, in Potchefstroom, South Africa, for his contributions to the field of Education Law.

Jennifer A. Sughrue is an associate professor in the Department of Educational Leadership at Florida Atlantic University. Her research interests center primarily on educational policy-to-practice studies, ethics and educational leadership, and international education. She has contributed chapters to various books on legal issues and the principalship and is a school law reporter for the Education Law Association. She currently sits on the executive board of ELA. Prior to moving to higher education, she was a teacher, counselor, and administrator in American K-12 schools in Africa and South America.

Acknowledgements

We would like to express our deep appreciation to those who have reviewed the transcript and provided exceptional support to the completion of the work; David Schimmel, Melissa Grubbs (who served as an Associate Editor), Sandy Walker, Rebecca Wilkins, Jennifer Vincent and Marie Hill. Each and every one of the chapter authors/co-authors deserves credit for their timely and appropriate accommodations to timelines and competence in their work. Also, this work could not have been accomplished without the support of the Education Law Association, in particular Mandy Schrank, Executive Director, and Jody Thornburg, Publications Editor.

We would also like to recognize the support of our "family" networks (Steve–Jacki, Rachel, Jennifer, Matthew; Ralph–Alice, Jonathan and James) whose understanding of our efforts and time commitment is deeply appreciated.

Dedication

To Joey, Nate, and others to follow. For Aunt Mary for her support.

Note on Reference Formats

This monograph uses two different citation systems: American Psychological Association (APA) style and A Uniform System of Citation. APA is frequently used in academic journals that deal with education. A Uniform System is usually used in writing about legal issues. Various disciplines have developed citation or style guidelines that most appropriately meet the needs of the specific discipline. Because education as a field of study draws from a number of disciplines, readers are likely to come across a variety of citation systems. However, when writing a thesis, students should use a style selected by their department or school.

Contents

1 School Law and Research in the 21st Century

Steve Permuth & Ralph D. Mawdsley

As the complexities of law dramatically increase in an age of explosive technology and new perspectives as to how and what research must/should be used in adding substance to studying the law, we are continually faced with an uncomfortable general shortcoming and reality in the study and context of legal research. That shortcoming is that legal research appears, at times, to limit the breadth and depth of inquiry (Schimmel, 1996).

As Schimmel notes,

> Most research in education uses only one method. Often it consists of comprehensive but relatively simple summaries of case law on a subject…, or surveys of attitudes and knowledge of teachers or administrators about a Supreme Court decision or a federal statute affecting education. Rarely do researchers combine several methods that would enable them to approach topics from multiple perspectives and with added depth and texture (p.1).

The purpose of this text is to provide a contemporary, albeit limited, view of research and law in a context of rich mutual meaning. The editors seek to explore and share a sense that the critical value of quality research, through a number of possibly interrelated paradigms and processes, produce for those of us interested in educational law, a new sense of the accumulation and interpretation of information to make our research more informed and of a higher standard. Further, whether one is a law student or a student studying to be a school principal or superintendent, a critical element of understanding law is the underpinning of the research used by attorneys, courts, and governments in making legal decisions that impact us. As such, this text is directed at law school students and professors, students studying education at the Master's level or beyond in programs such as educational leadership, as well as practicing attorneys, school administrators, etc.

This text can be viewed as both an update and expansion of the earlier 1996 publication from NOLPE, *Research That Makes a Difference: Complementary Methods for Examining Legal Issues in Education* (Schimmel, 1996). While chapters of the text can be reviewed as an entity, a far-more effective method is to view the monograph as one statement. The text includes an update on four chapters from the original text, described appropriately as "complementary methods of research" and three new chapters.

Chapter 2 starts with an initial summary of "traditional research" that addresses the context of law and points to the legal sources (e.g., primary–the cases and statutes themselves, secondary–juried and non-juried articles), which tend to serve as a basis for legal research.

Chapter 3 provides an exploration of the critical area of qualitative research, which is a rich and vibrant exploration of how to deal with "ambiguity, collect data, find patterns and connections, and write the story presented by your data."

Chapter 4 addresses a number of the key issues affecting law and qualitative research; these areas of research use data, move to statistical conclusion of deduction or inference, and direct research through a relationship among variables.

Chapter 5 is a new chapter addressing the essential directive that research in issues of legal education can be qualitative and/or quantitative and that there is no innate dichotomy between the two terms. Rather, as the title suggests, qualitative and quantitative research should be viewed as part of a continuum, not as separate strategies in order to produce the most accurate and clear information.

Chapter 6 is an updated text to be viewed as integrative within the context of the "continua" of research articulated as policy research. Policy research "has a broad scope and uses multiple methods to analyze options and provides comprehensive information to decision makers to help them make or improve legal and educational policies."

Chapter 7 addresses the critical area of technology and the support, as a matter of substance and process, that it provides to increase the accuracy, viability, and vitality of the research underpinning legal decisions and protocol.

Chapter 8 addresses an integral essential of research authorship in the description of the issues of language and legal writing in dealing with issues of school law in support of the assumption that, even with data, one has to be able to portray the data through contemporary writing and language skills appropriate not only to the author, but also the receiver of the message.

The authors and editors hope that this monograph serves as a fundamental base in the understanding of the mutually supportive roles which research and law have in common. If done well, with the clear understanding of the expanse of research opportunities, the quality of legal papers and work leads to an even better understanding of the empirical basis for sound legal judgments.

2 Legal Research: The "Traditional" Method

Charles J. Russo

Introduction

King George III of England is reputed to have said that a lawyer is not someone who knows the law but is someone who knows where to find the law.[1] By analogy, this approach applies to anyone interested in the law, regardless of an individual's specialty. More specifically, as educators, students, and attorneys throughout the world recognize the complex nature of the problems in which we share a common interest, the need to combine research methods and strategies should become increasingly apparent.[2]

The use of complementary methods can help bring research questions into clearer focus and can also offer solutions that might not have been considered had a single method been employed. As Gestalt psychology suggests, by applying a variety of complementary techniques, the sum of a researcher's efforts can exceed the whole of its parts. Moreover, each of the different methods of inquiry is particularly well suited to the nature of the questions it seeks to answer.

This chapter turns to the underlying source of our common interest, the law, and presents a brief overview of what might be described as traditional legal research. As noted in the other chapters, there are two topics running throughout this monograph. The first issue concerns search and seizure and the issue considered by legal research: whether school officials may conduct searches of students consistent with the Fourth Amendment, as enunciated by the Supreme Court in *New Jersey v. T.L.O.*,[3] or, more recently, in *Board of Education of Independent School District No. 92 of Pottawatomie v. Earls (Earls)*.[4] The second topic concerns religion and education, and the research addresses when, if ever, there can be prayers at public school graduation ceremonies in light of rulings such as *Lee v. Weisman* (*Lee*).[5]

Clearly, a knowledge gap exists between those who work with the law on a regular basis and those who do not. Faced with the realization of the massive amounts of material that would soon be at their finger tips, educators, unlike attorneys, are unnecessarily apprehensive and overwhelmed. This chapter seeks to allay concerns by pointing out that the legal method and other forms of research serve essentially the same purpose: they are interested in arriving at a better understanding of the question in hand. The difference is, of course, that in legal research the primary source of information is the law itself, even if the initial research begins with secondary sources such as articles and commentaries on the law.

The Nature of Legal Research

Systematic inquiry in the law can be described as a form of historical-legal research that is neither qualitative nor quantitative. In other words, it is a systematic investigation involving the interpretation and explanation of the law. Moreover, a legal dispute can begin with a single issue that has far-reaching implications. Perhaps the best example of how a legal controversy with massive social overtones can affect American life is the Supreme Court's 1954 decision in *Brown v. Board of Education (Brown)*,[6] striking down segregation in American public schools.

Aimed at dismantling *de jure* segregation in public education, it can be argued that *Brown* was not resolved on the basis of the law alone, for the Court relied on research data from the social sciences in addressing the plight of the African-American children who had been subject to segregation. Consequently, *Brown* served as the impetus for many systemic social changes in American society in a way that the parties may not have been able to anticipate. Justice Kennedy's discussion of peer pressure as it relates to school prayer in the majority opinion in *Lee* provides another example of how the Court has progressed in applying non-legal analyses in attempting to resolve the difficult issues it confronts on a regular basis. While *Brown* and *Lee* represent the exceptional cases in which the Court explicitly relied on the social sciences, these two rulings exemplify how these two distinct disciplines can interact.

As it attempts to make sense of the evolving reality known as the law, legal research employs a timeline that looks to the past, present, and future for a variety of purposes. By placing a legal dispute in perspective, researchers in education law hope not only to inform policymakers and practitioners about the meaning and status of the law, but also seek to raise questions for future research. Attorneys, on the other hand, typically engage in legal research as a means of arriving at a deeper understanding of the issue(s) confronting them so as to better represent the interests of their clients.

Rooted in the historical nature of the law and its reliance on precedent, legal research requires students to look to the past to locate authority that will govern the disposition of the question under investigation, whether school prayer, search and seizure, or another topic. This is due to the Anglo-American legal system being grounded in the principle of precedent or *stare decisis* (to abide by), the notion that an authoritative ruling of the highest court in a given jurisdiction is binding on lower courts within its purview. Moreover, the law by its very nature tends to be a reactive, rather than proactive, force that is shaped by past events that can help lead to stability in its application.

In light of the more-or-less reactive nature of law, when attorneys challenge adverse rulings or as researchers study emerging questions, they each look to see how past authoritative decisions have dealt with the same issue. If there is a case supportive of their respective points of view, then they can argue that it should be followed. However, if precedent is contrary to their position, then they will seek to distinguish their case by attempting to show that it is sufficiently different and inapplicable to the facts at hand. For example, an attorney arguing in favor of prayer at graduation on behalf of a university might maintain that insofar as an institution of higher education is different from a secondary school, *Lee* is inapplicable.[7]

Sources of Law

In examining a legal issue, three broad categories of information need to be considered: primary sources, secondary sources, and research (or finding) tools. Access to each of these can be obtained either manually, by locating the book that contains the desired information, or through subscriptions to electronic databases, namely Westlaw, Lexis, or on free websites.[8] In fact, in teaching courses on education law, professors are finding that heavy reliance is placed on electronic searches. Computer databases seem to be replacing the need for untold numbers of volumes of reporters, digests, and the like that are discussed later in this chapter. However, as the availability of electronic access may be limited, this chapter focuses on manual searches and operates on the assumption that once an individual is aware of how to conduct legal research, it matters little whether it is carried out manually or electronically. At the same time, if one has the opportunity to conduct electronic searches, these searches involve learning a number of new skills, especially with regard to framing search terms or questions. Needless to say, all searches, regardless of how they are completed, may be limited by resources available in a given library.

The source of law that one begins with is, in large part, a matter of preference, depending on how familiar one is with legal sources and research. Put another way, an experienced researcher should be able to go right to a primary source, such as a Supreme Court opinion. On the other hand, a novice who is unacquainted with the intricacies of legal research might be wise to start with a secondary source, such as an article in West's *Education Law Reporter*, a law review, or an entry in a legal encyclopedia since these should provide information that can help the researcher to develop a full understanding of the issue(s). Since these articles are likely to be well footnoted to the law and other secondary sources, they can lead to the cross-referencing of additional sources of information, not unlike the triangulation of data in qualitative analyses.

A. Primary Sources

As with inquiry in the social sciences, legal researchers rely heavily on primary sources, whether federal or state law. Included here are constitutions, statutes (and their legislative histories), regulations (along with administrative decisions and rulings that interpret them), and case law.

The United States Constitution is the law of the land. As the primary source of American law, the Constitution provides the framework within which the entire legal system operates. To this end, all actions taken by the federal and state governments, including state constitutions, which are supreme within their states as long as they do not contradict or limit rights protected under their federal counterpart, statutes, regulations, and common law, are subject to the Constitution as interpreted by the Supreme Court.

As important as education is, it is not mentioned in the Constitution. Under the Tenth Amendment, according to which "[t]he powers not delegated to the United States by the Constitution, nor prohibited by it to the States, are reserved to the States respectively, or to the people," education is primarily the concern of individual states. The federal government can intervene in disputes, such as *Brown*, when state action deprives individuals of rights protected under the Constitution. In *Brown*, the Supreme Court struck down state-sanctioned racial segregation because it violated the students' rights to equal protection under the Fourteenth Amendment.

Along with delineating the rights and responsibilities of Americans, the Constitution establishes the three co-equal branches of government that exist on both the federal and state level. The legislative, executive, and judicial branches of government, in turn, give rise to the three other sources of law.

The legislative branch makes the law. In other words, once a bill completes the legislative process, it is signed into law by a Chief Executive who has the authority to enforce the new statute. Federal statutes are located in the United States Code (U.S.C.) or the United States Code Annotated (U.S.C.A.), a version that is particularly useful for attorneys and other individuals working with the law. State laws are identified by a variety of titles.

Keeping in mind that a statute provides broad directives, the executive branch fleshes a law out by providing details in the form of regulations. For example, a typical compulsory attendance law requires that "[e]xcept as provided in this section, the parent of a child of compulsory school age shall cause such child to attend a school in the school district in which the child is entitled to attend school."[9] Insofar as statutes are typically silent on such matters as the content of the curriculum and the length of the school day, these elements are addressed by regulations that are developed by personnel at administrative agencies who are well versed in their areas of expertise. Given their extensiveness, it is safe to say that the professional lives of educators, especially in public schools, are more directly influenced by regulations than by statutes. Federal statutes are located in the Code of Federal Regulations (C.F.R.). State regulations are identified by a variety of titles.

From time to time the United States Department of Education issues policy letters, typically in response to inquiries from state or local educational officials, to either clarify a regulation or interpret what is required by federal law. These letters are generally published in the *Federal Register* and are often reproduced by loose-leaf, law-reporting services.

The fourth and final source of law is judge-made or common law. Common law refers to judicial interpretations of issues that may have been overlooked in the legislative or regulatory process or that may not have been anticipated when a statute was enacted. In the landmark case of *Marbury v. Madison*,[10] the Supreme Court asserted its authority to review the actions of other branches of government and, in so doing, established precedent. Although there is occasional tension between the three branches of government, the legislative and executive branches generally defer to judicial interpretations of their actions.

Common law is rooted in the concept of precedent, the proposition that a majority ruling of the highest court in a given jurisdiction, or geographic area over which a court has authority, is binding on all lower courts within its jurisdiction. In other words, a ruling of the United States Supreme Court is binding throughout the nation while a decision of a state supreme court is binding only in that state. Persuasive precedent, a ruling from another jurisdiction, is actually not precedent at all. That is, as a judge in Indiana seeks to resolve a novel legal issue, the judge would typically review precedent from other jurisdictions to determine whether it has been addressed elsewhere. A court is not bound to follow precedent from another jurisdiction.

The federal courts and most state judicial systems have three levels: a trial court, an intermediate appellate court, and a court of last resort. In federal court, trial courts are known as federal district courts; state trial courts employ a variety of names. Each state has at least one federal district court, and some densely populated states, such as California and New York, have as many as four.

Trial courts typically involve one judge and a jury. The role of the judge, as trier of law, is to apply the law by deciding, for example, whether evidence is admissible and to instruct the jury on how the law should be applied in a case. Federal judges are appointed for life, based on the advice and consent of the United States Senate; state courts vary, as some judges are appointed while others are elected.[11] A jury is the trier of fact to the extent that it decides what happened and enters a verdict based on the evidence presented at trial. As the trier of fact in a special education suit, the jury (or a judge in a non-jury trial) reviews the record of administrative or due process hearings as well as additional evidence and hears the testimony of witnesses.

Other than areas such as special education, which is governed largely by the IDEA, few education cases fall under the jurisdiction, or the legal authority, of the federal courts. Before a dispute can proceed to federal court, it must satisfy one of two broad categories. First, a case must involve diversity of citizenship, namely that the plaintiff and defendant are from two different jurisdictions, and the amount in controversy must be at least $75,000; this latter requirement is imposed because of the costs associated with operating the federal court system.[12] Second, a dispute must involve a federal question, meaning that it is over the interpretation of the United States Constitution, a federal statute, or a federal regulation.

A party[13] not satisfied with the decision of a trial court ordinarily has the right to appeal in order to seek discretionary review from an intermediate appellate court. There are thirteen federal judicial circuits in the United States. Under this arrangement, which is designed, in part, for administrative ease and convenience, each circuit is comprised of several states. For example, the Sixth Circuit consists of Michigan, Ohio, Kentucky, and Tennessee. State courts with a three-tiered system most often refer to this intermediate appellate level as a court of appeals. An intermediate appellate court typically consists of three judges and ordinarily reviews a case for errors in the record of a trial court rather than the facts.

A party not satisfied with the ruling of an intermediate appellate court may seek review from the high court in the jurisdiction. In order for a case to reach the Supreme Court, a party must file a petition seeking a writ of *certiorari* (to be informed). In order to be granted a writ of *certiorari*, at least four of the Court's nine Justices must agree to hear an appeal. Insofar as the Court receives approximately five thousand petitions per year, and takes, on average, perhaps one hundred cases, it should be clear that few cases will make their way to the Supreme Court. The denial of a writ of *certiorari* is of no precedential value and merely has the effect of leaving the lower court's decision unchanged. It is generally easier for a discretionary appeal in a state court to reach the court of last resort, typically composed of five, seven, or nine members, especially where a state law is at issue.

Legal citations are easy to read. The first number indicates the volume number where the case, statute, or regulation is located; the abbreviation refers to the book or series in which the material may be found; the second number indicates the page on which a case begins or the section number of a statute or regulation; the last part of a citation includes the name of the court, for lower court cases, and the year in which the dispute was resolved. For example, the citation for *Board of Education of the Hendrick Hudson Central School District v. Rowley*, 458 U.S. 176 (1982), the first Supreme Court case involving special education, reveals that it can be found on page 176 of volume 458 of the United States Reports. The earlier case between the parties, *Rowley v. Board of Education of the Hendrick Hudson Central School District*, 632 F.2d 945 (2d Cir.1980), which was decided by the Second Circuit in 1980, begins on page 945 of volume 632 in the Federal Reporter, second series. Similarly, the IDEA, 20 U.S.C. §§ 1400 *et seq.*, can be found starting in section 1400 of title 20 of the United States Code.

1. Constitutions

Constitutions, the most basic form of law, create the necessary governmental framework in a jurisdiction; they outline the rights and obligations of both the government and its citizens. Federal and state constitutions are published both separately and in a jurisdiction's statutory compilations.

2. Statutes

Just as judicial opinions can be found in a variety of sources, so also can statutes. Similar to the process involving cases, a new or revised statute first appears as an individual copy shortly after it is signed into law. A statute next appears as a session law, a chronological ordering of laws enacted by a given session of the legislature. A well-known illustration of this is the Individuals with Disabilities Education Act (IDEA),[14] formerly the Education for All Handicapped Children's Act, which is still often referred to as Public Law 94-142, indicating that it was the 142nd piece of legislation enacted by the 94th Congress in 1975. Finally, a statute is published in the official version of the jurisdiction's code.

The official version of federal statutes is found in the United States Code (U.S.C.). However, West's United States Code Annotated (U.S.C.A.), which includes brief summaries, or annotations, of cases that have applied or construed a statute, is more useful to researchers and practicing attorneys who are attempting to construe the meaning of a statute. State statutes appear under a variety of titles that typically include the name of the state in the title such as McKinney's Consolidated [Education] Laws of New York Annotated. The statutes are updated annually by means of a pocket part, a pamphlet that is placed in the rear of the main volume. The frequency with which a new hardbound main volume is issued depends on how many changes occur in a jurisdiction.

Along with seeking an understanding of a statute based on its judicial construction, an important tool is legislative history. A history traces the development of a statute through legislative hearings and can be useful to clarify its meaning because reviewing what a bill's author or others may have had to say about it can provide guidance as a court interprets a statute. Moreover, as with the IDEA, it is not uncommon for author(s) of a bill to include detailed findings and statements of purpose as a kind of preface that can further help to clarify the meaning of a statue.

Federal legislative histories are ordinarily found in the Congressional Record, which provides a nearly verbatim report of daily legislative and other proceedings in Congress. However, the Congressional Record does not include hearings and rarely contains committee reports unless they are read into the record. Another useful source is the United States Code Congressional and Administrative News, which publishes selected committee reports. In addition, copies of various hearings and reports can be obtained directly from the committee or subcommittee that conducted the proceeding or from libraries that serve as depositories of federal documents. State legislative histories vary from one location to another; for assistance in obtaining access to these records, it is best to seek the assistance of a librarian.

3. Regulations

Regulations, which flesh out the meaning of statutes, are developed by state and federal agencies having responsibility for enforcing the law. Consequently, in order to fully understand a statute such as the IDEA, it is important to consult the IDEA Part B Regulations since they provide additional detail concerning the implementation of the law. The Federal Register is a daily publication that publishes these regulations and also contains presidential proclamations, executive orders, and other documents by government agencies.[15] The Code of Federal Regulations is a permanent compilation of regulations, but depending upon when a revision was made may not be as up-to-date as the Federal Register. As with state statutes, locating state regulatory material is probably most accessible with the aid of a librarian.

4. Case Law

Insofar as a major focus of legal research and the Anglo-American legal system is case law, as found in precedent setting judicial opinions, this is a logical starting point in the examination of primary sources. Such an approach does not ignore the place of constitutions, statutes, and regulations. Rather, it is based on the recognition that as important as these other primary sources of law are, their meaning may not be clear until they are interpreted by judges or applied in particular circumstances. Also, to the extent that precedent occupies such a central role in the American legal system, it should be noted that most opinions sought by legal researchers are from appellate courts because these ordinarily have precedential effect beyond the two litigants. In other words, trial court rulings are limited to determinations based on fact between the two parties such as whether a school official actually searched a student's locker. On the other hand, appellate cases concern the interpretation and application of legal precedents such as whether a particular search was constitutionally permissible under the Fourth Amendment based on precedent set by *T.L.O.* or, perhaps, *Acton* or *Earls*.

a. Slip Opinions and Advance Sheets

On the day that a court renders judgment, it issues its ruling in the form of a slip opinion, typically available from the clerk of the court. A slip opinion is a bare-bones presentation of a court's decision, not containing a syllabus or any research aids commonly found in the reporter systems. Within a few weeks, the opinion is usually published in the softbound advance sheets of the appropriate federal or state reporter.

The benefit of advance sheets is that they include a variety of research aids and cross-references such as headnotes, which are explained later, to assist researchers. Once the bound volume of opinions appears, usually several months (or even years, as with the United State Reports) later, the advance sheets can be discarded since their page numbering is identical to that in the hardbound volume. Further, for purpose of citation, once a case is available in its official source, it is no longer necessary to include references to the other sources.

b. Published Opinions

Federal trial court opinions are found in the Federal Supplement (F. Supp.) Series.[16] Federal Circuit court rulings are published in the Federal Reporter (F.) Series;[17] Circuit Court rulings that are not accepted for publication in the Federal Reporter appear in the Federal Appendix (Fed.Appx.).[18] Even so, most of the opinions of federal courts are not published. Opinions of the United States Supreme Court are found in a variety of sources, both electronic and printed[19] United State Reports (U.S.).[20] Shortly after being handed down as a slip opinion, rulings of the Supreme Court appear in weekly looseleaf publications, United States Law Week (U.S.L.W.), published by the Bureau of National Affairs, and Supreme Court Bulletin, by Publishers Clearing House. A few weeks later, the opinions can be found in West's Supreme Court Reporter (S. Ct.), and the Lawyer's Edition (L. Ed.), produced by Lawyers Cooperative Publishing Company. At a later date, the text of these opinions can be located in their official source, the United State Reports (U.S.).

The published opinions of state court can also be found in several places, starting as slip opinions. Unlike their federal counterparts, most state trial court opinions are not published. Perhaps the most readily available location of state appellate court rulings is in West's National Reporter System. The National Reporter System divides the United States into seven somewhat arbitrarily defined regions: Atlantic, North Eastern, North Western, Pacific, South Eastern, Southern, and South Western. Moreover, in light of the volume of litigation they generate, West publishes separate reporters for more than thirty states besides California and New York. Although West is the official source of many state court opinions, a number of jurisdictions such as New Jersey and New York publish their own rulings. The distinct advantage to West's National Reporter System, along with all of its other publications, is that it provides a researcher with ready access into its key numbering system and its headnotes described below.

West also prepares topical reporters, such as the Education Law Reporter, which cull federal and state opinions on a specific subject, thereby making the lives of researchers a bit easier by placing most cases on a topic in one location. Along with the opinions of published cases, the Education Law Reporter includes peer-reviewed articles and book reviews on a variety of topics in school law.

Typically, a judicial opinion published in a reporter begins with a syllabus, which includes a brief summary of the facts of the case, a statement of the issue(s), and an outline of the court's rationale including references to precedent upon which the court relied in reaching its decision.

c. Citations

Faced with a legal citation such as *Lemon v. Kurtzman*, 403 U.S. 602, 91 S. Ct. 2105, 29 L. Ed. 2d 745 (1971), an important ruling on the Establishment Clause, the first task of a novice legal researcher is to make sense of this cryptic collection of numbers and abbreviations. Fortunately, there is a method to the madness of legal research.

The first set of numbers in a citation, those preceding the abbreviations, 403, 91, or 29, refers to the volume number in a series of reporters. The abbreviations, U.S., S. Ct., and L. Ed. 2d, identify the United States Reports, Supreme Court Reporter, and Lawyer's Edition, second series. The second set of number indicates the page on which the opinion begins. The date, set off in parentheses, also typically includes the name of the federal or state court that handed down the ruling.

B. Secondary Sources

Secondary sources are writings about the law rather than the law itself. These writings can be broken into two large categories. On the one hand, there are materials that summarize the law on a subject such as Rotunda and Nowak's five-volume *Treatise on Constitutional Law* that provides a summary of the law and its development. On the other hand, scholarly articles in law review often offer critiques of the law and advanced arguments about what the authors believe that the law should be.

These writings, although of no authoritative value in themselves, are sometimes used by the courts in reaching their decisions. In *Brown*, for example, the Supreme Court relied on psychological data to order an end to *de jure* segregation in public schools; also, as in *Board of Education of the Westside Community Schools v. Mergens*[21] and *Lee*, discussed earlier, it is not uncommon for a court to refer to articles in scholarly journals. Thus, secondary sources can, and do, provide the impetus for arguments to change the law.

Among the most commonly relied-upon secondary sources are articles in periodicals, encyclopedias and dictionaries, "restatements," and books and treatises. Secondary sources are particularly valuable to individuals who are neither familiar with nor comfortable with a search through the law itself since an informative article can present an overview of a topic and can open the door to the discovery of the appropriate primary sources.

1. Periodicals

Probably the most useful peer-reviewed journal for educators is West's *Education Law Reporter* (*ELR*). Articles in the *ELR* offer accurate, concise, and up-to-date analyses of current and emerging legal topics for academicians and practitioners. The *ELR* also occasionally includes book reviews. Articles in the *ELR*, although ordinarily not as voluminously footnoted as law reviews, are more user-friendly and appeal to a wider audience than many other scholarly legal publications. Two additional journals are the *School Law Bulletin*, published by the University of North Carolina at Chapel Hill's Institute of Government, and the *Illinois School Law Quarterly*, put out by Illinois State University. Although these journals usually focus on in-state issues, they frequently include articles with a national perspective.

Law reviews, on the other hand, edited by law students, tend to provide more comprehensive and extensively referenced analyses aimed primarily at academicians.[22] Yet, with the exceptions of the *BYU Journal of Law and Education*, published by the J. Reuben Clark Law School in conjunction with the Department of Educational Leadership, and the *Journal of Law and Education*, edited at the South Carolina Law Center and the University of Louisville School of Law, education-related topics generally are not a primary focus of law-review articles. In addition, the *Journal of College and University Law*, published by the National Association of College and University Attorneys, focuses on legal developments in higher education. Thus, even though articles in law reviews tend to focus on specific issues, they can serve as an excellent starting point by providing a researcher with a wealth of sources to assist in a search. Further, international education law journals, such as the *Australia & New Zealand Journal of Law and Education*, *Education and Law Journal* (Canada), *Education and the Law* (UK) and *Education Law Journal* (UK), and *European Journal for Education Law and Policy,* are having an impact on the field.

Last, but certainly not least, two ELA publications, the *ELA Notes* and the *School Law Reporter* can be useful. *ELA Notes* often contains short articles dealing with timely legal issues, and the *School Law Reporter* includes a lead essay before presenting a comprehensive digest of current legal opinions from around the country.

In addition to these periodicals, newsletter services, such as *Your School and the Law,* provide up-to-date useful information. Finally, professional publications including the *American Bar Association Journal*, and newspapers, such as the *New York Law Journal* and *National Law Journal*, although rarely referenced, can help in getting a search started.

2. Encyclopedias and Dictionaries

The two main encyclopedias are *Corpus Juris Secundum*, often referred to as *CJS*, published by West, and *American Jurisprudence*, often identified as *AmJur* by Lawyers Cooperative. As with encyclopedias in other disciplines, these works can provide a quick, general overview of a topic. While these encyclopedias do produce annual updates, or pocket parts, that highlight major changes in the law, they may not provide sufficient detail to allow a researcher to fully grasp a specific education-related topic.

3. Restatements of the Law

A useful and important commentary on the law, the American Law Institute's ten *Restatements of the Law*,[23] published by West, provide in-depth analysis. Although Education Law is not one of the topics covered, developments in the law of torts or contracts can have a profound impact upon the field and can provide assistance in researching background materials. Each restatement opens with a general comment on the law, is followed by an exhaustive examination of trends and developments in a particular subject area, and contains examples of specific cases and variations of the general rule. In light of the comprehensiveness of their coverage, restatements are perhaps the most persuasive secondary materials relied upon by the courts.

4. Books and Treatises

As in any field, a wide array of books and treatises can provide assistance to researchers. Contemporary[24] hornbooks contain such standard titles such as *Contracts* by Calamari and Perillo.[25] Additionally, West's *Nutshell Series* and various monographs, can provide a condensed overview of a given topic. Textbooks, designed for both undergraduate and graduate courses in school law along with casebooks designed more with the traditional law school approach in mind, can also provide assistance. Moreover, given the pace of change, ELA's *Yearbook of Educational Law*[26] provides a comprehensive review of developments. Finally, practitioner handbooks and commentaries prepared by the American Bar Association, the Practicing Law Institute, and their state affiliates, along with procedural manuals, can help to research a topic.

C. Finding Tools

As the legal database of some 3,000,000 cases adds at least 50,000 new decisions each year, a premium is placed on how to obtain the most up-to-date information. To this end, a variety of finding tools have been developed to allow ready access to the different sources of law. How or where a researcher begins investigating a topic is undoubtedly related to that person's familiarity with the law and with legal research. In other words, an experienced researcher who is acquainted with either the topic at hand or to the process of conducting a search might start with a case and work through the head notes, discussed below, at the start of the opinion or might rely on cases and secondary materials referred to by the court. On the other hand, a researcher who is less familiar with the law might start with a secondary source such as an article or an encyclopedia. In this way, the researcher can get an analysis of the topic along with a collection of cases and secondary materials to assist in further investigation of the subject matter.

Insofar as access to electronic databases such as Westlaw or Lexis may be limited, and costly, this discussion focuses on manual searches. However, a growing number of free electronic websites provide wide access to legislative, administrative, and judicial materials.[27] To the extent that cases, statutes, constitutions, and regulations may be uncovered by means of such secondary sources as articles, encyclopedias, and treatises, these methods are not discussed individually.

The most common means of accessing judicial opinions are by using case digests, annotated reports, and descriptive word searches. Cases may also be uncovered by combing through citators, such as Shepard's, which allow a researcher to verify the status of a ruling (or statute) as well as to find other opinions that have cited the main cause.

1. Digests

A digest is a comprehensive compilation, or index, to the law around major points in a judicial opinion, briefly summarized as paragraph length head notes or "squibs," thereby granting a researcher relatively easy access to a particular question. By far, the most comprehensive digest system is the key number digest developed by the West Publishing Company. Under this system, West has developed seven major headings[28] that digest the law into more than 400 numbered and keyed topics, including such education-related topics as schools, colleges and universities, civil rights, and labor relations, each of which is further organized and subdivided into manageable units. For example, if one wanted to find cases on search and seizure in schools, one would look under the major topic of schools, then to the major subheading of students, before turning to key 169.5, "Searches and Seizures." Moreover, to the extent that West has a uniform key system for all of its federal[29] and state[30] reporters, when searching through a digest, one can begin with a table (or alphabetical list) of cases that can be found as a separate volume at the end of a descriptive-word index, discussed below, providing examples of key concepts that can assist an individual in thoroughly researching a topic.

The head note, or keynote system, consists of a series of short, succinct summaries of the specific points of law in an opinion. These head notes are numbered sequentially in bold-faced print at the start of an opinion so that by turning to the appropriate identified key, in the ruling, a researcher can find the court's detailed discussion of that given point of law.

Turning, for example, to the question of prayer at public school graduations, a researcher could begin an inquiry by turning immediately to *Lee v. Weisman*. The head notes in the Supreme Court Reporter are Constitutional Law, key 84 (1), concerning religious liberty, in general, and 84.5 (3), concerning religious liberty in the public schools. Key number 84.4 (3) is also cross-referenced to schools key 165, "Religious instruction and reading of scriptures" and key 178, "Graduation and diploma or certificate." The genius of this system is that insofar as all of the opinions reported in West use key numbering or head notes, by looking in an appropriate case, one can find key points of law in all cases on a particular topic, from a variety of jurisdictions, within the period of time covered by a given digest.

2. Descriptive-Word Searches

Words and Phrases, also known as descriptive-word searches, is an encyclopedia set of forty-six volumes published by West containing alphabetical lists of words and phrases accompanied by summaries of opinions that have interpreted, defined, or construed them. The use of this system should be especially helpful to those new to legal research as the editors of these volumes cull key words describing pertinent facts about a case in order to assist in its being located.

3. Topic Method

A topical approach to finding cases can also be of great value to novice legal researchers. Perhaps the most useful tool here is the Index to Legal Periodicals, the Current Law Index, listings similar to the Education Index or the Guide to Periodical Literature. The Index to Legal Periodicals lists articles from law reviews by topic and author, so that an individual may search from a variety of perspectives. Thus, for example, an educational researcher interested in prayer at public school graduations would look for entries under "Education," "Religion," or "Schools and school districts" to name a few. Moreover, in addition to these more standard sources, a researcher might wish to search the database assembled and indexed by the now-dormant Educational Resources Information Center (ERIC) since it often cross-references with many legal and educational publications.

To summarize, if one has a relevant case in the West system, one can begin with head notes and the keynotes system to find other similar cases in a digest. If, on the other hand, one does not have a case, then the appropriate place to begin would be a journal or encyclopedia article for an overview of the topic.

Conclusion

This brief presentation, offering an overview of legal research, is not intended to be exhaustive. Rather, it is illustrative of how the "traditional" method is but one tool in the hands of educational researchers who seek a greater understanding of how the law is related to other disciplines, but most notably to education.

The traditional method, of course, seeks to predict how a court will rule based on precedent. What it does not, and cannot do, is go beyond the law to consider the attitudes, values, and beliefs of those affected by legal decisions. In light of the inherent limitations presented by the traditional legal perspective, researchers may wish to look to the other modes of inquiry to complement their findings. By using more than one approach, individuals who conduct systematic inquiry in the law can deepen their insight into their unique subject of study and can help others in their understanding of the relationship between law and education.

Then, as those who share a common interest in the law begin to appreciate how the various methods of systematic inquiry can be combined, perhaps the whole of researchers' labors will be greater than the sum of their parts.

Endnotes

1. Forward to the law. MILES O. PRICE & HARRY BITNER, EFFECTIVE LEGAL RESEARCH, (3d ed. 1969), page unnumbered.
2. *See, e.g.*, Charles J. Russo & Douglas J. Stewart, D. *The Place of Education Law in the International Community*. 2 EDUC. L.J. 18-25 (2001).
3. 469 U.S. 325, 105 S. Ct. 733, 83 L .Ed. 2d 720 [21 EDUC. L. REP. 1122] (1985).
4. 536 U.S. 822, 122 S. Ct. 2559, 153 L. Ed. 2d 735 [166 EDUC. L. REP. 79] (2002), *on remand*, 300 F.3d 1222 [168 EDUC. L. REP. 581] (10th Cir. 2002). [Case No. 112]. In *Earls*, the Court applied the same three-part test that it enunciated earlier when it upheld drug testing in *Vernonia Sch. Dist. 47J v. Acton* (*Acton*), 515 U.S. 646, 115 S. Ct. 2386, 132 L. Ed. 2d 564 [101 EDUC. L. REP. 37] (1995).
5. 505 U.S. 577, 112 S. Ct. 2649, 120 L. Ed. 2d 467 [75 EDUC. L. REP. 43] (1992).
6. 347 U.S. 483, 74 S. Ct. 686, 98 L. Ed. 873 (1954).
7. For cases upholding prayer at public universities, see *Tanford v. Brand*, 883 F. Supp. 1231 [100 EDUC. L. REP. 116] (S.D. Ind. 1995), 932 F. Supp. 1139 [111 EDUC. L. REP. 1203] (S.D. Ind. 1996), 104 F.3d 982 [115 EDUC. L. REP. 339] (7th Cir. 1997), *cert. denied*, 522 U.S. 814, 118 S. Ct. 60, 139 L. Ed. 2d 23 (1997); Chaudhuri v. State of Tenn., 886 F. Supp. 1374 [101 EDUC. L. REP. 126] (M.D. Tenn. 1995), 130 F.3d 232 [122 EDUC. L. REP. 573] (6th Cir. 1997), *cert. denied*, 523 U.S. 1024, 118 S. Ct. 1308, 140 L. Ed. 2d 473, (1998).
8. Supreme Court cases, for example, are available at http://www.supremecourtus.gov, the Court's own site, as well as http://supct.law.cornell.edu/supct and http://www.findlaw.com/casecode/supreme.html. Other federal cases are available at www.uscourts.gov.
9. OHIO REVISED CODE § 3321.03 (2005).
10. 5 U.S. 137 (1803)
11. U.S. CONST., art. III, § 1.
12. In suits based on diversity, "(a) … district courts shall have original jurisdiction of all civil actions where the matter in controversy exceeds the sum or value of $75,000, exclusive of interest and costs, and is between –

    (1) citizens of different States;

(2) citizens of a State and citizens or subjects of a foreign state;
(3) citizens of different States and in which citizens or subjects of a foreign state are additional parties; and
(4) a foreign state, defined in section 1603(a) of this title, as plaintiff and citizens of a State or of different States." 28 U.S.C. § 1332.

13. This sentence refers to a party based on the recognition that both parties may appeal in the same case on identical or different points of law.

14. The IDEA, which was recently re-codified as the Individuals with Disabilities Education Improvement Act, Pub. L. No. 108-416, 118 Stat 2647 (2004), has been located at 20 U.S.C. §§ 1400 *et seq.*

15. 1 C.F.R. § 1.1.

16. F. Supp. is now in its second series, F. Supp. 2d. A related series, Federal Rules Decisions (F.R.D.), includes opinions of federal trial court cases involving the interpretation of federal court rules that do not appear in the F. Supp. series.

17. The Federal Supplement is now in its third series, F.3d.

18. Labrum v. Wayne County Sch. Bd., 97 Fed.Appx. 882 [188 Educ. L. Rep. 187] (10th Cir. 2004) (holding that a school board's refusal to alter a bus route did not violate equal protection).

19. For example, the Supreme Court's recent decision upholding the constitutionality of drug testing all students who wish to participate in extracurricular activities, *Board of Educ. of Indep. Sch. Dist. No. 92, of Pottawatomie County v. Earls*, 536 U.S. 822, 122 S. Ct. 2559, 153 L. Ed. 2d 735 [166 Educ. L. Rep. 79] (2002), *on remand*, 300 F.3d 1222 [168 Educ. L. Rep. 581] (10th Cir.2002), was originally located at 2002 WL 1378649.

20. Once a case appears in the United States Reports, a parallel citation, such as the West's Supreme Court Reporter, is not necessary. However, such additional citations are typically included insofar as they assist researches in finding related information.

21. 496 U.S. 226, 110 S. Ct. 2356, 110 L. Ed. 2d 191 [60 Educ. L. Rep. 320] (1990).

22. For interesting discussions of the value, or lack thereof, and purpose of law reviews, *see* Richard A. Posner, *2004 Legal Affairs*, Nov.-Dec. 2004 57; Christopher Shea, *Students v. Professors: Law-Review Debate Heats Up as Student Editors Clash with Faculty Authors*, The Chron. of Higher Educ., June 2, 1995, at A 33-34.

23. The ten areas covered are agency, conflict of laws, contracts, foreign relations law, judgments, property, restitution, security, torts, and trusts.

24. As with contemporary restatements, multi-volume scholarly surveys include such classic historical series as *Wigmore on Evidence*, a work not unlike a restatement, and those exemplified by Blackstone's Commentaries on the Laws of England.

25. The Law of Contracts, 4th Ed. (1998).

26. In the interest of full disclosure, it is worth noting that the author of this article has served as editor of *The Yearbook of Education Law* since 1995.

27. *See* note 8.

28. The seven major headings are Persons, Property, Contracts, Torts, Crimes, Remedies, and Government. Schools, for example, are listed as subdivision of Government, under the subheading, Legislative and Executive Powers and Functions. *West's Law Finder: A Legal Research Manual* 16-17 (1989)

29. The federal practice digests include the U.S. Supreme Court reporter, Federal Digest, West's Federal Practice-3d, and U.S. Court of Claims Digest. Id.

30. Digests exist for all states except Delaware, Nevada, and Utah; in addition, North and South Dakota are in one volume as are Virginia and West Virginia. *Id.*

3 Qualitative Research Redux: Researching Contemporary Legal Issues Concerning Education

Joyce Lee & Louise Adler

Chapter Overview

This chapter introduces prospective qualitative researchers to legal issues in education most prone to litigation such as religion in the schools, freedom of expression, Fourth Amendment rights, law enforcement, educational equity, special education, and sexual harassment. Qualitative research, unlike traditional legal research, policy research, or quantitative research, provides interpretive insight into legal issues concerning education that other research methods cannot. In this chapter, readers are first introduced to representative cases identifying areas prone to litigation that would benefit from qualitative investigation. Qualitative methods are then contrasted with traditional methods for researching legal issues in terms of their advantages and disadvantages. The definitive features of qualitative research are revealed by examining two of the earliest qualitative approaches used by researchers: ethnography and case study. Contemporary approaches including action research, phenomenology, and discourse analysis are proposed as viable alternatives for researchers working within the qualitative paradigm. Field research techniques commonly used by qualitative researchers are explored, and pragmatic steps in the research process are enumerated. This chapter concludes with a list of supplemental resources that prospective researchers may consult to learn more about the application of various qualitative genres.

Introduction

Most research into legal issues in education consist of simple summaries of case law on a subject. Rarely do researchers take advantage of the wide range of complementary qualitative research methods or use mixed methods, a combination of qualitative and quantitative methods, to explore legal issues in education. Qualitative research methods can be used in tandem with case law to explore legal issues and policy decisions from an interpretive perspective. "A reorientation away from event decision making to process decision making necessitates looking at qualitative research as having an enlightening function" (Rist, 2003, p. 662).

Qualitative research has the to potential to enlighten, supplement, reinterpret, and validate our perspectives about legal issues pertaining to federal, state, and local legislative decisions concerning education. It assesses the impact that court decisions, constitutional laws, and rules enacted by regulatory and administrative bodies are having on those responsible for implementing and adhering to school policies. Researchers working in this paradigm find it especially effective for probing into the meaning people ascribe to politically charged legal issues concerning education. Prospective qualitative researchers will want to consider conducting research into these legal issues by first reviewing representative case laws in these areas.

Religion in the Schools

Historically, federal and state courts have held in many cases that school districts must remain neutral with respect to religion. Schools may not take any actions that establish or support religious beliefs and, likewise, school personnel must not require students to participate in religious activities during or after school. The following key laws continue to shape school policy on religious issues. *Engel v. Vitale* (1962) held that a twenty-two word prayer used daily in New York classrooms as an invocation at the beginning of the school day was unconstitutional. *Abington School District v. Schempp* (1963) delivered a landmark decision banning school prayer. *Wallace v. Jaffree* (1985) paved the way for a one-minute period of silence for meditation or voluntary prayer in school settings. *Mozert v. Hawkins County Board of Education* (1987) enabled petitioners to air their religious objections to curriculum content. *Board of Education of Westside Community Schools v. Mergens*

(1990) required the court to decide whether the Equal Access Act prohibited a high school from denying a student religious group permission to meet on school premises during non-instructional time. *Lee v. Weisman* (1992) questioned the legality of members of the clergy offering prayers as part of school ceremonies. *Santa Fe Independent School District v. Doe* (2000) permitted students to vote on whether to have student-led prayers at high school football games.

More recently, two noteworthy cases were settled. In *Donovan v. Punxsutawny Area School* (2003), the U.S. Court of Appeals for the Third Circuit concluded that the Equal Access Act applied to the school's activity period and that the school violated the First Amendment after refusing to permit a religious club access to the school's limited public forum solely because of its religious nature. Also, the U.S. Court of Appeals for the Eleventh Circuit issued a decision regarding the constitutionality of messages contained in student-painted murals inside a high school. In *Bannon v. School District of Palm Beach County* (2004), the court concluded that because the murals were sponsored and approved by the school, the administration could legally edit the religious content of the murals without engaging in unconstitutional viewpoint discrimination. Thus, the fundamental principle regarding religion in the schools is that individuals may pray privately at any time in a school setting, but prayers before an assembled school group or prayers sanctioned by the school are not legal under the Federal Constitution. Additional qualitative research regarding religion in the schools is needed to illuminate the impact of these school law cases on school practices.

Freedom of Expression

In legal precedents such as *Tinker v. Des Moines School District* (1969), the Court made it clear that constitutional protections apply to students both inside and outside of school. However, in *Bethel School District No.43 v. Fraser* (1986), the Supreme Court held that student speech was not protected by the First Amendment. Using profanity, appropriating the classroom as a forum for criticizing school administrators or policies, voicing political views unrelated to the curriculum, and wearing gang clothing and jewelry are all subject to proscription in order to protect the safety and welfare of students and faculty. Student publications also fall within the purview of the First Amendment's prohibition of censorship. Students are not free to publish articles in school newspapers without supervision and administrative review, as upheld in *Nicholson v. Board of Education* and, *Torrance County Unified School District* (1982), and reiterated in *Hazelwood School District v. Kuhlmeier* (1988).

Litigation regarding the Internet and free speech is rapidly proliferating as schools seek to implement Acceptable Use procedures and policies. While the Internet as a medium of communication is fully protected by the First Amendment, it does not fit neatly into First Amendment precedents. In *Killion v. Franklin Regional School District* (2001), the court engaged the *Tinker* rationale and held that a school district had violated a student's right of free speech when it suspended him for composing abusive remarks about a teacher, which he e-mailed to his friends from his home computer. The school could not provide evidence that the material caused substantial disruption to the school. Qualitative research methods are useful tools for investigating appropriate Internet use in educational venues.

Fourth Amendment Rights

Freedom from unreasonable searches and seizure of property is a Fourth Amendment right which also applies to searches conducted by public school administrators. In *New Jersey v. T.L.O* (1985), the Court determined that the Fourth Amendment's prohibition on unreasonable searches and seizures applied to searches conducted by public school officials. A decade after *T.L.O*, the U.S. Supreme Court took a major step in expanding the power of the school to search students. In *Vernonia School District 47J v. Acton* (1995), the court debated the district's Student Athlete Drug Policy which authorized random urinalysis drug testing, as to whether or not it violated the Fourth and Fourteenth Amendments. The Court interpreted the Fourth Amendment term "unreasonable" to permit school teachers and administrators to conduct random searches of students in certain circumstances without reasonably specific suspicion. Unreasonable searches and seizures by public school officials is an ongoing problem in education—a problem that could be solved through qualitative research.

Law Enforcement in the Schools

Many school law cases attempt to proscribe what constitutes a safe school environment. Bosher, et al (2004) point out that qualitative research studies were highly effective tools for investigating the impact of Columbine and 9/11 on the safety and security of educational institutions. In *Brownell v. Los Angeles Unified School District LAUSD* (1992), the court ruled that the LAUSD was not liable and did not have reason to forsee a gang-related shooting of a student. In *Wallmuth v. Rapides Parish School Board* (2002), the Supreme Court of Louisiana determined that the school board was not liable for injury to a student in a locker room fight when the teacher was not present. Many high schools across the country are adopting "zero tolerance" policies concerning students' use or possession of tobacco, alcohol, and drugs. One case on appeal, *Ette v. Linn-Mar Community School District* (2002), will decide whether the school district is justified for its decision to send a student home for smoking cigarettes on a school trip. Law enforcement is becoming increasingly necessary in school contexts. Future qualitative research studies in this area would enable school administrators to determine more explicitly what constitutes a safe, secure school environment.

Educational Equity

All persons are entitled to an education, irrespective of gender, race, ethnicity, or disability. For the past four decades, federal laws have ensured equity of access to educational opportunities. For example, Title IX of the Education Amendments of 1972 (which amended the 1964 Civil Rights Act) was created to protect the rights of individuals and to prohibit discrimination based on gender in educational programs or activities receiving federal funds. Gender-based discrimination involving any school program or activity jeopardizes federal financial assistance for the whole institution. However, President Bush's No Child Left Behind Act (NCLB)(2002) includes an amendment providing for single-sex schools. This policy change was initiated because educational research indicated that boys, especially African-American boys from underprivileged urban neighborhoods, performed better in schools that did not enroll girls. Challenges to the establishment of single-gender schools are anticipated.

In *McCormick v. School District of Mamaroneck* (2004), the U.S. Court of Appeals for the Second Circuit ruled on a Title IX lawsuit alleging that a school district precluded a girls' soccer team from post-seasonal regional and state competition by scheduling the games in the spring. This was in violation of Title IX because the boys' soccer season was conducted in the fall which afforded only the boys' team the opportunity to participate in competition. Gender discrimination applies to teachers as well. The *Franklin v. Gwinnett County Schools* (1992) decision rendered by the U.S. Supreme Court affirmed that any employee suffering gender discrimination may be entitled to compensatory and punitive damages against the school district. Title IX legislation spawned a plethora of qualitative research studies intended to erase gender bias; however, more qualitative research is needed to determine the impact of NCLB on educational equity practices in schools.

Special Education

A myriad of legislative activity in special education culminated with the Education of All Handicapped Children Act of 1975 (PL-142). This law mandates the least restrictive environment for disabled children and "mainstreams" them into settings previously limited to non-disabled children. The Individuals with Disabilities Education Act (IDEA) passed by Congress in 1990 requires that the educational placement of each disabled child is to be determined annually to ensure that the school makes an effort to find an inclusive solution. *Hartmann v. Loudoun County Board of Education (*1997) further upheld that disabled students must be educated to the maximum extent appropriate. Future qualitative studies are needed to monitor the impact of special education law on inclusive education practices and to ensure that schools conform to IDEA mandates.

Sexual Harassment

It is unfortunate that incidents of sexual misconduct are increasing dramatically in schools. Instances where teachers permit one student to sexually harass another, where a teacher becomes sexually involved with a student, where a teacher sexually molests a student, or where a teacher dates a student are on the rise. These profoundly serious issues confronting public education are further compounded by the failure of some school administrators to respond to allegations of sexual harassment. Fundamentally, the law states that any public sexual act by a teacher, whether heterosexual or homosexual, is normally grounds for dismissal given the court's ruling in the *Board of Education v. Jack M.* (1977). Discrimination against gay students is also prohibited as a result of *Nabozny v. Podlesny* (1996). In the *Davis v. Monroe* case (1999), the Supreme Court ruled that in the case of sexual harassment a student could sue under Title IX if it could be documented that school officials knew about sexual harassment and were indifferent to it. More qualitative research studies focusing on sexual harassment are needed to inform educators about how to alleviate sexual harassment and how to avoid the disruptive media attention that such infractions generate.

Comparing Qualitative Research with Other Research Methods

Every research approach, whether the traditional legal research discussed in the case laws above, quantitative research, qualitative research, or policy research, has a particular history and tradition and is uniquely suited to particular research questions or problems. All of these research approaches have value in studying the legal issues that surround education in the United States. Perhaps one way to differentiate among the approaches is to distinguish the scope of the territory each research approach proposes to investigate. Legal research in education covers those formal acts of government that shape public education, legal cases that involve educational agencies, and the development of legal precedents.

Traditional Legal Research

Traditional legal research focuses on a particular topic and asks, "What is the law?" Past cases and law review articles may be explored to trace judicial reasoning. Also, specific laws related to a topic may be explored. This is, to be sure, vital information, but it is not all of the information that may be helpful to lawyers, school administrators, teachers, and students of school law. The law, as we know, is a social construction and is suited to exploring the questions of *why* and *how* society, through its courts and legislative bodies, has created specific laws. Knowledge of *why* and *how* is crucial to those who must carry out laws in a democratic society. Also important are questions about the effects or consequences of the law that can be intended and unintended.

Quantitative Research

Quantitative research uses statistics to analyze data that answers questions about *who, where, why, how many*, and *how much*. It also investigates the relationships between specific variables. Counting cases and their outcomes is the most common type of quantitative research conducted in public education concerning legal issues. The quantitative approach usually starts with a clearly stated hypothesis, narrows the scope of the research as a way of controlling which variables are studied, and tests the hypothesis using data-gathering instruments such as surveys or questionnaires, to determine the relationships between variables.

Policy Research

Policy studies have a broader scope in the range of questions asked than traditional quantitative approaches. Policy studies often use mixed methods, both quantitative and qualitative, to frame the research issues. However, when researching policy issues, the focus is on evaluating the relative merits of specific sets of public policy options. According to Rist (2003), information needs for policy research cluster around three broad areas: (1) an understanding of the stages of studying the policy issue; (2) what has taken place previously in response to the condition or problem; and (3) what is known about the previous efforts and their impacts that would help one choose among present-day options (pp.619-627). Qualitative research fulfills more information needs during the third stage of the policy research cycle because it reveals "the intended and unintended consequences of policy instruments or tools that might be selected as a means to implement policy" (p.627).

Qualitative Research

Qualitative research is a research paradigm of organizing concepts and methods underpinned by certain philosophical assumptions all of which share a concern for probing and understanding how people process and interpret their world and how they assign meaning to their experiences and actions. Rossman and Rallis (2003) define qualitative research as "...approaches to inquiry that represent a lively and flourishing community of traditions" (p. 92). Crosscutting disciplines, fields, and subject matter and reflecting a complex, interconnected family of terms, concepts, and assumptions, qualitative research has become the preferred approach for conducting social science and human science research, despite initial resistance from positivists.

Qualitative researchers become research instruments by recognizing how their personal interests, talents, and skills have an important impact on the research process and outcomes. Researchers design a study, collect descriptive data in natural settings in the field, use inductive thinking, and present their findings from their subjects' points of view. According to Denzin and Lincoln (2003), qualitative research "…is a situated activity that locates the observer in the world. It consists of a set of interpretive, material practices that make the world visible. These practices transform the world. They turn the world into a series of representations, including field notes, interviews, conversations, photographs, recordings, and memos to the self" (p.5).

The results of qualitative research are presented in a language and terminology that reflect the words and actions of the people being studied. Researchers operating in this paradigm are reluctant to claim for their conclusions some form of universal generalizability or statistical validity. Qualitative research builds theory as researchers discern universal aspects of particular situations and common elements of unique events by identifying categories and/or themes that build a picture of a particular piece of the world. Rather than make a claim to rigid objectivity, qualitative researchers make the subjective involvement of the researcher explicit in reporting the research. During this process, researchers are challenged to deal with the ambiguity of the research process, to use multiple sources of data to formulate and analyze patterns, to construe meaning from these findings, and to communicate the results in publications that invite careful scrutiny by scholars. Qualitative research assumes that what is learned by researchers as they conduct their studies will shift what is studied and how the studies are conducted; thus, it is an evolutionary process.

Unlike quantitative research which deals with the figure-ground problem by focusing only on the figure (a carefully delimited hypothesis), qualitative approaches are concerned with the interaction between the figure and the ground. For example, a quantitative researcher might ask, "Are the number of cases increasing or decreasing?" and "How are school districts responding to the increase or decrease in the number of cases?" Qualitative researchers ask about the cases, but they cross the figure-ground boundaries by researching the social and cultural contexts that develop. They compose an interpretive narrative about why things happen.

Definitive Features of Qualitative Research

All qualitative research approaches employ an inductive approach, are naturalistic and holistic, are concerned with process, value subjective analysis, generalize from single or multiple instances, and search for meaning within experience (Bogdan and Biklen, 2003, pp.3-7). While there is infinite variability in the applications of qualitative research, all approaches rest on three basic assumptions:

1. Qualitative methods seek to understand phenomena in their entirety in order to develop a complete understanding of a person, program, or situation.
2. The researcher does not impose much of an organizing structure or make assumptions about the interrelationships among the data prior to making the observations.
3. It is a discovery-oriented approach in the natural environment (Rudestam and Newton, 1992, p. 32).

Five major qualitative genres, each reflecting the definitive features of qualitative research, are examined in the next section in terms of their efficacy for conducting research into legal issues concerning education. Prospective qualitative researchers may consider the strengths and limitations of ethnography, case study, new paradigm/action research, phenomenology, and discourse analysis. Such delineations are intended to orient qualitative researchers to select the most appropriate method for conducting research.

Ethnography

Ethnography is the most frequently adopted synonym for qualitative research because, historically, ethnography was where qualitative research began. The foundation upon which later varieties of qualitative research were constructed, ethnography is based on the classic field research methods developed in anthropology to convey a way of life of a group of people. Ethnographers have been known to immerse themselves in the culture they are studying ("going native") as a way of coming to appreciate the social order, meaning, and rituals from insiders' points of view. Whatever the focus of their research, ethnographers are concerned with the cultural context of the behavior they are observing. It would be inaccurate to assume that ethnographers only study groups existing in natural settings like the primitive Samoan cultures Margaret Mead studied. More than likely, ethnographic fieldwork is conducted in modern settings. Lightfoot's study of "good" high schools (1983), Peshkin's study of a fundamentalist Christian school (1986), and Rose's study (1988) of two different types of Christian schools are classic examples of ethnography.

While ethnographic studies have typically focused on descriptions of cultures (ethnos), more recently the method has been applied to researching small groups (classrooms), educational programs, and educational institutions, postmodern cultures affording rich sites for inquiry. Ethnographers use a wide angle lens to capture a holistic picture of a classroom, school culture, or educational program. Unlike empirical studies where variables are manipulated, ethnography is naturalistic because it gathers data from field settings without trying to manipulate what is being studied. To put it simplistically, rather than putting a rat in a maze to discover the strength of its desire to acquire food, a naturalistic design would follow the rat around in its natural habitat to discover how it satisfies its hunger.

Rather than starting with a hypothesis that is to be tested and proved or disproved, the ethnographer starts with some general questions. While visiting various field sites for long stretches of time (perhaps as long as a year to observe a full cycle of activity), the ethnographer collects data. As data emerges over time it suggests new avenues of inquiry. Ethnographic analysis methods are associated with what Glaser and Strauss (1967) called "grounded theory" because analytic induction is used to create categories. The most distinctive element of grounded theory is its approach to data analysis whereby researchers collect, code, and analyze data and then decide what data to collect next and where to find data in order to develop theory as it emerges. As substantive themes and central concepts emerge from the data, researchers decide who they need to interview or what they need to observe in a certain group of people, regardless of whether this group is representative of a larger population. Complex techniques of open coding, axial coding, selective coding, theoretical sampling and saturation, which are constant comparative methods of data analysis, are used by qualitative researchers using a grounded-theory approach.

Advocates of grounded theory believe that researchers must investigate a phenomenon without any preconceived theories. Bracketing off their assumptions and suspending them temporarily, ethnographers attempt to maintain openness in their perceptions so that their participants' perceptions assume center stage. They construct emergent themes that best fit the data. As themes are developed, researchers seek their fullest-possible generality and continually check these themes for relevance to the research question. The theory that results is grounded theory, because it is *grounded* in the direct apprehension of the participants' experiences.

The emphasis in grounded theory is on discovery, rather than on verification, as researchers seek to discover and perceive how their participants order their world. The respondents' own words and phrases often give rise to the terms and concepts used by researchers in reporting results. Grounded theory is particularly useful for producing substantive theory for change—theory developed for an area of practice such as teaching or educational administration. Researchers using grounded theory become highly attuned to the theories people use to guide their actions and the reasoning behind their decisions. Ethnographers also examine how people's belief systems and values guide their actions, seek to understand the meaning of those actions, and determine how those actions may impact other groups. Shared meaning is of primary importance because it teaches people how to behave in a cultural setting. It borrows from the traditions of semiotics, the study of signs and symbols in language, and relies on "thick descriptions" of a culture.

Wolcott (1988) argues that not every researcher who claims to be doing ethnography is actually producing an ethnographic study. "It is useful to distinguish between anthropologically informed researchers who do ethnography and educational researchers who frequently draw upon ethnographic approaches in doing descriptive studies" (p.202). Ethnography is much more than a set of techniques for gathering data. The written ethnographic account is not a verbatim transcript of every observation, interview, or document, but it tells the story of a culture that is understandable to others. "The ethnographer's task is not only to collect information from the emic or insider's perspective, but also to make sense of all the data from an etic or external scientific social perspective" (Fetterman, 1989, p.21).

In ethnography, the record produced becomes the focus of ethnographic investigation, rather than the particular methods used.

The written record conveys a well-rounded view of the context going beyond description into cultural and cross-cultural analysis. The purpose of ethnography is to compile a richly descriptive account of how members of a group or culture came to know the norms, values, traditions, beliefs, and stereotypes that governed their lives and gave meaning to their social order. Ethnographers set out to show how social norms in one world make sense from the point of view of another world.

According to Chambers (2003), the past two decades have seen changes and improvements in the development of ethnographic research methods which have included an increased sophistication in developing cultural models: greater diversification of research methods and techniques, including computer-assisted ethnographic research programs; more complete involvement of ethnographers in all stages of the research process; greater tendency for ethnographers to work as members of research teams; and the application of ethnographic methods to action research strategies (p.413). Ellis and Bochner (2003) propose that a new form of ethnography, autoethnography, is another useful research strategy reflecting an autobiographical genre of writing and research that "displays multiple layers of consciousness, connecting the personal to the cultural" (p.209). All new forms of ethnography can be applied to research legal issues concerning education, but must match the researcher's intent.

Ethnography and applied ethnography call into question the issue of the researcher's subjectivity or the research group's intersubjectivity. Issues of subjectivity in empirical research are diminished because all empirical research begins with a hypothesis based on a particular theory. However, even the most rigorously empirical research involves a subjective decision by the researcher. It would be impossible to separate out our human qualities from the research we conduct; hence, all research is to some extent subjective. In fact, many have argued that there is great danger in the assumption that research can be conducted in a value-free atmosphere. Human judgment is necessary when making decisions about the ethical implications of how we conduct and report research. When ethnographic researchers go to sites to collect physical data, they bring with them their own biographies including their values, physical appearance, preferences, language and all of the other complex personal traits that make them human. In ethnography, the issue of researcher bias or subjectivity is addressed in the proposal development stage where researchers "come clean" by disclosing their taken-for-granted assumptions, biases, and points of view. As the research progresses, they make a conscious effort to convey the impact of their own subjectivity on the research process.

The presence of the researcher has the potential to impact the events being observed. Ethnographers attempt to deal with this problem by visiting the site for extended periods of time. Ethnographers balance their need to become full participants in the events being observed with the necessity of being removed from the events as an observer. A continuum exists from non-responsive observation on one extreme to full participation on the other. Doing ethnographic research in one's organization poses a number of ethical dilemmas. One is that the researcher is so fully a participant that it is very difficult to separate roles and wear two hats simultaneously. It is also difficult to report the results and protect the anonymity of sources. One student conducted a "back yard" study and opted to have her master's project sealed because there was no way to report the data and keep her job.

Questions of validity and reliability in ethnographic research are not addressed in the same way as they are addressed in quantitative research. If one uses a quantitative method with a limited number of variables, it would be expected that if another researcher repeated the steps in the study, the results could be replicated. However, in ethnography, the research can never be repeated in exactly the same way. Concepts such as "dependability" or "consistency" are more useful tests of the quality of ethnographic research and for qualitative research in general.

Case Study Research

The case study method historically has been viewed as a detailed examination of one setting, a single subject, or a particular event (Merriam, 1988; Yin, 1989; Stake, 1995). A case could be a university department, a special education program, or even a child in a school setting. A case is considered from a specified perspective and with a special interest. It is unique and is one among others (Stake, 1995, p.2). Cases are empirical units subject to evaluation because scientific and practical interests are tied to them. They are used for purposes of demonstration and learning, both in education and in research. Case studies are generally considered an effective strategy for conducting research into a single instance. Historical case studies, observational case studies, life histories, and micro-ethnographies are subsets of this genre. Case studies can focus on a classroom, a teacher's room, the experience of a new administrator, or a gifted child. All are in-depth and detailed explorations of single examples of an event, group, or individual—an instance drawn from a class of similar phenomena. Case studies seek to understand larger phenomena through a closer examination of smaller, representative examples.

Case study researchers use context in much the same way that ethnographers use culture. Both are considered very important in the research and result in collecting data about the relationship between what is being studied and its surroundings. Context as it is used by the case study researcher could include cultural, social, economic, geographic, historical, or other factors that may impact on the entity being studied. This methodology should not be confused with "studying cases" or "briefing cases" in legal research. A more appropriate analogy would be the use of case studies in medicine or psychology where all the aspects of a patient's life are explored to better understand a medical or psychological problem. Once the "case" is defined, a holistic approach is taken to describe and analyze all factors that impinge on the case. Merriam (1988) suggests that case studies are often the best method if one is attempting to improve practice in education. She points to the usefulness of this method in conducting program evaluations and for informing the policy process. Case study research has been used to study various phenomena such as organizational performance, policy interventions, project implementation, and program development. In order to use a case study method, the researcher must be able to clearly define the boundaries of the case or cases.

Questions have been raised since the early use of this method in sociology about the extent to which the results of a case study can be applied beyond the specific study. One way to address this issue is to select a single group or phenomenon that is representative of the whole as the object of study. Thus, the selection becomes a critical step in the research design that must be clearly justified in the reporting. To be successful using this technique, the researcher must show that the characteristics of the global population are concentrated in the local object of the case study which is a difficult task. However, another option available is to avoid claiming that the results are generalizable, or that while the actual results may not be generalizable, patterns or themes identified may be generalizable to other settings.

New Paradigm Research

Qualitative research has been increasingly influenced by "post-experimental inquiry" (Denzin and Lincoln, 2003, p. 3) and the current theoretical scene reflected in critical theory, feminism, and postmodernism. Qualitative research from this philosophical stance is concerned with "moral discourse and asks that the social sciences and humanities become sites for critical conversations about democracy, race, gender, class, nation-states, globalization, freedom, and community" (p.3). Critical theory is an approach to thinking and researching that emphasizes research as an ethical and political act. Critical theory invites criticism of social organizations that privilege some people at the expense of others. Critical theorists argue that research should empower the powerless and work toward the elimination of inequality and injustice. Feminist theory focuses on the impact of gender as a central topic in qualitative research including how the experiences of girls and women are communicated and what methodologies are appropriate for exploring issues related to gender. Postmodernism, an abandonment of belief in science and rational thinking, is dominated by mass culture and technological communication. From a postmodern perspective, the world can only be known from an individual's unique perspective implying that there is no universal truth and that truth is relative. Qualitative researchers working from "new paradigm" perspectives reject the notion that the world is directly knowable and that knowledge is definite and unequivocal. They assert that research is a systematic process of building theory; however, building theory must include activities that do not silence or oppress members of marginalized groups. "Research always has political consequences," Bogdan and Biklen contend (2003, p.225). Thus, action research, participatory action research, political action research, and collaborative inquiry are but a few of the multiple forms of new paradigm research that foster social action as an outcome of the qualitative research process.

Action research is a new paradigm method applied to advance social, organizational, or institutional causes and to promulgate positive changes in existing practices. Action research is so named because of its orientation to the researcher or researchers who not only collect and analyze data but take action on the findings by altering some part of the world and effectuating immediate or long-term change. Action researchers illuminate problematic aspects of a situation and investigate disorienting dilemmas of practice in an effort to discover the root causes of a problem. Typical settings for action research (or collaborative action research when action research is conducted by a group) include schools and school systems, community development projects, political advocacy movements, health organizations, corporate and business settings, and public and private bureaucracies.

Action research has a political dimension in that research is conducted to surface underlying causes of oppression or discrimination and to explore alternative means by which people can become empowered individually and collectively to change some aspect of their lives. Increasingly, action research is becoming a more systematically conducted inquiry designed to bring about social change that involves subjects as participants who shape their worlds to improve the conditions under which they live. Action research is intended to improve practice, the understanding of practice by practitioners, and the situation in which practice takes place. As an action research project develops, it is expected that a widening circle of those affected by the practice will become involved in the research process. Action research is situational in the sense that it is concerned with diagnosing and solving a problem in a specific context. It is often collaborative so that artificial divisions between researchers and subjects are broken down and situations may be improved through cooperation. In participatory action research, the research subjects are involved in designing, conducting, and reporting the research, and they become self-evaluative. In action research and in participatory action research, co-researchers modify and improve the research activity as they encounter it in a cyclical way through action and reflection. Data gathering and data analysis often happen concurrently. The overall purpose of the research cycle is to generate knowledge for action in people, systems, and broader social structures—information that is usable and relevant, even transformational. Both quantitative and qualitative methods can be embedded in action research, collaborative action research, case study, or ethnography reflecting a "mixed methods" paradigm for researching legal issues related to education.

Phenomenological Research

The term phenomenology refers to the researcher's subjective experience with a phenomenon; it reflects the researcher's disciplined study of consciousness from a first-person perspective. Qualitative researchers using a phenomenological approach attempt to understand the meaning of events and interactions of ordinary people in particular situations and emphasize the subjective aspects of people's behavior. Phenomenology is not so much a methodology as it is a philosophical orientation, a way of thinking about how we come to know and construct our realities. The phenomenologist is concerned with describing a phenomenon precisely, representing the meaning of that phenomenon from the perspective of the people who experience it, and understanding the phenomenon in the way that the subjects do. The basic tenet of phenomenological research is that meaningful interpretation of human experience can only come first-hand from those persons who have thoroughly immersed themselves in the phenomenon they wish to interpret and understand. For example, religion in the schools, students' freedom of expression, search and seizure policies, law-enforcement issues, educational equity practices, and sexual harassment are all "phenomena" that can be better understood from the perspectives of individuals who experience them in various ways.

Phenomenological research involves a return to an experience for the purpose of observing and describing it in narrative form. These observations provide the basis for reflective analysis which is intended to reveal the essence of the phenomenon—that which makes the phenomenon what it is. Phenomenological studies seek to understand the lived experiences of a small number of people or a group through in-depth, exploratory engagement. Researchers working in this genre often wish to understand the nature of an experience, the meaning a person or a group of people make of that experience, and how reflection on the experience yields meaning.

Discourse Analysis

Similar to ethnography, discourse analysis explores the meaning participants make in social interactions and settings when the locus of these studies is communicative behavior. Researchers inquire into patterns and modes of communication, especially language, often captured in text, transcripts, or in audiovisual materials, as it occurs in social contexts. This genre departs from ethnography as researchers focus on fine-grained interactions, speech acts, body language and gestures, and signs and signals (semiotics) in a specific context. The words and actions people use to communicate and how they use these words and actions to communicate meaning is important. For example, the way teachers communicate with one another or with administrators through body position, hand gestures, dress, and choice of words are "texts" that can be read and interpreted by researchers. Discourse analysis requires the microanalysis of naturally occurring speech events and interactions within a context, as opposed to an interview set up by the researcher. Researchers may use video or audio taped events and analyze media for patterns in the discourse, the use of proxemics (space), kinesics (body motion), and conformance or deviance from the pattern.

Qualitative Research Techniques

Participant Observation

Ethnographic studies happen face-to-face using participant observation and interviewing. Ethnographers also use written sources and collect artifacts such as pictures, photos, maps, videotapes, digital images and text. Ethnography done in settings new to the researcher requires gaining access and becoming familiar with the lay of the land. Access to the site should be requested in advance unless it is open to the general public. Researchers will also need the help of a gatekeeper and one or more insiders to gain a better understanding of the events. Careful note taking with as much detail as possible is critical. In some settings tape recorders, cameras, or video cameras may aid in this process but informed consent issues must be addressed. The advantage of being a participant observer is to focus on an event with a fresh set of eyes. Yet, the process of observation means much more than watching what happens. It means watching purposefully to collect and then reflect on observational data that addresses the research question.

Interviews

There are many kinds of interview methods (key informant, life history, structured, semi-structured, informal, and questionnaires) that qualitative researchers employ. Interviews are an opportunity to learn about events the researcher cannot observe or to gather information about the subjects' opinions and perceptions. Key informants are insiders who have agreed to help the researcher. Structured and semi-structured interviews are used to gather specific information and are usually used after the researcher has studied the site long enough to develop some notions they want to test or explore. Informal interviews can take place serendipitously in the course of visits to a site. Interviewing is a craft that improves with practice and coaching. Questionnaires are used when it is not possible or advisable to speak directly to people who have information concerning a legal issue; however, qualitative researchers do not depend solely on data gathered from questionnaires.

Documents

While raw data consists of materials that researchers produce, such as field notes and interviews, qualitative researchers also obtain personal documents, diaries, personal letters, autobiographies, official documents from schools and educational organizations, policy documents, student records and personnel files, internal documents, external communications, and popular-culture documents connected with their research questions. Audio and visual materials such as photographs and video tapes produced by the researcher or culled from the mass media, electronic information downloaded from the Internet, and cultural artifacts are sources of data pertinent to researching legal issues concerning education.

Recommendations for Prospective Researchers

After carefully considering the advantages and disadvantages of the vast array of qualitative approaches, qualitative researchers researching school law issues should consider what pragmatic steps for conducting qualitative research should be taken. Qualitative research is a recursive and reiterative process involving research design and planning, data collection and analysis, reporting and communicating the findings for public testing. What follows are practical recommendations for the prospective qualitative researcher engaging in the research process.

Research Design and Planning

When you plan your research effort, you or your advisor may discover that there are aspects of your research question that cannot be addressed by traditional legal research about the law. If the information you seek is about how or why legal events take place, you should consider using a qualitative method in addition to traditional legal research. The first step is to determine that the information you seek could best be found using a qualitative method. Second, you will have to read enough about the methods so you can select an appropriate one and assure that you can completely apply the method. Identifying a mentor who is skilled in the use of this method is also valuable, even if that person is not an expert on your research topic. Third, you must approach this type of research with a mindset that is inductive rather than deductive. Fourth, you must specify in writing the research procedures that you will implement and how you will address the potential for researcher bias to influence the outcome. Outline all of the procedures that you will use to gather and analyze your data. You must provide evidence that you are using sound research techniques. To argue this successfully, you will need to make reference to experts on the particular methodology you select. You must also demonstrate that you have solutions to problems typical of qualitative research such as how to gain access, how to define the boundaries of the study, and how to accurately record the data. The focus of the study must be narrowed so the scope is not too large or too small and is worthy of investigation.

Data Collection

Only after careful planning, and with the approval of your advisor, should you gather the data. A variety of data collection methods are used in qualitative research such as observation, document and artifact analysis, open-ended questionnaires, interviews, and focus groups. While the predetermined procedures outlined in the proposal should be followed, qualitative research is not a rigid process. New insights into the research question gained, access to unanticipated sources of information, new research subjects, and unanticipated events necessitate revisions during the research process. You may also find that your plans need to be adjusted once you begin to gather data because your previous interpretations became insufficient and failed to disclose an important issue that you discovered once you began to collect the data necessitating a renegotiation of the research proposal.

Data Analysis

Data analysis is the most time-consuming step in qualitative research. No doubt you will begin to see patterns emerge in the data collected as you collect it. Or, you may structure the analysis of the data by the way interview protocols, surveys, or other instruments are constructed. Coding the data may be accomplished using colored highlighters, but advances in computer software make it possible to automate this laborious process of analyzing textual information.

Being at a site allows qualitative researchers to observe, to interview people, and to obtain records and artifacts. Each of these sources of data can be used to corroborate research outcomes, a process called triangulation. Qualitative researchers use multiple fieldwork techniques to gather data and may collect data from various sources such as parents, administrators, teachers, and students to bolster the validity of their study.

Writing the Report

Most of the data collected in qualitative research is in words or text so excellent writing skills are necessary to communicate the findings of a study in an interesting way. Telling the story presented by your data requires skillful use of language. The writing process often brings the researcher a deeper understanding of the meaning of the data. It is of paramount importance that qualitative researcher provide a clear connection between the data collected and their interpretation of the data. Qualitative researchers use "thick description" that goes beyond mere reporting to probe "the intentions, motives, meanings, contexts, situations and circumstances of action" (Denzin, 1988, p.39).

Given the steps outlined above, assume for a moment that you are a qualitative researcher conducting a case study on the implementation of a crisis-management plan for a school district. You could begin by doing traditional legal research to define the parameters of case law decisions related to school safety. Then you would select a site for conducting a case study and define its boundaries. Will you explore crisis-management implementation at only one site or at multiple sites? What are the characteristics of each site and do needs differ in terms of urban, rural, or suburban contexts? What are the socio-economic and the socio-cultural conditions? What kind of case study will you do? Will it be exploratory, explanatory, or descriptive? How will you gain entry to the site to do interviews, observations, and gather documents?

Only after you had assured yourself that you understood the case study method well enough to gather the necessary data would you actually visit the site. Careful recording of the data and its subsequent analysis are also critical and perhaps the most difficult steps in doing a quality case study. If the primary focus of your research project is to do traditional legal research, qualitative data can supplement your work. You may want to use press reports or letters to the editor to illustrate the public's reaction to particular decisions. Or, for a particularly interesting case, you might want to speak by phone or contact via e-mail key players such as the attorneys who argued the case or the plaintiff. They might give you valuable insights that would enhance your analysis of the case. How will you write up and report your study? How will you ensure that you get feedback from others, especially experts in this area?

Conclusion

This chapter introduced prospective qualitative researchers to case laws reflecting compelling legal issues in public education that beg additional scrutiny from a qualitative perspective. Objective approaches, employed by traditional legal research, policy research, and quantitative research, were compared and contrasted with subjective research approaches as a way of extolling the virtues of qualitative research methods. The underlying assumptions, procedures, and processes for employing ethnography and case study research, the earliest exemplars of qualitative research, were discussed. Action research, phenomenology, and discourse analysis, referred to as "new paradigm" approaches, were promoted as alternative ways for researchers to construct knowledge for practice. Pragmatic, step-by-step recommendations for "doing" qualitative research were included to encourage novice researchers to experiment with qualitative methodologies. The Supplemental Resources section below directs readers to references containing a wealth of information about these research genres. To conclude, qualitative research methods have the power and potential to truly enlighten our understanding of legal issues in education and, therefore, to engender more humane and democratic practices in schools.

Supplemental Resources

Qualitative Research

Boyatzis, R. (1998). *Transforming qualitative information: Thematic analysis and code development.* Thousand Oaks, CA: Sage Publications.

Delamount, S. (1992). *Fieldwork in educational settings: Methods, pitfalls and perspectives.* London: Falmer.

Denzin, N.K. & Lincoln, Y.S. (Eds.) (2003). *Collecting and interpreting qualitative materials* (2nd Ed.). Thousand Oaks, CA: Sage.

Lincoln, Y.S., & Guba, E.G. (1985). *Naturalistic inquiry.* Beverly Hills, CA: Sage.

Lincoln, Y.S., & Guba, E.G. (2000). Paradigmatic controversies, contradictions, and emerging confluences. In N.K. Denzin & Y.S. Lincoln (Eds.), *Handbook of qualitative research* (2nd ed., pp.163-188). Thousand Oaks, CA:Sage.

Mann, C. & Stewart, F. (2000*). Internet communication and qualitative research: A handbook for researching online.* Thousand Oaks, CA: Sage.

Marshall, C. & Rossman, G.B. (1999). *Designing qualitative research* (3rd. ed.). Thousand Oaks, CA: Sage.

Maxwell, J.A. (1996). *Qualitative research design.* Thousand Oaks: Sage.

Patton, M.Q. (2002). *Qualitative evaluation and research methods* (3rd ed). Thousand Oaks, CA: Sage.

Peshkin, A. (2000). *The nature of interpretation in qualitative research.* Educational Researcher, 29(9), 5-9.

Rossman, G. & Rallis, S. (2003*). Learning in the field: An introduction to qualitative research.* Thousand Oaks, CA: Sage Publications.

Seal, C., Gobo, G., Gubrium, J., Silverman, D. (2004). Handbook of data analysis. Thousand Oaks: Sage.

Silverman, D. (2004). *Qualitative research: Theory, method and practice* (2nd.Ed.). Thousand Oaks, CA: Sage Publications.

Strauss, A. & Corbin, J. (1990). *Basics of qualitative research: Grounded theory procedures and techniques*. Thousand Oaks, CA: Sage Publications

Weis, L. & Fine, M. (2000). Speed *bumps: A student-friendly guide to qualitative research.* Teachers College Press, New York, NY.

New Paradigm/Action Research

Anderson, G. & Jones, F. (2000). Knowledge generation in educational administration from the inside out: The promise and perils of site-based administrator research. *Educational Administration Quarterly*, 36, 3 428-464.

Anderson, G., Herr, K., Nihlen, A. (1994*). Studying your own school: An educator's guide to qualitative practitioner research.* Thousand Oaks, CA: Corwin Press.

Anderson, G. & Herr, K. (1999). The new paradigm wars: Is there room for rigorous practitioner knowledge in schools and universities? *Educational Researcher*, 28, 5, 12-21, 40.

Bray, J., Lee, J. Smith, L., and Yorks, L. (2000). *Collaborative inquiry in practice: Action, reflection, and making meaning.* Thousand Oaks, CA: Sage.

Calhoun, E. (1994*). How to use action research in the self-renewing school.* Alexandria, VA: Association for Supervision and Curriculum Development.

Coghlan, D. & Brannick, T. (2001). *Doing action research in your own organization.*

Greenwood, D. & Levin, M. (1998*). Introduction to action research: Social research for social change.* Thousand Oaks, CA: Sage.

Kemmis, S. & McTaggart, R. (2000). Participatory action research. In N.K. Denzin & Y.S. Lincoln (Eds.), *Handbook of qualitative research* (2nd ed., pp. 567-605). Thousand Oaks, CA: Sage.

McNiff, J., & Whitehead, J. (2002). *Action research: Principles and practice.* London, England: Routledge, Farmer.

Mills, G. (2000). *Action research.* Upper Saddle River, NJ: Merrill-Prentice Hall.

Reason, P., & Bradbury, H. (2001). *Handbook of action research: participative inquiry and practice.* Thousand Oaks, CA: Sage.

Sagor, R. (2000). *Collaborative action research for educational change.* Alexandria, VA: Association for Supervision and Curriculum Development Yearbook, 169-191.

Sagor, R. (2000). *Guiding school improvement with action research.* Alexandria, VA: Association for Supervision and Curriculum Development.

Discourse Analysis

Gee, J. P. (1999). *Introduction to discourse analysis: Theory and method.* New York: Routlege.

Labov, W. (1982). Speech actions and reactions in personal narrative. In D. Tanner (Ed.), *Analyzing discourse: Text and talk* (pp.219-247). Washington, DC: Georgetown University Press.

MacLure, Maggie (2003). *Discourse in educational and social research.* Philadelphia, PA: Open University Press.

Wodak, R. & Meyer, M. (2002). *Methods of critical discourse analysis.* Thousand Oaks, CA: Sage.

Ethnography

Atkinson, P., Coffey, A., Delamont, S., Lofland, J., & Lofland, L. (2001). *Handbook of ethnography*. Thousand Oaks, CA: Sage.

Campbell, M. & Gregor, F. (2002). *Doing institutional ethnography: A primer in mapping social relations*. Garamond Press

Emerson, R.M., Fretz, R.I., & Shaw, L.L. (1995). *Writing ethnographic field notes*. Chicago university of Chicago Press.

Pink, S. (2001). *Doing visual ethnography*. Thousand Oaks, CA: Sage.

Spradley, J.P. (1979). *The ethnographic interview*. New York: Holt, Reinehart & Winston.

Phenomenology

Gubrium, J.F., & Holstein, J.A. (2000). Analyzing interpretive practice. In N.K. Denzin & Y.S. Lincoln (Eds.*), Handbook of qualitative research* (2nd ed., pp. 487-508). Thousand Oaks, CA: Sage.

Van Manen, M. (1990). *Researching lived experience: Human science for an action sensitive pedagogy*. Albany: SUNY Press.

Case Study Research

Merriam, S. B. (1988). *Case study research in education*. San Francisco: Jossey-Bass.

Scholz, R. & Tietje, O. Embedded case study methods: Integrating quantitative and qualitative knowledge. Thousand Oaks, CA: Sage.

Travers, M. (2001). *Qualitative research through case studies*. Thousand Oaks, CA: Sage.

Yin, R.K. *Case study research: Design and methods* (3rd ed). Thousand Oaks, CA: Sage.

Field Methods and Techniques

Bernard, R. (2003). *Field methods*. Thousand Oaks, CA: Sage.

Gubrium, J, & Holstein, J. (2003). *Postmodern interviewing*. Thousand Oaks, CA: Sage.

Holstein, J. & Gubrium, J. (2003*). Inside interviewing: New Lenses, New Concerns*. Thousand Oaks, CA: Sage.

Krueger, R. & Casey, M. (2000). *Focus groups: A practical guide for applied research.* Thousand Oaks, CA: Sage.

Wengraf, T. (2001). *Qualitative research interviewing*. Thousand Oaks, CA: Sage.

References

Adler, L. (1990). Decisions fired with emotion. *Urban Education*, 25, 1, 3-13.

Abington School District v. Schempp, 374 U.S. 203, 83 S.Ct. 1560, 10 L.Ed.2nd 844 (1963).

Americans With Disabilities Act of 1990, 42 U.S.C.A. 12101 et seq. (West 1993).

Bannon v. School District of Palm Beach County, 2004 WL 2283490 (11th Cir. 2004).

Bethel School District No.43 v. Fraser, 106 S.Ct.3159 (1986).

Board of Educ. V. Jack M., 19 Cal. 3d 691, 139 Cal. Rptr. 700, 566 P.2d 602 (1977).

Board of Education, Island Trees Union Free School District No.26 v. Pico, 457 U.S. 853, 102 S. Ct. 2799,73 L.Ed. 2d 435 (1982).

Board of Education of Westside Community Schools v. Mergens, 496 U.S. 226, 110 S.Ct. 2356 (1990).

Bray, J. Lee, J., Smith, L. & Yorks, L. (2000). *Collaborative inquiry in practice: Action, reflection, and making meaning.* Thousand Oaks: CA: Sage.

Brownell v. Los Angeles Unified School District, 4 Cal.App.4th 787, 5 Cal. Rptr. 2d 756 (1992).

Bosher, W., Kamienski, K., Vacca, R. (2004). *The school law handbook: What every leader needs to know*. NY: Teachers College Press.

Chambers, Erve. (2003). Applied ethnography. In Denzin, N. and Lincoln, Y. (Eds.), *Collecting and interpreting qualitative materials* (pp. 389-418). Thousand Oaks, CA: Sage.

Davis v. Monroe County Board of Education, 120 F.3d. 1390, U.S. 629 (1999).

Denzin, N. (1998). *The research act*. New York: McGraw-Hill.

Donovan v. Punxsutawny Area School, 336 F.3d 211 (3rd Cir. 2003).

Education of All Handicapped Children Act of 1975 (PL-142).

Ellis, C. and Bochner, A. (2003). Autoethnography, personal narrative, reflexivity: Researcher as subject. In Denzin, N. and Lincoln, Y. (Eds.), *Collecting and interpreting qualitative materials* (pp. 199-258). Thousand Oaks, CA: Sage.

Engel v. Vitale, 370 U.S. 421, 82 S.Ct. 1261, 8Led.2nd601 (1962).

Ette v. Linn-Mar Community School District, 656, N.W. 2nd 62, S.Ct. (2002).

Fetterman, D. (1989). *Ethnography step by step*. Newbury Park, CA: Sage.

Glazer, M. & Strauss, A. (1967). *The discovery of grounded theory: Strategies for qualitative research*. Chicago: Aldine.

Hamel, J. (1993). Case study methods. Newbury Park, CA: Sage.

Hartmann v. Loudoun County Board of Education, 118 F.3rd 996 (4th Cir. 1997).

Hazelwood School District v. Kuhlmeier, 108 S.Ct. 562 (1982).

Killion v. Franklin Regional School District, 136 F. Supp. 2d 446 (2001).

Lee v. Weisman, 505 U.S. 577, 11 S.Ct. 2649 (1992).

Lightfoot, S. (1983). *The good high school.* New York: Basic Books.

McCormick v. Sch.District of Mamaroneck, 370 F.3d 275 (2nd Cir. 2004).

Merriam, S. (1988). *Case study research in education: A qualitative approach.* San Francisco: Jossey-Bass.

Mozert v. Hawkins County Board of Education, 527 F.2d 1058 (6th Cir.1987).

Nabozny v. Podlesny, 92 F. 3d 446 (7th Cir. 1996).

Nicholson v. Board of Education, Torrance County Unified School District, 682 F. 2nd 858 (9th Cir.1982).

New Jersey v. T.L.O, 469 U.S. 325, 105 S.Ct. 733, 83 L.Ed.2d 720 (1985).

No Child Left Behind Act. PL107-110-January 8, 2002, 115 STAT.1425.

Peshkin, A. (1986). *God's choice: The total world of a fundamentalist Christian school.* Chicago, IL: University of Chicago Press.

Rist, R. (2003). Influencing the policy process with qualitative research. In Denzin, N. and Lincoln, Y.(Eds.), *Collecting and interpreting qualitative materials*. Thousand Oaks, CA: Sage.

Rudestam, K., & Newton, R. (1992). Surviving your dissertation: A comprehensive guide to content and process. Newbury Park, CA: Sage.

Rossman, G. & Rallis, S. (2003*). Learning in the field: An introduction to qualitative research*. Thousand Oaks, CA: Sage Publications.

Santa Fe Independent School District V. Doe, 530 U.S. 290, 120 S.Ct. 2266 (2000).

Stake, R. (1988). Case study methods in educational research: Seeking sweet water. In R.M. Jaeger (Ed.), *Complementary methods: For research in education* (pp. 254-278). Washington, DC: American Educational Research Association.

Silverman, D. (2003). Analyzing talk and text. In Denzin, N. and Lincoln, Y.(Eds.), *Collecting and interpreting qualitative materials*. Thousand Oaks, CA: Sage.

Tinker v. Des Moines Independent Community School System, 393 U.S. 503, 89 S.Ct. 733 (1969).

Title IX Prohibition of Sex Discrimination of the Education Amendments of 1972, Pub. L. 92-318, 86 Stat. 373, 20 U.S.C. 1681 et seq.

Vernonia School District 47J v. Acton, 515 U.S. 646, 115 S. Ct. 2386, 132 L.Ed.2d 564 (1995).

Wallace v. Jaffree, 472 U.S. 38, 105 S.Ct. 2479, 86 L.Ed.2nd29 (1985).

Wallmuth v. Rapides Parish School Board, 813 So.2d 341, S.Ct. (2002).

Wolcott, H. (1988). Ethnographic research in education. In R.M. Jaeger (Ed.), *Complementary methods: For research in education* (pp.188-249). Washington, DC: American Educational Research Association.

Yin, R. (1989). Case study research: Design and methods. Newbury Park, CA: Sage.

Yin, R. (1993). *Applications of case study research*. Newbury Park, CA: Sage.

4 Quantitative Research Strategies

Grover H. Baldwin & John M. Ferron

Introduction

Imagine a researcher who uses a survey to measure the current attitudes of students concerning the *Lee v. Weisman* decision banning graduation prayer in public schools. Descriptive research, such as this, is commonly utilized in studies of educational law (Schimmel, 1996). Quantitative research also includes strategies, which go beyond description, to examine associations between variables (e.g., the correlation between the proportion of the community belonging to specified religious groups and the number of lawsuits over school prayer) and to study causes and effects (e.g., the impact a new policy has on the number of lawsuits filed).

This chapter shows how quantitative methods can study these issues, add to the findings, and build upon and share in the work of other research methodologies. The intent of this chapter is to provide individuals, particularly graduate students, with some ideas on how to use quantitative research methodology in the study of school law issues. Quantitative methodology does connect to other research methodologies, as detailed by the chapter by Kromrey, Onwuegbuzie, and Hogarty. For instance, data from a quantitative study may well provide information useful for triangulation as reviewed in Lee and Adler's chapter in this volume. Such support increases the power of the findings and substantiates the work of qualitative researchers. What is the connection between quantitative research methodology and school law? Where do the concepts, issues, questions, values, and concerns of school law "fit in" with the research methodology of education?

School law is about the relationships of people and organizations concerned with issues dealing with children in the enterprise we call education. Because it is a public enterprise for public schools, everyone who has been through education knows about it and has an opinion. Parents, taxpayers, teachers, administrators, siblings, the business community, and the students themselves are directly affected by decisions of policymaking bodies (the school boards) and the implementation of these policies (by administrators and teachers). Current issues of outcome-based education, school prayer, latchkey programs, inclusions of handicapped and gifted individuals in all classrooms, and violence in the schools, are all grist for the research mill as the various parties try to provide the best education possible for the students, the school districts, and the nation. For instance, why, and how, did a group of individuals from the community gain control over a district school board so that no grant for any additional funds to aid and improve the education of the children would be permitted to be filed until it had the approval of that special interest group? More importantly, what does such an action say about the democratic process and the fiduciary and legally mandated responsibilities of the school board when it allows its authority to be abrogated?

It is in these contexts, when the various players believe they are harmed or deprived, that school decisions end up as court cases. As a result, these individuals and groups challenge the system and seek to have their voices heard. Thus, conflicts arise between these affected individuals and the elected officials (school board members) and the school professionals who are charged with operating the system for the benefit of all students. These challenges, to the implementation of programs that would benefit the majority of students or that are in compliance with state and federal mandates, can diminish the effectiveness of education. The challenges also set new precedents for the operation and organization of schools.

There are two investigative strands that will be used in this chapter. The initial strand is the issue of First Amendment rights governing church/state relations, including the effects of *Lee v. Weisman* (1993), the graduation prayer case. This issue will be used in the first five research strategies. For the last two methods, decision trees and cost-benefit analysis, the issues surrounding search and seizure decisions will be the focal point. In both strands, there will be illustrative examples of how quantitative research methodology might be conceived and implemented.

Research into the issues, the ideas, and the various aspects of school law (including the people and groups that make up education) is important for those who lead the educational enterprises.

Quantitative research methods can provide a solid database upon which effective and rational decisions can be made and questions answered. Beyond this, quantitative methodology provides a framework that allows greater understanding of the parts and the whole of the system.

Key Elements

As in any research methodology, there are certain key elements that must be considered when conducting a study to assure that the results are not contaminated with bias and other confounding elements, i.e., when the researcher's own beliefs prejudice the findings. These key elements should guide the planning of research studies: (a) the conceptualization of the problem, (b) the research design, (c) the issues of internal and external validity, and (d) the appropriateness of the statistical analyses.

Conceptualization of the problem. The conceptualization of the problem, including the statement of the problem and the hypothesis, is critical for the researcher. The opening thrust of the study must clearly demonstrate that the researcher has a firm grasp of the issues involved, the variables that are under investigation, and the associations and relationships that can logically proceed from the general questions being asked by the study. The problem statement must clearly delineate these issues. For example, a problem is more than the annoyance caused by some students who want a space to read the Bible and pray before school. The problem is how to protect the rights of the students who want that activity and to protect the rights of students who do not want to participate nor want to feel that they are different or who might be coerced into such activity.

Hypotheses. A hypothesis is "a tentative, reasonable, testable explanation for the occurrence of certain behaviors, phenomenon, or events" (Gay. 1987. p. 545). There are two types of hypotheses: research and statistical. The research hypothesis states the expected relationship between two or more variables. For example, there is a relationship between the use of school prayer and the level of swearing by students in school. Since a study is based on a sample of students and schools, one can question whether an observed relationship was due to a true relationship between the two variables, or was simply a chance relationship due to the peculiarities of the sample that was selected. To differentiate between these two possibilities, researchers often state a statistical hypothesis. For this example, the null hypothesis would be that there is no relationship between the use of school prayer and the level of swearing by students in school. A statistical test could then be used to determine the probability of obtaining a relationship as large as the one obtained by chance. If this probability is small, say $p<.05$, the null hypothesis would be rejected, and the researcher would conclude there is a relationship between the two variables.

Research design. The research design is the way in which any study is conceived and conducted (Gay, 1987. pp. 81-88). For example, if the question under investigation involved the perceptions of the impact of school prayer decisions on school operations, then the researcher would have to decide which case decisions to use in the study and which individuals in the schools would be affected. The researcher might provide subjects a brief synopsis of each landmark school prayer decision and determine if there were any differences in perceptions of the impact of these decisions among school board members, school administrators, class advisers, teachers, or other school individuals likely to be directly affected by the decisions. A description of the research design lets the reader know how the researcher made the comparisons, examined the relationships, and assured that the data collected were accurate and unbiased.

As the researcher considers the various research strategies, it is suggested to use (a) a random selection of participants (i.e., by picking the individuals from a hat or using a table of random numbers) and (b) a random assignment of individuals to groups (i.e., picking the individuals from a hat and then randomly placing them in alternative piles until the groups are formed). Further, the use of control groups (testing people who are similar to those in the study, but who have not been affected by the study) to check against the possibility of contamination of the data is recommended.

Internal and external validity. Among the major concerns for quantitative researchers are the elements of internal and external validity. Internal validity addresses the questions that arise concerning the conduct of the study itself and the extent to which the study is reproducible (can be duplicated) with similar results being expected. This element deals with the extent to which the independent, dependent, and extraneous variables are "controlled by the researcher so that the observed changes in the dependent variable are due to the treatment and not an extraneous variable" (Borg & Gall, 1983, p. 634). The researcher must demonstrate control over the variables that may interfere with the interaction of the independent and dependent variables.

The *independent variable* is the one that affects (or is assumed to affect) the dependent variable under study and is included in the research design so that its effect can be determined (Wiersma, 1995, p. 35). Such variables may include the location of school districts (urban, suburban, rural), the size of school districts (small, medium, large), the socioeconomic status of school districts (lower, middle, upper class), the roles of individuals (teacher, principal, superintendent, school board member), and the like.

Dependent variables are defined as "the variable being affected or assumed to be affected by the independent variable" (Wiersma, 1995, p. 465). Examples of dependent variables might include attitudes, perceptions, actions, or policy changes of school districts.

Extraneous variables are those things, other than independent and dependent variables, that might affect the outcome of the study due to lack of control. Extraneous variables might include decision-making processes in school districts, the climate of the district, the status of the budget and tax rates as these might influence the attitudes, and perceptions and beliefs of individuals responding to some question of change in district policy.

External validity. External validity addresses questions as to the value of the findings to the larger or different groups. The researcher should confirm that the findings are applicable to specific and larger groups other than those used in the study. Here, such things as population and ecological validity are key elements. (The reader is encouraged to see the Bracht and Glass, 1968, article.) This includes whether the respondents accurately represent the larger population on such items as age, sex, race, etc., a complete description of all procedures, and an accounting for the Hawthorne Effect (i.e., just being in the study may increase the individual's sense of importance and thus change the study's results) to name just a few. (For a more detailed explanation of internal and external validity, the reader might consider the works of Borg and Gall, 1989, Bracht and Glass, 1968, Campbell and Stanley, 1968, and Shadish, Cook, and Campbell, 2002).

Statistical analysis. The issues involved in the statistical analysis call for the researcher to assure that the most appropriate analytic techniques are used and that the appropriate level of significance was established when designing the study. While specific examples will be provided within each of the research strategies that are reviewed, for detailed examination of these issues, the reader is guided to *Reasoning with Statistics* as noted in the references (Williams, 1992).

Access to the data set is one limitation that all quantitative studies in school law must address. As those who are familiar with the workings of the legal system and the courts well know, many cases do not reach the courts but are settled within the administrative structures of the school boards using their quasi-judicial functions. Further, there are many cases that are decided by the courts at various levels that are not recorded. There are many reasons for these actions, but the result is that the researcher does not have access to the total data set. This limits the ability to generalize to the entire universe of education and the impact of decisions on education. However, even recognizing these limitations, the researcher does provide a benchmark, a starting point, for further exploration and examination of the issues involved in providing education.

In all the key elements, it is a question of balance. The researcher must address each of the areas and devise the best solution, or at least the solution that maintains the most credibility, before conducting the research.

A Journey Through Research Strategies

What follows are specific examples of the various quantitative strategies. Each strategy follows traditional quantitative methodology procedures. Each begins with an introduction, a statement of a problem, a brief synopsis of what a review of literature might deal with, the research design and methodology, and the statistical analysis procedures (where appropriate). The strategies presented are not the only ones that could be devised, but rather show some possibilities for those interested in school law research. While the research methods flow from historical to quasi-experimental, the researcher may begin the research process with any of these strategies. There is no presumption, nor necessity, to move from historical to descriptive to correlation, causal-comparative, and quasi-experimental in a linear fashion to plan and conduct research.

All research studies begin with a question about relationships between things. These are the "what if" questions that raise the level of consciousness and pervade the search for knowledge. For example, one question might address what factors affect the provision for student bible-reading and prayer groups in school. Questions constitute the key element that dictates the use of sound quantitative research. They lead to the exploration of specific independent variables (things that affect outcomes) that affect the dependent variables (the desired outcomes). Flowing from the question listed above, the independent variable might be how the success of those who want to have religion in the schools is changing school policy by the school board. The dependent variable would be the number of policy decisions by school boards that agree or disagree with the demands of those seeking prayer and Bible reading in the schools. These relationships are explored under careful conditions so that the results will yield useful knowledge and provide baseline data on the issues involved.

Research Strategy #1: Studies of the Past

Where do the research "questions" come from? Researchers might look to the past to see what has occurred. This leads to a historical strategy that examines documents, diaries, letters, oral history, and case law to determine what went on in the past. This database allows quantitative researchers to make connections between variables (accuracy and age of the documents) without the danger of contaminating the field of study with extraneous and irrelevant variables (what the writer had for lunch or dinner). One example might be a review of case decisions concerning student challenges to the policies and practices of school officials regarding their request for Bible study/prayer groups in schools and the court's reasoning in their decisions on these issues.

Within this strategy of historical research, the simple box scoring of decisions is one means to quantify the numerical data. Below is an example of the "planning" process that might occur for such a study.

Introduction

There appears to be a rise in the concern for the moral fiber of the United States that is sweeping the country today. Expressions of concern by various members of society—clergy, politicians, parents, taxpayers—focus on the rising levels of crime, violence, drugs, teen pregnancy, AIDS, welfare costs, and a host of other social ills viewed as prevalent in society today. Various groups have set themselves up as "moral watchdogs" of these growing trends. Blame has been laid at a variety of doorsteps: the government, families, churches, kids in general, and the schools. Time and again, there are calls for a return to school prayer and religious/moral teachings in schools so that "our children" will grow up right. The dilemma facing school personnel is the tradition of separation of church and state begun in *Everson v. Board of Education* (1947) and continuing through the *Lee v. Weisman* decision. Just what is the court history concerning this separation of church and state, and what might be the guiding principles the school administrator might glean from the Supreme Court's decisions?

Statement of the Problem

The historical study proposed here examines the history of decisions concerning separation of church and state, particularly as they pertain to the schools, via the resulting court challenges at the Supreme Court level within a set time period. Specifically, by decades of Supreme Court decisions, the study traces the win/loss ratio in separation of church and state cases and the reasons for the success or failure of the lawsuits. The hypothesis for this study might be that there are no significant differences between decades of Supreme Court decisions and the rationale used to decide the cases (e.g., the child benefit theory versus the parochial school benefit theory).

Review of Related Literature

Here, the researcher would examine the legal history of litigant challenges and defendant appeals, the courts' varying interpretations of the separation of church and state under the First Amendment, and the precedents that might be useful to support or deny school district approaches to religious activities in the schools. Issues such as Bible reading, religious dress, moments of silence, state-established or student-initiated prayer, invocations/benedictions, and parochial aid come to mind as a beginning place for a theoretical foundation of the study.

Research Design and Methodology

The research design for this proposed study is that of a simple box score approach to the positions of the courts on the issues of church/state relations. All the major church/state relationship decisions would be identified from the first major decision (as determined by the researcher) through 1973 or another significant date. The case decisions might be divided into various categories:

by the win/loss record, by court reporting area, by types of issues, by decades, etc. A frequency count is prepared for each of these categories and reported in a lengthy table similar to the one that follows.

Table 1
Tabulation of Court Decision

	1850-1875		1876-1900		1901-1925		1926-1956		1957-1975	
Court Reporter	Win	Lose	Win	Lose	Win	Lose	Win	Lose	Win	Lose
Atlantic	5	1	2	4	6	5	3	4	3	3
Northeast	4	3	5	1	4	2	2	4	2	5

Statistical Analysis

This tabulation of data can be used in analytic reports. The researcher could provide analysis of decade by decade across circuit courts, decade by decade within each circuit, by issues by decade across and within circuit court areas, and each decade individually across circuit courts. The data could be treated by a chi-square analysis that measures frequency of responses by category (i.e., how many cases fall within each of the win/loss columns for each of the case law reporters) and could produce significant/nonsignificant differences across and between the categories. In order to provide accurate data analysis, each of the "boxes" should be expected to have a minimum of five observations. If the researcher found that there were less than five responses expected in each box, then the researcher could collapse similar categories, or in the example in Table 1 above, group by larger periods of time, e.g., a fifty year period.

An alternative analysis strategy would be to conceptualize the outcome of the case as a dichotomous dependent variable (win versus lose). Logistic regression (e.g., Hosmer, 2000) could then be used to test whether the odds of a case being won varied as a function of the year of the decision. More complex models could then be considered by including additional variables, such as the reporting area of the court, and the type of issue being considered. One may find, for example, that the odds of winning changed over time and that the degree to which the odds of winning changed over time depended on the type of issue being considered.

The results of such a study would yield a careful delineation of the issues involved in church/state relations and the parameters within which school officials might begin to develop an approach to school religious activities. For example, the results would also point to major areas of concern and conflict within the decisions and the tensions between the culture and courts at various times in history.

Research Strategy #2: Studies of Current Conditions

The most common quantitative research methodology is descriptive research (Schimmel, 1996). Here, the researcher examines the current status of some condition or phenomenon. For instance, the researcher might be concerned with the attitudes of students concerning the *Lee v. Weisman* decision banning graduation prayer in public schools. These studies are useful as a benchmark, or set of base data, for future reference and provide a platform for other quantitative methodologies. The results of these studies do not predict what the various courts will do next but provide a backdrop against which local school decisions can be made. Descriptive research illustrates what the current conditions are and opens the inquisitive door to other questions of how and why.

Introduction and Review of Related Literature

In this example, the introduction and review of related literature deals with a historical review of the policy changes, court decisions and responses to the change in graduation prayer in schools, and the background of church/state prayer and Bible reading in the schools. The researcher would have to review the opinions and articles about each of the landmark case decisions dealing with religion in the schools. Then, the researcher ascertains how, and in what direction, attitudes might have changed. This latter part is important as it provides a guide to the development of a questionnaire, or interview protocol, which the researcher might use to determine the current state of attitudes regarding the *Weisman* decision.

Statement of the Problem

The statement of the problem might be expressed as follows: With the 1993 Supreme Court decision concerning the ban on the use of prayer at public school graduations, this study seeks to determine the current attitudes of students concerning the banning of prayer at school graduations. The hypothesis for this study would be that there is no difference in the attitudes of various groups of students with respect to the banning of prayer at school graduation exercises.

Research Design and Methodology

The research design and methodology for this study might entail the use of a survey or, if the groups were small enough, a structured interview to gather the data. The researcher would review the points of law and decision points found in *Weisman*, and construct the survey or interview instrument that would address these issues. Instrument development tends to be a multistage process, where data are gathered to refine the instrument and bolster arguments regarding the reliability and validity of inferences made from the resulting data. One may wish to show that experts agree that the items do address the issues over which individuals would have developed specific positions and that the attitude scores are temporally stable (i.e., an individual's attitude measured today does not differ notably from the attitude measured a week ago). The process of developing instruments and gathering data for reliability and validity arguments can be complex and has been presented in detail elsewhere (e.g., Crocker & Algina, 1986; Moss, 1992).

In addition to constructing the survey, the researcher would construct a sampling plan. The researcher would define the various groups in terms of race, gender, religious background, section of the state, or whatever criteria might be useful, and devise a sampling plan that would lead to obtaining a representative sample from each group, as well as a large enough sample from each group to support the planned statistical analyses. For instance, the researcher might use the local high school graduating class in various regions of the state in which the researcher lived. After constructing a list of all the high schools, the researcher would randomly select a sample of the high schools in each of the regions. Then, the researcher might randomly select a smaller sample of the graduating seniors from each of the selected high schools that represented the larger population. This form of sampling would be referred to as cluster sampling. Fink (2003) provides details on a variety of sampling strategies. In addition to determining the method of sampling, the researcher would determine the sample size. Power analysis (Cohen,

1992; Murphy & Myors, 1998) is often used to determine sample size. This approach finds the number of observations needed to ensure the researcher has a reasonable chance of detecting differences that may exist between groups.

Following the delineation of the sampling plan, the researcher would "issue" the survey to the students and ask for their responses to the items. The researcher would carefully track the response rate and determine whether follow-up procedures were needed to raise the response rate. After the surveys were returned, the researcher would initially screen the data to determine the extent to which those who responded were representative of the population that was sampled, or systematically different from those who did not respond. The researcher would then compile the results and analyze them for the attitudes held by the students toward the banning of prayer at graduation. This analysis could aggregate the data by race, gender, religious background, region of the state, or the other variables that the researcher found that might lead to differences.

Statistical Analysis

Initially the researcher would analyze the data to determine the number and nature of the attitudinal variables underlying the responses to the survey items. If a single latent variable is adequate for explaining the responses, the researcher may combine items from the survey to create a global attitude measure. If attitudes are found to be multidimensional, the researcher will likely create scales to represent each of the attitudinal dimensions. This initial work is often carried out using factor analysis (e.g., Fabrigar, Wegener, MacCallum, & Strahan, 1999; Gorsuch, 1983). The researcher would then construct the attitudinal variable (or variables), estimate reliability by computing the internal consistency (Cronbach, 1951), and describe the distribution of attitude scores for each group. To make inferences about the mean attitude scores in the population, the researcher would construct a confidence interval, which would produce an interval that is likely to contain the population mean for a specific group.

A researcher may also wish to examine differences among groups. Where there are two categories of an independent variable (i.e., gender: male or female), the t-test for independent samples might be used. A t-test is a comparison of the averages of two groups, i.e., males/ females, urban/rural, Protestant/Catholic. Where there are three or more categories of a variable (i.e. race: Caucasian, African-American, Oriental, Native-American), an analysis of variance, which allows for comparison of three or more groups, would be used. These analyses could be conducted on a global measure of attitude or on each attitudinal dimension. If multiple attitudinal dimensions were being considered, an alternative would be to turn to a multivariate analysis of variance (e.g., Bray & Maxwell, 1982; Stevens, 2002), which allows group differences to be explored for a set of outcome measures.

The results would point to specific attitudes and beliefs that would be important for further study. For example, if the data analysis indicated significant differences in the attitudes over the banning of school prayer at graduation by gender, race, religious background, or section of the state, then the researcher might use that data to build additional research studies that would examine these factors more closely.

Research Strategy #3: Studies of Relationships

A third quantitative research methodology is that of correlation studies that begin to examine the strength of relationships between two or more variables. Variables of interest could be drawn from the historical and descriptive studies and placed in juxtaposition to test their association to one another. This could mean an examination of the relationship between a court decision banning prayer in schools and the variables of "religiosity" of various segments of society in upholding the ban on prayer in schools. The segments could also be separated into religious groups, parts of the country, or some other significant variable found to influence prayer in schools.

The correlation research may uncover a positive relationship, a negative (inverse) relationship, or no relationship between the variables. In demonstrating the difference of these relationships, we will assume that the ban on graduation prayer is in effect. As an example of a positive relationship, we might find that when specific groups of religions are equally represented that the ban on graduation prayer tends to be upheld. Thus, high levels of religious balance correspond with high levels of ban adherence. For a negative relationship, we might find that when certain religious groups are present in the community, there tends to be a denial of the court's ban and graduation prayers are used. Thus, a high proportion of community membership in a particular denomination corresponds with a low level of ban adherence. Lastly, a finding of no relationship might indicate that the presence of certain religious groups and the degree of religious balance does not alter the likelihood that the ban on graduation prayer will be upheld. The results of the study would state the relationship between the variables and the strength of those associations.

Continuing the example of school graduation prayer, certain religious groups might be thought to have a propensity to sue school districts that fail to provide opportunities for children to pray at graduation. Thus, one may hypothesize a strong positive relationship between the proportion of the community belonging to these religious groups and the number of lawsuits over school prayer.

Introduction

The researcher begins by looking for emerging patterns regarding the issues, the plaintiff/defendant groups, and other variables that impact on both lawsuits and decisions. As indicated above, relationships can be a key element in providing guidance to school personnel in school prayer issues. Variables such as location (rural, suburban, or urban), intensity of religious activity, political culture as set forth by Elazar (1973), socioeconomic grouping, ethnic and religious makeup of the community, and school district policies and past practices may all have a profound impact on the attitudes and practices of school districts. The extent of the relationships may provide guidance to similar districts and administrative personnel who face school prayer/religious issues, i.e., whether to have graduation prayer, whether to permit student-initiated prayer, what to do about the peer relationships that are created by the exclusivity of prayer groups. Yet, the strength of the relationship between and among these variables is unknown. This is why the researcher seeks to determine the strength and the direction of that relationship.

Statement of the Problem

This study examines the relationship of the variables of location (rural, suburban, or urban), intensity of religious activity, political culture, socioeconomic grouping, ethnic and religious makeup of the community, and attitudes and school district policies on the issue of school prayer.

The hypotheses for this study include separate statements of relationships between the variables under consideration and the court decisions. For example, there is no relationship between the location of a school district (rural, suburban, or urban) and the school district policies on the issue of school prayers.

Research Design and Methodology

The research design for this study calls for a careful examination of the potential variables and their relationship to the policies of the local school boards. These variables include the independent variables of location, intensity of religious activity, political culture, socioeconomic grouping, ethnic and religious makeup of the community, and the dependent variables of the school district's policies and attitudes regarding prayer at school. The researcher then selects the group to be surveyed, designs a sampling plan, constructs the survey, and collects the data much like the procedures used in descriptive research.

Statistical Analysis

The statistical analysis for a correlation study seeks to point out the strength and direction of relationships between the independent and dependent variables. As previously mentioned, a variety of statistical analyses may be applied. For a pair of continuous variables, one may use Pearson's product moment correlation (e.g., intensity of religious activity and attitudes regarding prayer at school). For a situation where one of the variables is dichotomous (e.g., whether or not prayer bands have been upheld) and another is continuous (e.g., intensity of religious activity), a point-biserial correlation could be used. When the variables are rank ordered, the Spearman rank correlation may be used to index relationship (e.g., socioeconomic status of the communities and the level to which prayer bands have been upheld). It is also possible to look at the relationships among more than two variables at a time. For example, multiple regression (Pedhazur, 1997) could be used to examine relationships among two or more independent variables (e.g., location, religious activity, political culture, socioeconomic grouping, ethnic and religious makeup of the community) and a continuous dependent variable (e.g., attitude about prayer at school). Logistic regression could be used to examine relationships among independent variables and a binary dependent variable (e.g., whether or not the ban on school prayer had been upheld). For more complex patterns of relationships, one may use structural equation modeling (e.g., Bollen, 1989; Raykov & Marcoulides, 2000). For example, one may be interested in the relationship of multiple variables (e.g., religious activity, political culture, religious makeup of the community) with other variables (e.g., attitudes in the community about prayer at school) that in turn relate to other variables (e.g., amount of court cases filed, and the how frequently bans on school prayer are upheld).

A key element for the researcher is to determine the viability of different statistical methods for examining relationships among variables and to select the most appropriate. A good source for that decision is found in *Reasoning with Statistics* (Williams, 1992). The analysis will often produce a measure of association, which falls between –1.0 (perfect negative relationship) and +1.0 (perfect positive relationship). A zero would indicate no relationship between the variables. The researcher typically hopes that the association is strong (i.e., close to the ends of the scale), but a low correlation of +/- .10 or .20 may be statistically significant and warrant concluding that a relationship exists. Yet, merely accepting or rejecting the hypothesis is not enough. The researcher also must address the level of practical significance of the findings (Robinson & Levin, 1997; Thompson, 1993). The coefficient of correlation (.20 in our example) is a "mathematical way of expressing the degree to which the variables relate to one another and not an indication of the degree to which the variables share some common characteristics" (McMillan & Schumacher, 1984, p. 197). The degree of shared characteristics is found by squaring the coefficient of correlation (in our case, .20 squared equals .04). Here, if the researcher found a statistically significant relationship of .20 between intensity of religious activity and attitudes regarding prayer at school, the researcher could state that 4 percent of the variation in attitudes is associated with variation in the intensity of religious activity. While the .20 correlation may be statistically significant, in a practical sense the researcher might well look elsewhere to determine the reasons for attitudes regarding school prayer as 96 percent of the variation may be explained by other variables. If the researcher finds both statistical and practical significance between the variables, then the researcher could move to a deeper exploration of this specific variable. This is a key element to moving to the following two strategies of traditional educational research.

Research Strategy #4: Studies of What Has Occurred

Once the researcher has established the relationship between independent variables and dependent variables, the researcher might use this data to fashion a research study using causal-comparative methodology. Here, the researcher studies differences among groups in an attempt to determine the causes for the differences. By carefully selecting and simultaneously examining multiple independent variables, the researcher can look at the effect of one variable while holding the other relevant independent variables constant. For example, in dealing with graduation prayer in the schools, the researcher may want to address the question of the effect of pastoral, ministerial, or rabbinical influence on issues of school prayer. Do pastors, ministers, or rabbis of specific religious denominations lead the challenges to school prayer? Do these individuals follow their parishioners' wishes and create the challenges? Or, is there some other variable at work that interferes with the first two variables, such as the national movement that is challenging outcome-based education that affects the local policies on school prayer, even if graduation prayer is unrelated to outcome-based education? It should be noted that, although there is a clear intention on the researcher's part to move toward causal explanations, this type of research is another type of non-experimental research (i.e., the researcher does not manipulate the independent variables in any way). Consequently, it has much in common with the descriptive and correlation strategies previously discussed (see Johnson, 2001, for elaboration on this point), and effect inferences are very limited.

Introduction

Over the past decade, various state and federal courts have rendered decisions concerning various aspects of school policies within the church/state debate. For example, let us assume that location (rural, suburban, and urban), political culture (moralistic, traditionalistic, and individualistic), and religious denominations are found to have very strong relationships regarding school prayer in the correlation study outlined above. Using a causal-comparative methodology, the researcher might examine the effects of these variables on school prayer decisions and policy developments in the school districts.

Statement of the Problem

This study examines the effects of the location, political culture, and religious denominations on the "implementers" of policy as specified by Johnson and Canon (1984). There are several hypotheses for this study. First, there is no significant difference between the location of the school district and the school prayer policies of the district. Second, there is no significant difference between the political culture of the school district and the school prayer policies of the district. Third, there is no significant difference between the types of religious denominations in the school district and the school prayer policies of the district. Fourth, there is no significant interaction between the variables of location, political culture, and religious denominations within school districts and school prayer policies of the district.

Review of Related Literature

In this scenario, the researcher would review a body of related literature dealing with the establishment of the school officials as implementers of policy as distinct from the school board members who make the policy. This would follow the basic structure established by Johnson and Canon (1984) in their work, *Judicial Policies: Implementation and Impact.*

The researcher must provide a detailed description of each of the independent variables (location, political culture, and type of religious denominations), what they are, why they are the key independent variables, and how they are expected to impact school districts. The specifics of these variables might include location (by regions of the country), political culture (individualistic, moralistic, traditionalistic) (Elazar, 1973), and type of religious denominations (Lutheran, Baptist, Methodist. etc.).

Research Design and Methodology

This research strategy calls for causal-comparative methodology. We now have established the independent variables (location, political culture, and religious denominations) that can operate on a dependent variable (school prayer policies). The researcher develops a procedure for obtaining location, political culture, religious denominations, and the school prayer policies within a district. The researcher could develop a survey, examine documents, conduct interviews, or use some combination of these methods. The researcher will also need to develop a method for quantifying the information on school policies. Can a single variable be created that indicates the degree to which the district policies allow for school prayer? Or do several variables need to be developed to capture the policy differences among school districts? As with other research designs, the researcher will need to pilot test and gather data to construct arguments regarding the reliability and validity of inferences made from the resulting data.

This study could be conducted at the state or national level, though the national level would open up greater options for the researcher. As with other research designs, a sampling plan must be developed. For instance, the researcher could stratify by state and then randomly select within each state. This stratified random sampling would ensure all states were represented. Fink (2003) provides details on a variety of other sampling strategies that may be useful. With the sampling plan and procedures in place, the researcher would be ready to collect, compile, and submit the data for statistical analysis.

Statistical Analysis

For each school district, a score on the policy variable (or variables) would need to be determined. Each district would also be classified by location (region of the country), political culture (individualistic, moralistic, traditionalistic), and religious denomination profile (primarily Lutheran, primarily Baptist, religiously balanced, etc.). Groups of school districts would be made that had the same location, political culture, and religious denomination profile. For each group, the distribution of values on the policy variable(s) would be examined, and an average score would be computed. Differences among group averages could then be analyzed using the three-way analysis of variance (e.g., Stevens, 1999) with the independent variables being location, political culture and religious denomination profile. The dependent variable would be the policy variable. If there were multiple policy variables, a three-way multivariate analysis of variance could be used (e.g., Stevens, 2002). These analyses may reveal that, after controlling location and political culture, there tends to be differences in policies depending on the religious denomination profile of the community (i.e., a main effect for denomination), and that the size of these differences depends on the political culture (i.e., an interaction between denomination and political culture). Follow-up analyses (e.g., Stevens, 1999, 2002) could be used to examine which denomination profiles led to policies that differed, where this analysis could be done separately for each type of political culture. The results of this study would point to potential causal relationships between the variables that would lend themselves to further examination.

Research Strategy #5: Studies That Disclose Differences

The fifth research strategy addresses the cause-effect relationships between independent and dependent variables. This endeavor leads to the use of either experimental or quasi-experimental research strategies. The distinction between these two strategies lies in the degree of control of the independent variables. Experimental strategies use random assignment of individuals within the study to the levels of the independent variable (e.g., the experimental or control group). Quasi-experimental strategies typically are not able to use random assignment due to the use of intact groups (such as intact classrooms or intact school boards) (Gay, 1989). While quasi-experimental strategies do not allow for the level of control as found in true experimental strategies, there are specific designs that provide adequate control of potential sources of invalidity that still allow for the examination of questions of cause and effect (Gay, 1987, p. 289). The primary means of controlling this potential invalidity are the use of matching criteria for the selection of the individuals or groups, or the use of analysis of covariance as a means to statistically adjust for initial differences among the groups.

Once the researcher has the sense of what specific independent variables affect the dependent variables (in our case, graduation prayer), a study can be designed that will examine the cause-effect relationship between the independent and dependent variables. For instance, in the example we will use below, there are two general groups in the population: those school districts that had policies preventing the use of graduation prayer before the *Weisman* decision and those school districts who established policies banning graduation prayer after the *Weisman* decision. The districts to be tested might be randomly drawn from each of these groups as they do represent different mindsets regarding graduation prayer. However, as they cannot be randomly assigned, the use of a quasi-experimental design is appropriate. There are many types of quasi-experimental designs that a researcher might use in this study. The reader is referred to volumes by Campbell and Stanley

(1968); Cates (1986); or Shadish, Cook, and Campbell (2002) for a detailed explanation of the specific research designs and the drawbacks of each design.

In planning the study, the researcher would first isolate the independent variable. Then, the researcher selects the school districts from the different groups (perhaps done randomly) and manipulates some condition to determine its effect on the dependent variable. In addressing the issues of *Weisman*, the astute school law researcher might have had an inkling of the direction of the Supreme Court as the dynamics of the court had changed and the challenge brought by *Weisman* seemed to be addressing a particular concern of society as shaped by the politics of the nation. Many school law researchers do follow the trends of the court and are aware of potential changes in the court's direction. Thus, for our example, assuming the researcher anticipated a change in school prayer policy and assuming a lead-time of one year before the implementation of a policy that eliminated school prayer from graduation exercises, what might this quasi-experimental study look like?

Introduction

School prayer is an issue that pervades school districts at several junctures during the school year, but particularly at graduation. For many years, school districts across the nation have allowed, encouraged, or arranged invocations and benedictions at graduation ceremonies regardless of the religious makeup of the community or the audience. With the *Lee v. Weisman* decision, what effect would such action create on the part of the public and the graduating class? In the year following the *Weisman* decision, there were attempts to circumvent the decision by school district personnel, by parents, and by students. Some of the reactions to the *Weisman* decision are illustrated by reports of behavior on the part of the valedictorian of the graduating class who sneezed at the end of the address, with the resulting action of the entire class standing and in unison saying, "God Bless You," to districts allowing student-led prayer after being voted on by the graduating class. In other districts, the decision in *Weisman* had no effect on attitudes as policies prohibiting school prayer had been in effect for some time.

Statement of the Problem

This study examines the attitudes of parents and students where, due to *Weisman*, the use of graduation prayer had been eliminated.

The hypothesis for this study is that there is no significant difference between the attitudes of parents and students in school districts that permitted, and in school districts that did not permit, school prayer in 1992, following the 1993 *Weisman* decision eliminating school prayer at graduation ceremonies.

Review of Related Literature

The review of related literature would deal with the background of school prayer issues in education, a review of the case law regarding school prayer, and a review of the policies that districts had in effect. Attitudes toward religious and school prayer issues on the part of various groups—parents, students, staff, administrators, religious leaders—would be reviewed to form a basis on which to derive the expected attitudes toward the elimination of school prayer at graduation.

Research Design and Methodology

In this study, the researcher might use a nonequivalent control group design with random selection of respondents within each of the two categories. The categories are the pre-existing condition of policies and practices permitting, or not permitting, school prayer in the school districts. This research design is one of the most frequently used in educational research due to the fact that the researcher has "intact groups that would make it impractical to randomize or where educational officials would be unreceptive to the demands of randomization" (Cates, 1985, p. 78). The design would look like that found in Figure 1 below.

Figure 1.
Nonequivalent Control Group Research Design

Random Selection	Pre-Condition	Pre-Test	Intervention (*Weisman*)	Post-Test
District Permitting Graduation Prayer Prior to *Weisman*	School Prayer 1992	X	No School Prayer 1993	X
Districts Not Permitting Graduation Prayer Prior to *Weisman*	No School Prayer 1992	X	No School Prayer 1993	X

For this example, we also assume that the researcher anticipated the potential change in school prayer by the Supreme Court and gathered pretest data from high school juniors and their parents in the year prior to the *Weisman* decision. This is not an unusual occurrence for those interested in school law research who are cognizant of the activities and potential trends of the courts.

The independent variables would be whether the districts permitted graduation prayer prior to *Weisman* and the various groups in the school districts (students and parents). The dependent variable would be the attitudes espoused and exhibited by the respondents. The researcher would first list those districts, by state or region, that had a policy permitting school prayer at graduation and those that had a policy prohibiting school prayer at graduation prior to 1992. From this list, the researcher would randomly select districts of similar size, location, and other controlling variables, selecting an equal number of districts that were as equivalent as possible from each of the two categories. Once that was completed, the researcher would arrange lists of current students due to graduate the following year. From that list, the researcher would randomly select students (and their parents) for inclusion within the study.

The researcher would devise a survey instrument, pilot test the survey, and assure validity and reliability. Then, in 1992, the year preceding implementation of *Weisman*, the researcher would visit these school districts immediately following the graduation ceremony, administer the survey, and gather data on attitudes of students and parents in school districts that did and did not have prayer at graduation. This would entail gathering survey information from the individuals within the groups listed above. This would be the pretest portion of the study.

The intervention of the *Weisman* decision in 1993 would be expected to change the attitudes of these individuals in those districts that are now faced with eliminating prayer at graduation. The researcher would visit the same school districts and individuals in 1993 at the graduation ceremony and gather survey information concerning the attitudes from the same groups and individuals (students and parents) regarding the lack of prayer at graduation. This is the posttest portion of the research study.

Statistical Analysis

The researcher would compile the data from the surveys, both pre and post. Attitudinal variable(s) would be made, averages would be calculated, and appropriate statistical tests would be applied. In this example, inclusion of the pretest attitudes as a covariate would be appropriate to account for initial differences of the nonequivalent groups. More specifically, the statistical analysis would examine the effects of the intervention (implementation of *Weisman*) on attitudes, after controlling for 1992 initial attitudes. Interest in both student and parent attitudes leads to some choices in the statistical modeling. If there were no way to link the information of students to parents, the respondent group would simply become another predictor of the dependent variable attitudes. If one could link students with their parents, one could capitalize on the possible interrelationships. One alternative would be to use a hierarchical modeling strategy (Raudenbush & Bryk, 2002), where the nesting of students and parents within families, and the nesting of families within schools, could be explicitly modeled. The findings of the study would reveal differences between the experimental (the districts that changed their policy in response to *Weisman*) and control group (the districts that prohibited prayer even before *Weisman*). With these results, the researcher could further study whether the attitudinal effects of the *Weisman* decision were the same for students and for parents.

Alternative Quantitative Methods

Beyond the standard educational research methodologies, a researcher might consider the development of a research strand, using management science techniques. These methodologies allow for the merging of several areas and permit the researcher to produce a useful model or series of suggested guidelines for both school administrators and policymakers to develop both policies and plans of action. The techniques proposed here are decision-tree modeling and cost-benefit analysis. Due to the nature of these techniques, the examples used will be issues of search and seizure in the schools.

Research Strategy #6: Decision Theory and Decision Trees for Practitioners

The decision-tree methodology is explained by Anderson, Sweeny, and Williams (1983). Decision trees are a subsets of decision theory that allow for the "determination of optimal strategies for use when a decision maker is faced with several decision alternatives and an uncertain or risk-filled pattern of future events" (Anderson, Sweeny, & Williams, 1983. p. 414). What might be more fraught with risk than improper search and seizure procedures and decisions by school officials? Think of the possibilities of risk involving a bomb threat to a school of 2,000 pupils. Do we get the students out of school or not? Do we search all, some, or none of the lockers of the school? How do we account for the variable of time between the call and the alleged detonation time? Who should do the search—school officials, police or fire department personnel—and under what conditions? Having been personally involved in these activities, there are several decision points and alternatives that must be considered.

Introduction to the Problem

Over the past two decades, there have been many court decisions regarding search and seizure actions of school officials. These court decisions have yielded specific guidelines for the conduct of searches. However, while these decisions have given us guiding principles to follow, there are a number of practical decision points and alternatives that must be considered by each school administrator when contemplating a school search. These decision points include the legal aspects of searches as well as (for lack of better terms) the ethical, moral, and administrative decision points. Just what alternatives do administrators use, and what alternatives should they consider in contemplating and carrying out a search of lockers, student property, student persons, and the school? This study examines the legal and administrative decision points and builds a set of decision theories useful to school administrators in the conduct of searches within schools.

Review of Related Literature

The review of literature would contain the standard legal guidelines found within the court decisions that allow for, and prohibit, certain actions while conducting a search within a school. In addition, the literature search would review the nature of decision theory, the nature and extent of probability theory usage where there is uncertainty, and the best way to determine the appropriate levels of probability. Further, the review of related literature would deal with the actions reported in the literature (and court decisions) that administrators took under various search conditions.

Research Design and Methodology

The research design for this strategy could best be described as a blend of descriptive, correlational, and causal-comparative methods, using educational research parlance. First, it is suggested that the researcher develop a decision theory scenario that would include the various aspects of the decision confronting the administrators. The researcher would have to describe the conditions of the search, the alternatives that face the school administrator, and the consequences (in probability terms) of each action. This would entail the researcher producing a decision tree, acquainting practitioners with the notion of decision theory, and surveying administrators for the actions they would take under each scenario and why they would act as they did. The researcher would glean the decision strategies used by these experts, redesign the scenario, recalculate the probabilities, and reduce the scenario to the single best based on the results. The researcher could then submit the final decision tree to practitioners in the field and reach a consensus on the best set of alternatives for each scenario.

The example in Figure 2, which is a decision tree over the issues involved in search and seizure, may help clarify the planning that goes into the construction of a decision tree. The decision to be reached is whether or not to conduct a search and the probability of success if the search is conducted. The square represents the starting point: to conduct the search or not. The diamonds, marked "Yes" and "No", are the initial decision points. If the decision is to conduct the search, then the three aspects (for this example) of where to conduct the search (randomly, selectively, or all); the time needed or devoted to the search (less than ten minutes, between ten and twenty minutes, or greater than twenty minutes); and the cost in terms of salary, public relations, good will, and inconvenience of students (low cost, medium cost, or high cost) must be considered. The researcher would hypothetically establish the parameters for these aspects and label them. The researcher then needs to consider the probability (marked by the specific criteria in the diagram) for success in finding the contraband (the "High" or "Low").

To interpret and to choose the appropriate strategy to use in this search and seizure example, both the practitioner and the researcher examine the place to search, the time it would to take to conduct the search, and the cost of that search to choose the best approach that fits their situation. For example, in order to reach the 90 percent chance of finding the contraband, the search would include all locations, take more than twenty minutes, and would cost the most. To search all the lockers would yield a 90 percent chance of finding the contraband. However, the time to conduct the search to reach the 90 percent chance of finding the contraband would be in excess of twenty minutes and disrupt the school day, the students, and the educational process. Also, the cost of the search (time of salary, public relations, good will within the community) would be high to reach the 90 percent chance of finding the contraband. While this might be the ideal solution if past successes yield promise of future success, there might be other, more suitable solutions. For instance, using a selective search, with a ten to twenty minute time span, and using only administrators (for salary cost purposes), the chance of finding the contraband drops to 60 percent. Yet, given the selective nature of the search and the use of specific personnel who know where to look, the probability might go higher while the cost is reduced. There are many variations that can be used to reach the desired probability of success ("High" or "Low"). The success of the decision tree approach depends on the depth of criteria used at each level and the ability to make the decision that best fits the desired goal.

Figure 2.
Decision Tree for Search and Seizure

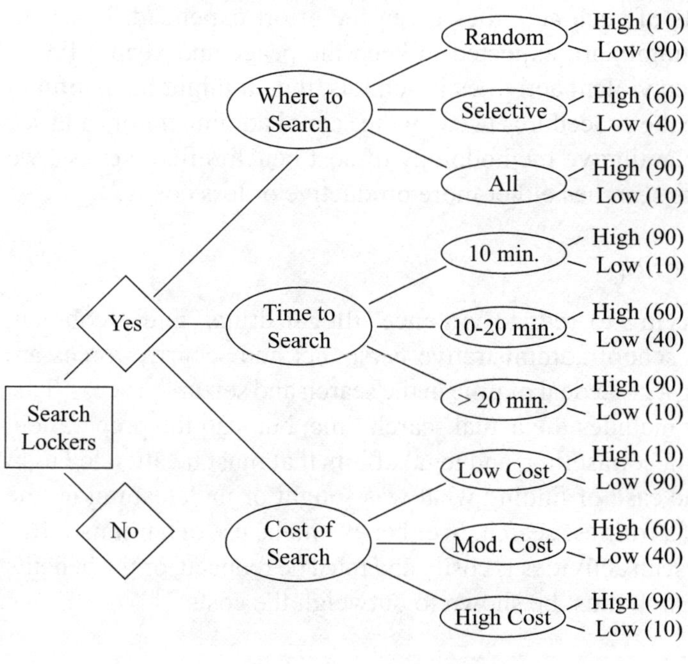

Once the initial decision tree is established, the model is tested with practitioners in the field as indicated above. With the responses from the field answering the questions of where, time, costs, and probability of success, the researcher can reconstruct the decision tree to more closely model reality.

Statistical Analysis

Due to the nature of the decision theory/decision tree development and refinement, there is no statistical analysis in this research strategy that complements the first five research strategies. However, if the researcher was of such a mind, a descriptive survey with attendant statistical analysis of responses from the administrators could be conducted. Such an exercise might not test a theory per se, but it may produce a product that would enable the practitioner to move to preventive law practices.

Research Strategy #7: Cost Benefit/Effectiveness Analysis

The last research strategy proposed is that of cost benefit/effectiveness (CB/E) of search and seizure efforts of school administrative personnel. Speaking from experience, one of the hallmarks of search and seizure activities of school administrators is the lack of results of such activities given the effort expended. If school administrators are expected to keep the peace and keep a lid on illegal and violent activities in schools, then it might be helpful to examine the procedures used by the school administrators and see if, via quantitative methodology of cost benefit/effectiveness, we can make searches either more productive or less costly.

Introduction

In trying to reduce violence, illegal drugs, and alcohol in schools, school administrative personnel and security forces are spending a great deal of time in the search and seizure process. This not only includes the actual search time, but also the preparation, aftermath, counseling, and legal affairs that must be attended to in either the case of finding what was sought or in "cleaning up the mess" of a fruitless search. In either event, the use of administrative time for such activities is costly and must be reduced, or the benefits of the search must be shown to outweigh the costs.

The proposed study examines the cost benefit/effectiveness relationships found in using school personnel for search and seizure activities. Specifically, the study calculates the costs of such activities by a variety of school personnel and examines the benefits of such activities.

Review of Related Literature

The review of related literature for this research strategy would include several sections. First, there would be a section on the growing concern for time and effort expended by school administrators with the search and seizure process. This would include literature from school administrators, school board, and central office individuals, as well as the general opinion literature. Second, there would need to be a detailed examination of the strengths, weaknesses, and methodology involved in cost benefit/effectiveness procedures. This section would draw heavily of the work of Levin (1983) and studies that have used these techniques. Third, there might be a section on the development of a "Cost of Search Index" and the variables that must be considered in determining the cost of administrative time and effort in search and seizure practices. This would include the issues of salaries, time, and stress factors associated with search practices. Fourth, there would be a section on the benefits and effectiveness of a search and the criteria used to determine whether a search had been beneficial and/or effective.

Research Design and Methodology

Here the researcher returns to a design and methodology that more closely approximates traditional quantitative educational research. The design is somewhat like a descriptive research design in that the researcher gathers data regarding various searches that were conducted. This would follow a structured interview design, as well as data collection for items such as salary, time involved in the search, effects on administrators and students, and the climate/culture of the organization. The structured interview would deal with a limited population of school administrators, preferably selected for their direct involvement with the search process. Two extremes could be considered in this study: those administrators who infrequently conduct searches and those administrators who frequently conduct searches. In that manner, not only can costs and benefits be described, but also efficiencies associated with repetitive action might be taken into consideration. The benefits of the search must also be considered. This would entail calculation of specific benefits of specific searches.

With this data in hand, the researcher could then construct a cost benefit/effectiveness analysis for specific search strategies for specific searches. This could be for both those frequently involved and those not frequently involved in searches. Comparisons could be made and the appropriate CB/E techniques could be replicated and disseminated throughout districts and states.

Statistical Analysis

Due to the nature of cost benefit/effectiveness research strategies, no standard statistical analysis using educational statistics would be needed. The numbers and data generated by the CB/E analysis would be sufficient to determine the best set of techniques to use.

Uses of Quantitative Methodology in Educational Law

There are many research questions that can be addressed by quantitative methodology in the area of educational law. These should not be limited to merely counting cases: they also deal with the attitudes, opinions, and effects of specific and multiple court decisions on issues facing school personnel. A sampling of questions might include:

> Who are the specific groups that oppose banning prayer in schools, and why do they object?
>
> What effect does inclusion of special education students have on school students, patrons, personnel, and budgets?
>
> What are the perceptions of school administrators toward issues of educational reform and school restructuring?
>
> What is the relationship between state proficiency tests, the rate of graduation/dropout, and the skills needed for work?
>
> What is the difference between gender and age views of title IX and violations concerning sexual harassment?

Any of these questions can be addressed using quantitative research methodology that can provide useful data and knowledge to the profession. It should be emphasized that the results of such efforts will only form the basis for potential action by school personnel. The results of quantitative studies are not stand-alone, fixed answers to the problems faced by educators. Rather, they are additional data points that the educator can draw upon to render a decision. In a sense, the results of the data analysis and the conclusions drawn should be neutral and should allow for interpretation by the individual implementing the decision. The key element is that in quantitative methodology, the user of the information has sound data on which to base a decision because of the use of control and the effort to eliminate bias and confounding variables. All data, whether quantitative, qualitative, or from whatever methodology used, can and should be viewed with a critical eye. All data are just information for the individual decision maker to put into the mix of the decision-making process. Quantitative research methodology tries to assure that the data are accurate and reproducible, thus allowing for consistency that aids the decision-making process.

In addition, quantitative research methodology can provide a base of both qualitative research methods and policy study methods that examine similar problems from different perspectives as reviewed elsewhere in this volume. Quantitative methods can provide information for qualitative research methods necessary for triangulation of data. Quantitative methods also provide a database that a policy studies researcher can use to render decisions on specific issues. The findings from quantitative research provide another vehicle by which researchers can view the issue; the legal concern; or the knowledge, attitudes, beliefs, and actions taken by school administrators, students, parents, and community members. Knowledge and use of all the complementary research methods can only aid the school administrator and policymaker in rendering decisions appropriate for the schools. No one method alone can provide the information needed for decision making. Several methods combined, however, can produce a stronger decision and course of action.

Conclusion

This chapter sought to develop live research strategies that might be useful for researchers and graduate students within the arena of school law. The authors have suggested that while traditional analysis of school law issues and topics might serve the purpose of continued examination of these issues, there are other strategies that the researcher may consider. These have included not only simple box scoring, but also in-depth analysis of the actors within school law—the implementers and the policymakers—as they react to the notions of court decisions and changes in philosophy. The authors have also suggested that proper grist for the school law research mill may be practitioner/practical research topics that examine how to do a better job in the arena of school policy development and school operation. Better decision making, better policies, and better practices are the aim of all educational research.

References

Anderson. D. R., Sweeney. D. J., & Williams, T. A. (1983). *An introduction to management science: Quantitative approaches to decision-making* (3rd ed.). St. Paul, MN: West.

Bollen, K. A. (1989). *Structural Equation Modeling with Latent Variables*. New York: John Wiley & Sons.

Borg. W.. & Gall. M. (1989). *Educational research: An introduction* (5th ed.). New York: Longman.

Bracht. G. H., & Glass, G. V. (1968). The external validity of experiments. *American Education Research Journal, 5*, 437-474.

Bray, J. H., & Maxwell, S. E. (1982). Analyzing and interpreting significant MANOVAs. *Review of Educational Research, 52*, 340-367.

Campbell, W., & Stanley. J. (1968). *Experimental and quasi-experimental designs for research.* Chicago: Rand McNally.

Cates, W. M. (1986). *A practical guide to education research.* Englewood Cliffs. NJ: Prentice-Hall.

Cohen, J. (1992). A power primer. *Psychological Bulletin, 112*, 155-159.

Crocker, L., & Algina, J. (1986). *Introduction to Classical and Modern Test Theory*. New York: Holt, Rinehart, and Winston.

Cronbach, L. J. (1951). *Coefficient alpha and the internal structure of tests. Psychometrika, 16*, 297-334.

Elazar. D. (1973). *American federalism* (3rd ed.). New York: Harper Row.

Fabrigar, L. R., Wegener, D. T., MacCallum, R. C., & Strahan, E. J. (1999). Evaluating the use of exploratory factor analysis in psychological research, *Psychological Methods*, *4*, 272-299.

Fink, A. (2003). *How to Sample in Surveys*. Thousand Oaks, CA: Sage.

Gay. L. R. (1987). *Educational research: Competencies for analysis andapplication* (3rd ed.). Columbus: Merrill.

Gorsuch, R. L. (1983). *Factor analysis* (2nd ed.). Hillsdale, NJ: Lawrence Erlbaum.

Hosmer, D. W. (2000). *Applied Logistic Regression*. New York: Wiley.

Johnson, B. (2001). Toward a new classification of nonexperimental quantitative research. *Educational Researcher*, *30*, 3-13.

Johnson. C. A., & Canon. B. C. (1984). *Judicial policies: Implementation and impact*. Washington: C.Q. Press.

Lee v. Weisman, 112 S. Ct. 2649 (1992). *Lemon v. Kurtzman. 403 U.S. 602* (1971).

Levin, H. M. (1983). *Cost-effectiveness: A primer*. Newbury Park. CA: Sage.

McMillan, J. H.. & Schumacher. S. (1989). *Research in education: A conceptual approach* (2nd ed.). Glenview. IL: Scott. Foresman.

Moss, P. A. (1992). Shifting conceptions of validity in educational measurement: Implications for performance assessment. *Review of Educational Research*, *62*, 229-258.

Murphy, K. R., & Myors, B. (1998). *Statistical power analysis: A simple and general model for traditional and modern hypothesis tests*. Mahwah, N. J.: Erlbaum.

Pedhazur, E. J. (1997.) *Multiple regression in behavioral research: Explanation and prediction* (3rd Edition). Fort Worth: Harcourt Brace.

Raudenbush, S. W., & Bryk, A. S. (2002). *Hierarchical linear models: Applications and data analysis methods* (2nd Edition). Thousand Oaks: Sage.

Raykov, T., & Marcoulides, G. (2000). *A first course in structural equation modeling*. Mahwah, NJ: Lawrence Erlbaum.

Robinson, D. H., & Levin, J. R. (1997). Reflections on statistical and substantive significance, with a slice of replication. *Educational Researcher*, *26*, *5*, 21-26.

Schimmel, D. (1996). *Research that makes a difference: Complementary methods for examining legal issues in education.* Topeka, Kansas: National Organization on Legal Problems in Education.

Shadish, W. R., Cook, T. D., & Campbell, D. T. (2002). *Experimental and quasi-experimental designs for generalized causal inference*. Boston: Houghton Mifflin Company.

Stevens, J. P. (1999). Intermediate statistics (2nd Edition). Mahwah, N. J.: Lawrence Erlbaum.

Stevens, J. P. (2002). *Applied multivariate statistics for the social sciences* (4th Edition). Mahwah, N. J.: Lawrence Erlbaum.

Thompson, B. (Ed.). (1993). Statistical significance testing in contemporary practice: Some proposed alternatives with comments from journal editors. *Journal of Experimental Education*, *61*, 285-393.

Wiersma. W. (1995). *Research methods in education: An introduction* (6th ed.). Boston: Allyn & Bacon.

Williams, F. (1992). *Reasoning with statistics* (4th ed.). Ft. Worth. TX: Harcourt. Brace. Jovanovich.

5 The Continua of Disciplined Inquiry: Quantitative, Qualitative, and Mixed Methods

Jeffrey D. Kromrey, Anthony J. Onwuegbuzie, & Kristine Y. Hogarty

Introduction

Disciplined inquiry related to the history, the issues, and the consequences of school law is critical for educational leaders and practitioners. In contrast to the historical-legal investigations of the interpretation and application of case law that characterize much of legal research, a variety of research methods are both appropriate and necessary for comprehensive inquiry related to school law. Critical issues in contemporary education such as class size, accommodations and access for the disabled, segregation, special education programming, changing graduation requirements, and school accountability legislation require rigorous inquiry from a variety of perspectives to provide comprehensive understanding that will guide policy makers and others involved in modern educational systems.

Unfortunately, the formal treatment of research methods that often groups approaches to inquiry into the ostensibly distinct categories of *qualitative* and *quantitative* methods. Such a dualistic perspective reflects the early growing pains that led to the paradigm wars in educational research during the 1980s and 1990s. This chapter presents a more productive view of research as continua rather than dualisms. The realization that individual studies may incorporate aspects of both qualitative and quantitative methods gives rise to mixed methods of inquiry and coherent approaches that combine desirable aspects of multiple approaches to empirical study. Such blended methods build on the strengths of the individual components, creating a composite that yields more information and higher-quality information than would be obtained through inquiry rooted in a single approach.

The purpose of this chapter is to delineate the traditionally viewed dualism of *quantitative* vs. *qualitative inquiry* in the context of legal research. Fundamentals of mixed methods of inquiry are then described as recent efforts to combine these formerly separate approaches to research. Finally, the controversial six principles of scientific research, advanced by the National Research Council (National Academy of Sciences, 2002), are used to develop a set of dimensions upon which individual studies may be described. These dimensions represent the context of continua that more clearly represent a comprehensive view of empirical inquiry.

A Traditional View of Quantitative Inquiry

Many scholars equate quantitative inquiry with experiments, statistics, and mathematics. Proponents of such a narrow view should be reminded of Kerlinger's (1964) definition of research: "systematic, controlled, empirical and critical investigation of hypothetical propositions about the presumed relations among natural phenomenon" (p. 13). Similarly, the teachings of Guba and Lincoln (1994) suggest that scholars adopt assumptions based on binary choices in three areas that classify them into paradigm-based groups. The first of these three assumptions is ontological. For those trained in the tradition of quantitative inquiry, there exists a single, independent reality that is relatively constant across time and settings, that is, an absolute truth that the researcher can *potentially* discover. The second assumption is epistemological, with positivists investing in the belief that the researcher can remain objective in the search for such truth. The last assumption is methodological and concerns the ways in which researchers conduct inquiry and investigate the world. Methods that lend themselves to quantitative inquiry include *a priori* designs, random sampling, deductive analysis, and hypothesis testing.

The breadth and depth of inquiry pursued using quantitative methods often begins with a vague sense of uncertainty or a desire to more fully explore a particular topic (see Figure 1). An examination of the previous research in the field and the existing theories gives rise to research questions and hypotheses. These questions and hypotheses will determine the selection of a research design and requisite data analysis. Once a well-articulated research question has been advanced, an appropriate research design can be determined. This part of the process will involve critical decisions regarding the selection of participants, situations, observations, measurements, and procedures.

This type of inquiry often involves some type of probability-sampling technique to ensure that the chosen group is *representative* of the target population (a term often referred to as generalizability). An unrepresentative sample will make it difficult to generalize the results of a given study. In addition to obtaining a representative sample, researchers are also keenly aware of issues regarding precision; that is, larger samples tend to yield more precise inferences. If, for example, the research question or hypothesis was related to issues of school accountability, an informed researcher could either conduct a census (for example, gathering information from all schools in Florida), or draw a stratified random sample of schools across the country. When choosing a stratified random sample, sampling occurs from within a pre-identified set of strata, striving to select a random sample of participants that represents important variables that if ignored, may potentially cloud conclusions and interpretations. Quantitative inquiry is often described as context free, with researchers holding universal principals, operating in a value-free environment according to a pre-specified methodology. Further, these types of studies are often designed with the expressed goal of explanation and prediction. These aspects of traditional quantitative inquiry are juxtaposed against those that are characteristic of traditional, qualitative approaches in Table 1.

Research Design

A host of research designs are available to investigate research problems of a quantitative nature. These designs are categorized according to the way in which the variables of interest are, or are not, manipulated. An experimental design requires the manipulation of an independent variable, whereas a causal comparative or correlational design does not. For example, research on the effectiveness of magnet schools (e.g., Dickinson, Holifield, Creer, & Holifield, 2000) may involve the random selection of students from a pool of school applicants (an experiment) or the comparison of achievement of students who attend a magnet program with students who do not (a causal comparative design). Each approach has its inherent strengths and weaknesses. The strength of a true experiment is found in the control of extraneous variables through the random assignment of participants to treatments, resulting in a strong case for causality or internal validity. This control at times comes at the cost of introducing artificiality to the inquiry that may compromise the generalizability or external validity of a research effort. In contrast, causal-comparative designs lack the control obtained via experiments, yet have the advantage of occurring in more naturalistic settings and allowing for the examination of natural variation, enhancing external validity. Similarly, correlational designs often occur in natural settings. The inability to control extraneous variables in causal-comparative and correlational designs limits the ability to make causal inferences and, hence, diminishes internal validity. Lastly, descriptive and survey research round out the set of designs often implemented in the quantitative realm (for example, the analysis of trends in Black and Hispanic achievement gaps presented by Lee, 2004). Exploration of issues critical to school law may be addressed with any of the aforementioned designs, depending on the nature of the variables of interest, the ability to control extraneous variables (i.e., in a true or quasi-experiment), and the point in time of the inquiry (i.e., does the inquiry involve established groups, and have the data already been collected).

Issues of Measurement

Of the utmost importance to researchers are notions related to the credibility of the data, which includes issues of measurement and the attendant matters of reliability and validity. Unlike the physical sciences, many researchers in the social sciences do not have the luxury of having access to direct means of measuring hypothetical constructs. Observations or measures will be imperfect or imprecise as they may incorrectly include elements of a particular construct of interest or may inadvertently neglect to include something of importance. Messick (1995) refers to these problems as construct-irrelevant variance and construct under-representation, respectively. In order to circumvent such problems, carefully designed reliability and validity studies are critical.

Evidence of the reliability and validity of the inferences of the scores obtained from measurement instruments can take many forms, and there is not a single-prescribed method or combination of methods advanced in the literature. The approaches available to establish the credibility of a newly created measure vary with respect to the intention of the instrument. Measures that are employed to investigate issues such as school accountability must withstand intense scrutiny, suggesting rigorous reliability and validity studies. Content experts would be called upon to speak to adequate coverage of the various domains representing the distinct disciplines (e.g., math, reading, science), while measurement specialists would need to insure the stability or reliability of the scores from which potentially high-stakes decisions would be made.

Data Collection, Analysis, and Reporting

The collection of data in the conduct of quantitative inquiry may involve standardized measures, researcher-constructed instruments, or a combination of both. Researchers are often concerned with a host of demographic variables or specific constructs that may interact or influence the central variables under investigation. For example, in pursuit of answers regarding issues of school accountability, the informed investigator may collect information related to individual schools (e.g., minority representation, socioeconomic status, class size, average salary), as well as scores on particular measures of academic achievement. The majority of the data collected comprises numbers that may be analyzed in a variety of ways.

Initially, descriptive statistics are often computed to provide a sense of the representativeness of the sample, certain group characteristics, and other pertinent information. Data are then often analyzed according to the stated research questions and hypotheses. An arsenal of inferential statistics is available to conduct analyses of a univariate, bivariate, and multivariate nature.

Quantitative data are often described in the narrative of a research report and supplemented by tables representing prescribed elements of statistical tests. For example, in the analysis of minority achievement gaps, Lee (2004) graphed time trends in standardized mean differences between minority and majority students, illustrating the initial narrowing then widening of such gaps. Regardless of the support or contradiction of the results, ethical researchers report both results that are statistically significant and results that fail to obtain statistical significance. More recently, estimates of practical significance (e.g., effect sizes) are provided alongside tests of null hypotheses.

A Traditional View of Qualitative Inquiry

In contrast to quantitative research, most qualitative inquiry is *inductive* in orientation, with the researcher beginning with few preordinate hypotheses or formal expectations. Qualitative research may be further distinguished by its focus on detailed description of a particular phenomenon occurring at a particular time within a particular context. As Krathwohl (1998) points out, the strategies of qualitative research are ideal for the study of complex phenomena about which there is little certain knowledge. Further, qualitative inquiry typically seeks answers to questions about the *how* and *why* of phenomena.

A variety of research designs comprise the traditional domains of qualitative inquiry, including ethnography, oral history, phenomenology, and case study. While these designs offer critical distinctions in approaches to research structure and data collection, common threads among the methods provide the distinguishing features of qualitative research.

Research problems and hypotheses. In the choice of a research problem, most qualitative research uses an "emergent design." In such a design, rather than establishing an *a priori* statement of research questions or hypotheses, the particular questions to be addressed are developed in the course of conducting the study. That is, the researcher begins with an idea for an area of study and a general problem to be investigated, then becomes immersed in the study's setting (e.g., conducting preliminary observations or initial interviews, reviewing documents and other artifacts, or just "hanging out" at the research site). For example, Gersti-Pepin (2002) spent four years at a magnet school, allowing her "to observe the effects of the policy implementation from within the culture and from a perspective that is almost inaccessible to non-students" (p. 48).

Subjectivity and objectivity. In qualitative research, the role of the researcher in the arena is often explicitly analyzed and documented (for example, the researcher may be described as an integral part of the research "instrumentation"). In contrast to quantitative research that relies on the greater objectivity (separation of researcher from research participants) that results from the data collection strategies, the subjective involvement of the researcher in the qualitative study is incorporated into the study design and the data analysis. For example, in the study of inner-city high schools, the researcher's sensitivities may lead to noting certain postings on bulletin boards (leading to interviews and other inquiries) but ignoring others. Similarly, the conduct of interviews and the observations of teachers' and administrators' behaviors are "flavored" by the researcher's involvement.

Data collection. A variety of data types may be collected in qualitative inquiry. For example, Harmon (2002) used classroom observations, group discussions, student and teacher interviews, as well as interactive fieldwork in her analysis of the perceptions of gifted African-American inner-city students. Additionally, text data from diaries, documents (such as meeting minutes, official records, and other artifacts), and personnel logs yield raw data for qualitative research. Regardless of the source of these data, the majority of data gathered in qualitative research consists of words or text that reflects the perspectives and experiences of the research participants. Further, in many studies, considerable effort is required to gain entry to the setting. Months of effort may be required to establish trust with research participants and to become privy to the critical sources of data.

Data analysis. Data analysis typically begins with a search for patterns and connections among the data yielding broad, fluid, working hypotheses. Data may be coded and organized according to these hypotheses. For example, a researcher may note that new administrators appear to suggest a broad range of strategies for raising student achievement, providing ideas for teachers to pursue with little direct supervision. In contrast, more professionally experienced administrators may appear to offer fewer strategies, but pursue them with greater vigor—insisting that the faculty implement and evaluate the efforts within set timelines.

Further, gaps in the data or contradictory results may suggest the need for additional data collection, analysis, and interpretation (the "grounded theory" methods described by Glaser & Strauss, 1967). Critical considerations for the dependability of the data suggest that researchers should develop multiple sources of evidence (triangulation), search for negative cases, and explicitly seek disconfirming evidence.

Data reporting. The presentation of the data derived from qualitative inquiry is typically in the form of organized, verbatim quotes from the primary data sources, as the researcher tells the story of the inquiry. Extended selections from conversations with administrators and teachers may be interspersed with quotes from meetings of the Parent Teacher Association (PTA) or formal memos from the local school district or the state department of education.

Such thick descriptions provide a voice for the research participants and allow the reader to validate the researchers' interpretations of these data. As Denzin (1978) indicates, such description "goes beyond the mere or bare reporting of an act (thin description), but describes and probes the intentions, motives, meanings, contexts, situations and circumstances of action" (p. 39).

An Emerging View of Mixed-Methods Inquiry

In a myriad of fields, including the field of legal research and policy studies, quantitative research is viewed as the first methodological wave (circa the nineteenth century) inasmuch as it represented the first research paradigm that contained a complete and formal set of ontological, epistemological, axiological, rhetorical, and methodological assumptions and principles. The turn of the twentieth century witnessed the second methodological wave, namely, qualitative research, which arose from a rejection of positivism. Denzin and Lincoln (2000) define the period 1900 to 1950 as the first historical moment for qualitative research. The 1960s saw the emergence of a research school of thought that advocated the combining of quantitative and qualitative approaches, termed mixed-methods research. This was the birth of the third methodological wave. Since the 1960s, this third-wave methodology has become popularized in many disciplines including education (Johnson & Onwuegbuzie, 2004; Onwuegbuzie & Johnson, 2004; Rocco et al., 2003), psychology (Waszak & Sines, 2003), nursing (Dzurec & Abraham, 1993; Morse, 1991; Sandelowski, 2001; Twinn, 2003), sociology (Hunter & Brewer, 2003), health sciences (Forthofer, 2003; Morgan, 1998), management and organizational research (Currall & Towler, 2003), library and information science research (Onwuegbuzie, Jiao, & Bostick, 2004), and program evaluation (Greene, Caracelli, & Graham, 1989; Rallis & Rossman, 2003).

In recent years, mixed-methods research has received increased recognition and credibility in a variety of fields and is beginning to play a major role in influencing and informing educational practice. Indeed, the last decade has seen a proliferation in the number of mixed-methods articles published in scholarly journals, particularly educational research journals. Several journals now routinely publish mixed-methods research (e.g., *Field Methods*, *Educational Evaluation & Policy Analysis, Quality & Quantity*, *Evaluation, Evaluation Practice, Research in Nursing & Health*), and the list is growing. Some of these published works have been the basis of educational reform in many settings. The mixed-method movement has been boosted by the recent publication of a handbook (Tashakkori & Teddlie, 2003a), and a special issue on mixed-method research is being planned for publication in an upcoming issue of *Research in the Schools*, an internationally referred journal (Onwuegbuzie & Daniel, in press).

Although pragmatism, which represents the major philosophy that underpins mixed-methods research, has received attention in legal areas such as bioethics and health law (Wolf, 1994), mixed-methods research has yet to permeate the field of legal research. Thus, in what follows, we demonstrate how mixed-methods approaches can improve the quality of legal research. In so doing, we present mixed-methods research as the third research paradigm in the study of legal issues.

Strengths of Quantitative and Qualitative Research

Quantitative research. The previous two sections have presented a general overview of traditional quantitative and qualitative inquiries. When a study exclusively uses quantitative or qualitative approaches, it is referred to as monomethod research. Both quantitative and qualitative research methods have unique strengths. In particular, quantitative research is very useful for identifying prevalence rates, relationships, and cause-and-effect relationships, which under certain conditions (e.g., large and random samples), can be generalized from the sample to the population. For example, descriptive research can be used to determine the average proportion of minority students in a school or school district. Correlational research could be utilized to examine the relationship between minority representation and achievement. Experimental research could be used to determine the effect of increasing minority representation on academic performance. In any case, if designed in an optimal way, in which rigor is maximized, quantitative research can inform educational policy and legal decisions.

Qualitative research. In contrast, qualitative research is very useful for obtaining insights into the routine and problematic experiences and the meaning attached to these experiences of individuals (e.g., biography, auto-biography, life history, oral history, auto-ethnography, case study) and groups (e.g., phenomenology, ethnography, grounded theory), which under certain conditions (e.g., data saturation, theoretical saturation, informational redundancy), can achieve *Verstehen* or understanding. For example, a case study can be used to study how desegregation of a school affects a particular student. An ethnographic study can be used to describe and interpret the cultural behaviors, customs, and experiences of African-American students or another cultural group of students who attend a desegregated middle school. A phenomenological inquiry can be utilized to describe the meaning of the lived experiences for teachers of a desegregated high school. Grounded theory research could be employed to generate or expand a theory of the effects of desegregation. Regardless of the research design or method used, qualitative research can inform policy development if it is conducted in a way that leads to insights into particular educational, social, and/or familial processes and practices that exist within a specific setting, location, context, time, event, incident, activity, and/or experience.

Limitations of Quantitative and Qualitative Research

Unfortunately, both quantitative and qualitative research methods have unique weaknesses. In particular, quantitative research studies typically yield data that do not explain the prevalence rates, differences, or relationships that have been identified by the researcher. Simply put, quantitative research does not lend itself to answering *why* and *how* questions. Quantitative research is better suited to "answering questions of who, where, how many, how much, and what is the relationship between specific variables" (Adler, 1996, p. 5). Conversely, with respect to qualitative inquiries, as noted by Onwuegbuzie and Johnson (2004), "Qualitative research is typically based on small, nonrandom samples ... which means that qualitative research findings are often not very generalizable beyond the local research participants" (p. 410). A list of strength and weaknesses of quantitative and qualitative research is presented in Table 2 and Table 3, respectively.

Because of the strengths and weaknesses inherent in both quantitative and qualitative research, in recent years, an increasing number of researchers, many of whom call themselves pragmatists, are advocating conducting studies that utilize both quantitative and qualitative techniques within the same inquiry. Such investigations represent what is often termed mixed methods, although other terms have been used such as mixed research, multimethods, blended methods, and integrated methods. However, mixed-methods research is the most common phrase used. Generally speaking, mixed-methods research represents inquiry that involves collecting, analyzing, and interpreting quantitative and qualitative data in a single study or in a series of studies that investigate the same underlying phenomenon.

The Context for Mixed-Method Research

Since the latter part of the nineteenth century, a heated debate has taken place regarding quantitative and qualitative research paradigms. Both quantitative purists (i.e., positivists) and qualitative purists (e.g., post-modernists, post-structuralists) have remained on the opposite ends of the research methodological spectrum, both sides arguing for the superiority and exclusivity of their paradigms. Indeed, both schools of thought have advanced the incompatibility thesis (Howe, 1988), which stipulates that quantitative and qualitative research paradigms and methods cannot and should not be mixed under any circumstance. As such, many graduate students and other non-purists from many fields have viewed research as representing a strict dichotomy between quantitative and qualitative choices. Yet, as contended by several pragmatist researchers (e.g., Johnson & Onwuegbuzie, 2004; Newman & Benz, 1998; Onwuegbuzie, 2002; Tashakkori & Teddlie, 1998), rather than representing a dichotomy, quantitative and qualitative research paradigms and methods lie on an epistemological continuum, with mixed-methods research situated at the center and quantitative and qualitative research placed at the end points. Such re-framing allows researchers to focus more on research methods rather than on paradigmatic concerns. Indeed, although many research methods are typically linked to certain paradigms (e.g., numeric data only representing quantitative research, interview data only representing qualitative research), there is no fixed direct correspondence between research paradigm and research method. Therefore, for example, qualitative data can be collected in experimental studies, while quantitative data can be collected in grounded-theory research and ethnographic studies. Mixing and matching research strategies that best address the research question(s) of interest is the essence of mixed-methods research.

A Blueprint for Conducting Mixed-Methods Studies in Legal Research

The mixed-methods research process in the legal field contains the following nine distinct steps: (1) determine the goal of the study, (2) formulate the research objective(s), (3) determine the research purpose, (4) select the research design, (5) collect the data, (6) analyze the data, (7) validate the data, (8) interpret the data, and (9) write the research report. These steps are presented in Figure 2. This figure shows that the first four steps (all represented by rectangles) are linear. That is, the study's goal leads to the research objective(s), which in turn, leads to a determination of the research purpose, which is followed by the selection of the research design. Conversely, the subsequent four steps, namely, data collection, data analysis, data validation, and data interpretation (all represented by oval shapes), are cyclical and interactive steps in the chain. Specifically, once data from at least one phase are collected, the data are next either analyzed or validated. If data analysis is the next step in the process, then the findings that emerge from these analyses are validated. Once validated, the data are then interpreted, or more data are collected if the mixed-methods research design is sequential in nature. Alternatively, findings from the first data analysis might be used to design the data-collection method for the subsequent phrase. These new data then are either analyzed or validated. In any case, once all data have been collected, analyzed, and validated, interpretation takes place. Writing the research report, as is the case in quantitative and qualitative research, is the last step in the research process of a single study. However, this step leads back to the first three steps, wherein the study's goal(s), research objective(s), and/or research purpose(s) are reformulated in subsequent studies, and Steps 4-9 are repeated until all research goals, objectives, and purposes are adequately addressed. Each of these steps is discussed in more detail below.

Step 1: Determine the goal of the study. This first stage involves the investigator deciding on the form of legal research of interest. In particular, as noted by Kjervik and King (1990), the researcher should decide which of the following four types of legal research is most pertinent: (1) conventional research, which identifies, analyzes, organizes, and synthesizes legal authority; (2) legal theory method, which represents a descriptive and evaluative approach to understanding legal rules; (3) fundamental research, which attempts to understand law as a social phenomenon examining historical, political, linguistic, or socio-political implications of law (i.e., policy study); and (4) law reform research, whereby the goal is to bring about change in legal obligations.

Step 2: Determine the research objective. In this step, the researcher should determine which five major standard research objectives are pertinent for the quantitative and qualitative phases of the study: (1) exploration, (2) description, (3) explanation, (4) prediction, and/or (5) influence (Johnson & Christensen, 2004). Specifically, exploration involves using mostly inductive methods to explore a concept, construct, phenomenon, or situation for the purpose of developing tentative hypotheses or generalizations. Description involves identifying and describing the nature and etiology of a phenomenon. Explanation represents developing theory in an attempt to elucidate the relationship among concepts or phenomena and to determine reasons for occurrences of events. Prediction relates to using pre-existing knowledge or theory to forecast what will occur at a later point in time. Finally, influence involves the manipulation of the setting or variable to produce a desired outcome. Both the qualitative and quantitative phases of each mixed-methods research study can be linked to one or more of these five research objectives.

We also recommend that the mixed-methods researcher determines which of the following nine mixed-methods research objectives, conceptualized by Newman, Ridenour, Newman, and DeMarco (2003), is most appropriate for the study: (1) predict; (2) add to the knowledge base; (3) have a personal, social, institutional, and/or organizational impact; (4) measure change; (5) understand complex phenomena; (6) test new ideas; (7) generate new ideas; (8) inform constituencies; or (9) examine the past. Making such a decision would help mixed-methods researchers to design their studies.

Step 3: Determine the research purpose. Once the research goal and objective(s) have been determined, the next step in the mixed-research process is to determine the research purpose. We recommend that you use Greene et al.'s (1989) framework. These methodologists identified the following five general purposes of mixed-methods studies: (1) triangulation (i.e., seeking convergence and corroboration of findings from different methods that study the same phenomenon); (2) complementarity (i.e., seeking elaboration, illustration, enhancement, and clarification of the findings from one method with results from the other method); (3) initiation (i.e., discovering paradoxes and contradictions that lead to a re-framing of the research question); (4) development (i.e., using the findings from one method to help inform the other method); and (5) expansion (i.e., seeking to expand the breadth and range of inquiry by using different methods for different inquiry components). As documented by Greene et al. (1989), every mixed-methods study can be classified as having one or more of these five purposes. Identifying the research purpose helps the researcher to select an appropriate mixed method research design. For instance, if the purpose of the research is development, then a sequential design is appropriate, involving the quantitative phase followed by the qualitative phase or the qualitative component followed by the quantitative component.

Step 4: Select the research design. Over the last several years, mixed-methods researchers have identified a myriad of research designs. In the Tashakkori and Teddlie (2003a) book alone, thirty-five research designs are presented. However, the simplest and most classic way to arrange research designs is to classify them as representing either mixed-methods deigns or mixed-model designs (Tashakkori & Teddlie, 1998). When utilizing mixed-method designs, the researcher systematically uses the quantitative research paradigm for one phase of a research study and the qualitative research paradigm for another phase of the study. That is, both the quantitative phase and the qualitative phase are kept intact and separate from one another until both sets of data have been analyzed. However, to be considered a mixed-method design, mixing must take place at some point in the study. The mixing generally occurs at the data interpretation stage, wherein meta-inferences (i.e., both sets of inferences are combined into a coherent whole; Tashakkori & Teddlie, 2003b) are made. Consequently, mixed-method designs incorporate qualitative and quantitative phases that, in effect, are conducted as part of a larger, overall study.

Most mixed-method designs utilize the following two dimensions as a base: time orientation and paradigm emphasis. Time orientation refers to whether the qualitative and quantitative phases of the study occur at approximately the same point in time (i.e., concurrent) or whether these two components occur one after the other (i.e., sequential). Paradigm emphasis pertains to whether both qualitative and quantitative phases of the study have approximately equal emphasis (i.e., equal status) with regard to answering the research question(s) or whether one phase clearly has more weight than the other phase (i.e., dominant status). Accordingly, in order to select a mixed-method design, the researcher must make two primary decisions: whether one wants to conduct the phases concurrently or sequentially, and whether one wants to operate largely within one dominant paradigm or not.

Crossing the two dimensions (i.e., time orientation and paradigm emphasis) produces a 2 (concurrent vs. sequential) x 2 (equal status vs. dominant status) matrix with four cells (Figure 3). In order to understand the specific designs shown in these four cells, some basic notation, credited to Morse (1991), needs to be introduced. The notation system works as follows:

- the letters quan or QUAN represent quantitative research;
- the letters qual or QUAL represent qualitative research;
- uppercase letters indicate highest priority;
- lowercase letters indicate lowest priority;
- a plus sign ("+") represents a concurrent collection of data;
- an arrow ("→") represents a sequential collection of data.

For example, the combination of symbols "QUAN + QUAL" summarizes a design wherein the quantitative and qualitative approaches are given equal status (i.e., both use uppercase letters) and are conducted concurrently (cf. the "+" sign). The combination of symbols "QUAN→qual" indicates that the quantitative phase is dominant (i.e., "QUAN" is in uppercase and "qual" is in lowercase), and a follow-up qualitative component is included in the study (see the arrow between "QUAN" and "qual"). Using this notational system yields the nine mixed-methods designs shown in Figure 3. As you can see, some of the cells include more designs than others (e.g., there is only one equal status concurrent design, but there are four sequential dominant status designs). We recognize that in legal research practice some designs will be more commonly used than others. For example, because many legal researchers (as are many other researchers) are trained in a single research paradigm, they will tend to use one of the dominant status designs. For example, predominantly quantitative researchers typically will design studies in which the quantitative component is the dominant phase.

Similarly, predominantly qualitative researchers will implement mixed-methods designs in which the qualitative component is given the most weight.

The second class of research designs is called mixed-model designs. In general, mixed-model designs involve mixing components or stages from qualitative and quantitative research (Tashakkori & Teddlie, 1998). There are two basic ways in which quantitative and qualitative components can be mixed. The first technique involves the use of both quantitative and qualitative research within one or more of the stages of a single research study (e.g., research objective, data collection, data analysis). The second procedure involves the use of both quantitative and qualitative research across any of the three stages. These two classes of mixed-model designs are called, respectively, "within-stage" and "across-stage" mixed-model research (Onwuegbuzie & Johnson, 2004).

In within-stage mixed-model research, the researcher mixes quantitative and qualitative research approaches at one or more of the major research stages (e.g., research objective, data collection, data analysis). That is, mixing occurs within at least one stage of a single study. For example, a legal researcher could mix within the data collection stage by gathering data that represent both qualitative and quantitative data types (e.g., responses to open- and closed-ended questionnaire items). Also, a researcher could mix within the data analysis stage by examining narrative data both qualitatively (searching for major themes) and quantitatively (counting the number of times key words or themes occur), or by analyzing numeric data both quantitatively (e.g., computing descriptive statistics) and qualitatively (forming categories based on the descriptive statistics).

In across-stage mixed-model research, the researcher mixes quantitative and qualitative research approaches across at least two of the major research stages in a single research study. For instance, a legal researcher could use a deductive approach as the research study's objective (quantitative), collect qualitative data (qualitative), but then analyze the data using quantitative techniques (quantitative). Figure 4 illustrates eight ways in which qualitative and quantitative components can be mixed across three major stages of the research process: (1) selecting the research objective, (2) collecting the data, and (3) analyzing the data. For example, Design 4 in Figure 4 represents a mixed-methods study that combines a quantitative research objective (i.e., explanation, prediction, and description) with a qualitative data collection (e.g., interview data) and qualitative data analysis (e.g., method of constant comparison; Glaser & Strauss, 1967). In contrast, Design 5 represents a mixed-methods study that combines a qualitative research objective (i.e., exploration and description) with a quantitative data collection (i.e., numeric data) and quantitative data analysis (e.g., correlation coefficient, t-test). It should be noted that whereas Designs 2-7 represent mixed-model designs, Design 1 and Design 8 represent monomethod designs. Specifically, Design 1 represents a quantitative design because all phases involve quantitative approaches, while Design 8 represents a qualitative design because all phases involve qualitative approaches.

The exciting aspect of mixed-methods research is that a legal researcher can create more tailored and/or more complex designs than the ones outlined here. (For additional mixed-methods designs, see Creswell, Plano, Clark, Guttmann, & Hanson, 2003; Maxwell & Loomis, 2003.) Also, it is possible for a design to emerge during a study in new ways, depending on how the research evolves. As such, mixed-methods research has the potential to open up new frontiers in research.

Step 5: Collect the data. Although qualitative and quantitative data can be collected using the same sample or sub-samples, this is often not the case. In fact, most of the time these data types are collected on different samples. Samples can be selected in one of two ways: randomly or non-randomly. Onwuegbuzie and Leech (2004) identified twenty-four sampling schemes that can be used in mixed-methods research, comprising five random sampling schemes (simple random sampling, stratified random sampling, cluster random sampling, systematic random sampling, and multi-stage random sampling), and nineteen purposive (i.e., non-random) sampling schemes (maximum variation sampling, homogeneous sampling, critical case sampling, theory-based sampling, confirming and disconfirming cases sampling, snowball/chain sampling, extreme case sampling, typical case sampling, intensity sampling, politically important cases sampling, random purposeful sampling, stratified purposeful sampling, criterion sampling, opportunistic sampling, mixed purposive sampling, convenience sampling, quota sampling, multi-stage purposeful random sampling, and multi-stage purposive sampling). Conveniently, any combination of random sampling and non-random sampling can be used in mixed-methods research. For example, random sampling can be used in the qualitative phase and non-random sampling in the quantitative phase. However, the generalizability of a mixed-methods research study typically is maximized when both phases utilize random sampling techniques, assuming of course, that the samples are sufficiently large.

Mixed-methods researchers can also use any of the available data-collection methods. Specifically, tests, questionnaires, focus groups, observations, interviews, and secondary data should be considered viable data sources. Again, any combination of data-collection methods can be used, depending on the research objective(s) and research purpose.

Johnson and Turner (2003) outlined six major data-collection strategies in mixed-methods research. These six methods are (a) mixture of open- and closed-ended items on one or more questionnaire; (b) mixture of depth and breadth interviewing; (c) mixture of *a prior* and *emergent/flowing* focus group strategies; (d) mixture of standardized open- and closed-ended pre-designed tests; (e) mixture of standardized/confirmatory and less structured/exploratory observation, alternating between participatory and nonparticipatory researcher roles; and (f) mixture of non-numeric and numeric documents, consisting of archived data based on open- and closed-ended items.

Step 6: Analyze the data. Mixed-methods researchers have at their disposal the whole range of quantitative (i.e., descriptive, inferential) and qualitative data-analysis techniques to consider. The choice of analysis, however, should be driven by the research goal, research objective(s), research purpose(s), research questions/ hypotheses, research design, and type of data collected. Uniquely, mixed-methods researchers can undertake quantitative analyses of qualitative data (i.e., *quantitizing*; Tashakkori & Teddlie, 1998), as well as perform qualitative analyses of quantitative data (i.e., *qualitizing*; Tashakkori & Teddlie, 1998). An example of quantitizing is determining the prevalence of words, concepts, or themes (cf. Onwuegbuzie, 2003b). Conversely, an example of qualitizing is the formation of profiles or categories based on numeric scores.

Onwuegbuzie and Teddlie (2003) have provided a comprehensive framework for conducting mixed-research data analyses. These researchers identified seven stages of the mixed-research data analysis process, as follows: (1) data reduction, (2) data display, (3) data transformation, (4) data correlation, (5) data consolidation, (6) data comparison, and (7) data integration. Data reduction, the first stage, includes reducing the dimensionality of the quantitative data (e.g., via descriptive statistics) and qualitative data (e.g., via exploratory content analysis). The second stage is data display, which involves describing pictorially the quantitative data (e.g., tables, graphs) and qualitative data (e.g., charts, lists, matrices, and Venn diagrams). Data transformation, the third stage, involves converting qualitative data into numerical codes that can be represented statistically (i.e., *quantitized*) and/or converting numerical data into narrative data that can be analyzed qualitatively (i.e., *qualitized*). The fourth stage involves data correlation, in which the quantitative data are correlated with the qualitized data or the qualitative data are correlated with the quantitized data. Next is data consolidation, the fifth stage, whereby both quantitative and qualitative data are combined to create new or consolidated variables or data sets. Data comparison is the sixth stage, which involves comparing data from the quantitative and qualitative data sources. Data integration is the seventh stage, whereby both quantitative and qualitative data are integrated into a coherent whole, or two separate sets (i.e., quantitative and qualitative) of coherent wholes. According to Onwuegbuzie and Teddlie, although these seven stages are somewhat sequential, they are not linear.

Step 7: Validate the data. Assessing validity in mixed-methods research is much more difficult than in monomethod studies because the validity or legitimation of inferences stemming from both the quantitative and qualitative phases must be assessed. That is, for the quantitative phase of a mixed-research study, internal validity (e.g., instrumentation, mortality) and external validity (e.g., population validity, ecological validity) should be evaluated. For the qualitative phase, validity (e.g., descriptive validity, interpretive validity) should also be examined.

With respect to quantitative research, Campbell and Stanley's (Campbell, 1957; Campbell & Stanley, 1963) seminal validity framework that delineates numerous threats to internal validity and external validity could be used (but see also Bracht & Glass, 1968; Cook & Campbell, 1979; and Smith & Glass, 1987). Another validity framework that could be utilized is Onwuegbuzie's (2003a) *Quantitative Legitimation Model*, which specifies fifty threats to internal and external validity that occur at the research design/data collection, data analysis, and/or data-interpretation stages of the quantitative research process. Several other validity frameworks could be used (e.g., American Educational Research Association,

American Psychological Association, and National Council on Measurement in Education, 1999; Messick, 1989, 1995; Onwuegbuzie, Daniel, & Collins, 2003; Shadish, Cook, & Campbell, 2001).

In terms of the qualitative research paradigm, legitimating models include those of Onwuegbuzie (2000), who conceptualized the *Qualitative Legitimation Model*, which contains twenty-nine elements of legitimation for qualitative research at the research design/data collection, data analysis, and data-interpretation stages of the research process. Onwuegbuzie identified threats to internal credibility in qualitative research, including ironic legitimation, paralogical legitimation, observational bias, and confirmation bias, among others. Also in this model, threats to external credibility were identified as being pertinent to qualitative research, including catalytic validity, communicative validity, action validity, and investigation validity.

Another useful qualitative legitimation framework is that of Maxwell (1992), who identified the following five types of validity in qualitative research: descriptive validity (i.e., factual accuracy of the account as documented by the researcher), interpretive validity (i.e., the extent to which an interpretation of the account represents an understanding of the perspective of the underlying group and the meanings attached to the members' words and actions), theoretical validity (i.e., the degree to which a theoretical explanation developed from research findings is consistent with the data), evaluative validity (i.e., the extent to which an evaluation framework can be applied to the objects of study, as opposed to a descriptive, interpretive, or explanatory one), and generalizability (i.e., the extent to which a researcher can generalize the account of a particular situation, context, or population to other individuals, times, settings, or context). With regard to the latter validity type, Maxwell differentiates internal generalizability from external generalizability, with the former referring to the generalizability of a conclusion within the underlying setting or group and the latter pertaining to generalizability beyond the group, setting, time, or context. According to Maxwell, internal generalizability is typically more important to qualitative researchers than is external generalizability. Other useful sources on legitimation in qualitative research include Creswell (1998), Glaser and Strauss (1967), Kvale (1995), Lather (1986, 1993), Lincoln and Guba (1985, 1990), Longino (1995), Maxwell (1996), Miles and Huberman (1984, 1994), Schwandt (2001), Strauss and Corbin (1998), and Wolcott (1990).

As can be seen in Figure 2, in mixed-methods research, assessment of legitimation or validity often is a cyclical, interactive process. In particular, an initial assessment of legitimation may lead to more data being collected (e.g., member checking). In any case, where possible, validity/legitimation strategies should be built into the research design.

Step 8: Interpret data. Although data interpretation may take place throughout the research process, holistic data interpretation occurs after most (if data saturation has been reached) or all data have been collected, analyzed, and validated. At this data-interpretation stage, the qualitative and quantitative data can be interpreted separately or simultaneously, depending on the research goal, objective(s), and purpose. However, most of the time, some integration or comparison occurs at the data-interpretation stage because this type of mixing leads to meta-inferences. Further, integrated data-interpretations can help the researcher to identify convergence, inconsistency, contradiction, and gaps in the data. Regardless of the extent to which mixing occurs at this stage, the ultimate goal of the legal researcher is to make inferences after ruling out as many rival hypotheses as possible. Therefore, data validation and data interpretation are inextricably intertwined.

Step 9: Write research report. Once all interpretations and inferences have been made and assessed for validity/legitimation, the legal researcher is in a position to write the report. The researcher can write separate reports for the quantitative and qualitative phases. Alternatively, the two sets of findings and interpretations could be written up in separate sections of a single research report. However, a more comprehensive, holistic, and integrated picture of the underlying phenomenon can be provided by fully integrating the quantitative and qualitative findings in the same section. Such integrated reports contain the same components as do most monomethod reports, including the review of the related literature, methods, results, and discussion sections. In these mixed-methods reports, the results section usually is thc longest section because it contains both the quantitative and qualitative results. A well-written report will be highly descriptive of all phases of the mixed-methods research process outlined in this chapter. Even when the quantitative phase is dominant, mixed-methods researchers always should contextualize their reports. That is, they should report and interpret all findings in their appropriate context. Contextualization should prevent the most important consumers (e.g., stakeholders, policy makers, judges) of the report from over-generalizing the findings and meta-inferences.

In writing a mixed-methods report, at least four methodological problems come to the fore that must be addressed (Onwuegbuzie & Johnson, 2004). First, the legal researcher must integrate the quantitative (i.e., typically impersonal and formal) and qualitative (i.e., typically personal and informal) styles of writing without unduly affecting the integrity of either quantitative or qualitative sections of the report. Second, all sections of the report should be as understandable as possible to the many readers who are not adequately trained in both qualitative and quantitative techniques. Third, the legal researcher has the difficult challenge of writing a mixed-methods report that is long enough to describe adequately all stages of the research process but short enough that is readable for busy stakeholders and policymakers, as well as fitting within any document length requirements for the target outlet. Writing both a full report and an executive summary may be useful here. Finally, because mixed-methods research is still an emerging field, they must convince consumers who are skeptical of this pragmatist paradigm of the credibility of their report. Thus, it is essential that these reports exhibit the highest degree of organization, coherence, and rigor.

The Continua of Educational Research

The rejection of the early dichotomization of research methods into incompatible camps of qualitative and quantitative paradigms and the advocacy of inquiry choices representing continua lead, naturally, to questions about the number and nature of such continua that will provide a context for a comprehensive view of empirical inquiry. An ample, thorough treatment of such a topic would fill many volumes and clearly lies beyond the scope of this chapter. However, the controversial six principles of scientific research advanced by the National Research Council (National Academy of Sciences, 2002) provide an initial view of the set of dimensions upon which individual studies may be described. Such dimensions represent a preliminary consideration of the continua that should be the focus of researchers' thinking and should provide a framework for methodological discussion and critique.

The six principles are:

1. *Pose significant questions that can be investigated empirically*. Among the plethora of questions that are asked in contemporary societies, only a subset represents viable candidates for empirical inquiry. Of this subset, some questions are of critical importance while others are trivial.
2. *Link research to relevant theory*. A broad goal of science is to generate and improve theories that explain phenomena. Inquiry that is contextualized within appropriate theoretical and conceptual frameworks leads to cumulative knowledge that refines and builds upon that which has come before.
3. *Use methods that permit direct investigation of the question*. The appropriateness of methodological choices can only be determined in the context of the specific research questions being asked. As illustrated earlier, questions about the extent to which increasing minority representation in schools causes improvements in student achievement require specific methodological approaches to allow the control of potentially confounding variables. Such approaches, however, constrain the ability to answer a variety of other, equally compelling research questions.
4. *Provide a coherent and explicit chain of reasoning*. The clear delineation of a logical chain of reasoning from theory and previous studies to research design and data analysis, then back to theory and previous studies requires researchers to critically evaluate their work. Further, explicit treatments of limitations and potential biases, the potential for counter-explanations, and detailed, public descriptions of procedures and analyses pave the way for coherent and compelling research.
5. *Replicate and generalize across studies*. All studies are conducted with finite samples and are limited in terms of settings, instrumentation, and other contextual factors. The reproduction of crucial findings across a variety of such contexts strengthens the extent to which arguments are supported and increases the potential impact of a study.
6. *Disclose research to encourage professional scrutiny and critique*. The dissemination of the results of inquiry and the subsequent critique and peer review is critical to the advance of knowledge. Public discourse on research methods and findings leads to clarification of implications and, ultimately, to the improvement of inquiry.

Such principles clearly represent characteristics that differ in extent or degree rather than yes/no dichotomies. Further, these principles are applicable across a range of methodological choices and provide a compelling context for the planning, conduct, and evaluation of investigations. As an example, the first principle suggests two dimensions upon which an instance of inquiry may be placed: the significance of the question addressed and the extent to which such a question may be answered empirically (Figure 5). Research that is low on both dimensions (being placed in the lower left area of Figure 5) suggests a study that is addressing a trivial question that cannot be adequately answered through empirical inquiry (e.g., "What color should school lunch boxes be?"). Conversely, a question, such as "What is the impact of minority representation on student achievement?" is both important and subject to empirical study (that is, research addressing such a question would be placed in the upper-right area of the plot). Further, research addressing "What proportions of minority students should be in each primary grade classroom?" is certainly high in importance, but "should" questions cannot be answered by empirical study. Such a study would be placed in the upper-left area of Figure 5. Finally, a study seeking to answer a question, such as "What is the relationship between teacher absenteeism and annual rainfall?" is certainly amenable to empirical investigation but is probably of little practical or theoretical importance (being placed in the lower-right area of Figure 5).

Similar treatments of the other principals will reveal that each represents a set of continua and that such continua may be conceptualized concurrently, yielding a multidimensional space within which research may be planned, conducted, and deliberated without the need for artificial dichotomization. Such a strategy, focusing on critical issues for all empirical inquiry, will lead to healthy, fertile debate about research methods, rather than channeling our energies to the limited and barren fields that are characteristic of the dualist landscape.

Conclusion

As can be seen from the research described in this chapter, mixed-methods studies are not only able to answer research questions that are more typically associated with the quantitative paradigm (e.g., who, where, how many, what is the relationship among variables), but they are also able to address research questions that are more commonly associated with the qualitative paradigm (i.e., why, how). Thus, as noted by Newman et al. (2003), mixed-methods investigations are able to address much more far-reaching research purposes in legal studies than are quantitative or qualitative research alone. Indeed, clearly, the best rationale for conducting mixed-methods research is its ability to capitalize on the strengths of both quantitative and qualitative research paradigms. In fact, according to the fundamental principle of mixed methods research, legal researchers should collect multiple data types utilizing different approaches and methods in such a way that the ensuing mixture or combination is likely to result in complementary strengths and nonoverlapping weaknesses (Brewer & Hunter, 1989; Johnson & Turner, 2003). For instance, experimental studies can be made more powerful, in terms of quality of data and inferences, if supplemented by or complemented with qualitative data (e.g., observational data, interview data). Similarly, the quality of data and inferences can be improved in ethnographic studies, grounded theory research, and the like by also collecting numeric information. As stated earlier, there is no fixed direct correspondence between research paradigm and research method. The mixing and matching of research strategies that best address our research questions should be paramount if our efforts are to result in a coherent program of disciplined inquiry. Thus, it is our firm belief that all researchers studying legal issues in education should critically examine the six principals of scientific research advanced by the National Research Council, and, when appropriate, consider the advantages of mixed-methods approaches in the conduct of empirical investigations.

References

Adler, L. (1996). Qualitative research of legal issues. In D. Schimmel (Ed.), *Research that makes a difference: Complementary methods for examining legal issues in education*, NOLPE Monograph Series (No. 56) (pp. 3-31). Topeka, KS: NOLPE.

American Educational Research Association, American Psychological Association, & National Council on Measurement in Education (1999). *Standards for educational and psychological testing* (rev. ed.). Washington: American Educational Research Association.

Bracht, G. H., & Glass, G. V. (1968). The external validity of experiments. *American Educational Research Journal, 5*, 437-474.

Brewer, J., & Hunter, A. (1989). *Multimethod research: A synthesis of styles*. Newbury Park, CA: Sage.

Campbell, D. T. (1957). Factors relevant to the validity of experiments in social settings. *Psychological Bulletin, 54*, 297-312.

Campbell, D. T., & Stanley, J. C. (1963). *Experimental and quasi-experimental designs for research*. Chicago: Rand McNally.

Cook, T. D., & Campbell, D. T. (1979). Quasi-experimentation: Design and analysis issues for field settings. Chicago: Rand McNally.

Creswell, J. W. (1998). *Qualitative inquiry and research design: Choosing among five traditions*. Thousand Oaks, CA: Sage.

Creswell, J. W, Plano Clark, V. L., Guttmann, M. L., & Hanson, E. E. (2003). Advanced mixed-methods research design. In A. Tashakkori and C. Teddlie (Eds.), *Handbook of mixed methods in social and behavioral research* (pp. 209-240). Thousand Oaks, CA: Sage.

Currall, S. C., & Towler, A. J. (2003). Research methods in management and organizational research: Toward integration of qualitative and quantitative techniques. In A. Tashakkori & C. Teddlie (Eds.), *Handbook of mixed methods in social and behavioral research* (pp. 513-526). Thousand Oaks, CA: Sage.

Denzin, N. K. (1978). *The research act: A theoretical introduction to sociological methods* (2nd ed.). New York: McGraw-Hill.

Denzin, N. K., & Lincoln, Y. S. (2000). Introduction: The discipline and practice of qualitative research. In N. K. Denzin & Y. S. Lincoln (Eds.), *Handbook of qualitative research* (2nd ed.) (pp. 1-28). Thousand Oaks, CA: Sage.

Dickinson, G. B., Holifield, M. L., Creer, D. G., & Holifield, G. (2000). Elementary magnet school students' interracial interaction choices. *Journal of Educational Research, 93*, 391-394.

Dzurec, L. C., & Abraham, J. L. (1993). The nature of inquiry: Linking quantitative and qualitative research. *Advances in Nursing Science, 16,* 73-79.

Forthofer, M. S. (2003). Status of mixed methods in the health sciences. In A. Tashakkori & C.

Teddlie (Eds.), *Handbook of mixed methods in social and behavioral research* (pp. 527-540). Thousand Oaks, CA: Sage.

Gersti-Pepin, C. (2002). Magnet Schools: A retrospective case study of segregation. *High School Journal*, *85*, 47-52.

Glaser, B. G., & Strauss, A. L. (1967). *The discovery of grounded theory: Strategies for qualitative research.* Chicago: Aldine.

Greene, J. C., Caracelli, V. J., & Graham, W. F. (1989). Toward a conceptual framework for mixed-method evaluation designs. *Educational Evaluation and Policy Analysis, 11,* 255-274.

Guba, E. & Lincoln, Y. (1994). Competing paradigms in qualitative research. In N. K. Denzin & Y. S. Lincoln (Eds.), *Handbook of qualitative reserach* (pp. 105-117). Thousand Oaks, CA: Sage.

Harmon, D. (2002). They won't teach me: The voices of gifted African American inner-city students. Roeper Review, 24, 68-75.

Howe, K. R. (1988). Against the quantitative-qualitative incompatibility thesis or dogmas die hard. *Educational Researcher, 17*, 10-16.

Hunter, A., & Brewer, J. (2003). Multimethod research in sociology. In A. Tashakkori & C.

Teddlie (Eds.), *Handbook of mixed methods in social and behavioral research* (pp. 577-594). Thousand Oaks, CA: Sage.

Johnson, R. B., & Christensen, L. B. (2004). *Educational research: Quantitative, qualitative, and mixed approaches*. Boston, MA: Allyn and Bacon.

Johnson, R. B., & Onwuegbuzie, A. J. (2004). Mixed methods research: A research paradigm whose time has come. *Educational Researcher*, *33*(7), 14-26.

Johnson, B., & Turner, L. A. (2003). Data collection strategies in mixed methods research. In A. Tashakkori and C. Teddlie (Eds.), *Handbook of mixed methods in social and behavioral research* (pp. 297-319). Thousand Oaks, CA: Sage.

Kerlinger, F. N. (1964). *Foundations of behavioral research*. New York: Holt, Rinehart, and Winston.

Krathwohl, D. R. (1998). *Methods of educational and social science research* (2nd ed.). New York: Longman.

Kjervik, D. K., & King, F. E. (1990). The legal research method: An approach to enhance nursing science. *Journal of Professional Nursing, 6*, 213-220.

Kvale, S. (1995). The social construction of validity. *Qualitative Inquiry, 1*, 19-40.

Lather, P. (1986). Issues of validity in openly ideological research: Between a rock and a soft place. *Interchange, 17*, 63-84.

Lather, P. (1993). Fertile obsession: Validity after poststructuralism. *Sociological Quarterly, 34*, 673-693.

Lee, J. (2004). Multiple facets of inequity in racial and ethnic achievement gaps. *Peabody Journal of Education*, *79*, 51-73.

Lincoln, Y. S., & Guba, E. G. (1985). *Naturalistic inquiry.* Beverly Hills, CA: Sage.

Lincoln, Y. S., & Guba, E. G. (1990). Judging the quality of case study reports.*International Journal of Qualitative Studies in Education, 3*, 53-59.

Longino, H. (1995). Gender, politics, and the theoretical virtues. *Synthese, 104*, 383-397.

Maxwell, J. A. (1992). Understanding and validity in qualitative research. *Harvard Educational Review, 62*, 279-299.

Maxwell, J. A. (1996). *Qualitative research design.* Newbury Park, CA: Sage.

Maxwell, J. A., & Loomis, D. M. (2003). Mixed methods design: An alternative approach. In A. Tashakkori and C. Teddlie (Eds.), *Handbook of mixed methods in social and behavioral research* (pp. 241-272). Thousand Oaks, CA: Sage.

Messick, S. (1989). Validity. In R. L. Linn (Ed.), *Educational measurement* (3rd ed., pp. 13-103), Old Tappan, N.J.: Macmillan.

Messick, S. (1995). Validity of psychological assessment: Validation of inferences from persons' responses and performances as scientific inquiry into score meaning. *American Psychologist, 50*, 741-749.

Miles, M. B., & Huberman, A. M. (1984). *Qualitative data analysis: A sourcebook of new methods*. Beverly Hills, CA: Sage.

Miles, M., & Huberman, A. M. (1994). *Qualitative data analysis: An expanded sourcebook* (2nd ed.). Thousand Oaks, CA: Sage.

Morgan, D. L. (1998). Practical strategies for combining qualitative and quantitative methods: Applications to health research. *Qualitative Health Research, 3*, 362-376.

Morse, J. M. (1991). Approaches to qualitative-quantitative methodological triangulation. *Nursing Research, 40*, 120-123.

National Academy of Sciences (2002). *Scientific research in education*. Washington, DC: National Academy Press.

Newman, I., & Benz, C. R. (1998). *Qualitative-quantitative research methodology: Exploring the interactive continuum*. Carbondale, IL: Southern Illinois University Press.

Newman, I., Ridenour, C. S., Newman, C., & DeMarco, G. M. P. (2003). A typology of research purposes and its relationship to mixed methods. In A. Tashakkori & C. Teddlie (Eds.), *Handbook of mixed methods in social and behavioral research* (pp. 167-188). Thousand Oaks, CA: Sage.

Onwuegbuzie, A. J. (2000, November). *Validity and qualitative research: An Oxymoron?* Paper presented at the annual meeting of the Association for the Advancement of Educational Research (AAER), Ponte Vedra, Florida.

Onwuegbuzie, A. J. (2002). Positivists, post-positivists, post-structuralists, and post-modernists: Why can't we all get along? Towards a framework for unifying research paradigms. *Education, 122*(3), 518-530.

Onwuegbuzie, A. J. (2003a). Expanding the framework of internal and external validity in quantitative research. *Research in the Schools, 10*, 71-90.

Onwuegbuzie, A. J. (2003b). Effect sizes in qualitative research: A prolegomenon. *Quality & Quantity: International Journal of Methodology, 37*, 393-409.

Onwuegbuzie, A. J., & Daniel, L. G. (Eds.). (in press). Special issue on mixed methods research [Special issue]. *Research in the Schools, 12*(2).

Onwuegbuzie, A. J., & Daniel, L. G., & Collins, K. M. T. (2004, February). *Problems associated with student teaching evaluations*. Paper presented at the annual meeting of the Southwest Educational Research Association (SERA), Dallas, TX.

Onwuegbuzie, A. J., Jiao, Q. G., & Bostick, S.L. (2004). *Library anxiety: Theory, research, and applications*. Lanham, MD: Scarecrow Press.

Onwuegbuzie, A. J., & Johnson, R. B. (2004). Mixed method and mixed model research. In R.B.

Johnson & L.B. Christensen, *Educational research: Quantitative, qualitative, and mixed approaches* (pp. 408-431). Needham Heights, MA: Allyn & Bacon.

Onwuegbuzie, A. J., & Leech, N. L. (2004, February). *A call for qualitative power analyses*. Paper presented at the annual meeting of the Southwest Educational Research Association, Dallas, TX.

Onwuegbuzie, A. J., & Teddlie, C. (2003). A framework for analyzing data in mixed-methods research. In A. Tashakkori & C. Teddlie (Eds.), *Handbook of mixed methods in social and behavioral research* (pp. 351-383). Thousand Oaks, CA: Sage.

Rallis, S. F., & Rossman, G. B. (2003). Mixed methods in evaluation context: A pragmatic framework. In A. Tashakkori & C. Teddlie (Eds.), *Handbook of mixed methods in social and behavioral research* (pp. 491-512). Thousand Oaks, CA: Sage.

Rocco, T. S., Bliss, L. A., Gallagher, S., Perez-Prado, A., Alacaci, C., Dwyer, E. S., Fine, J. C., &

Pappamihiel, N. E. (2003). The pragmatic and dialectical lenses: Two views of mixed methods use in education. In A. Tashakkori & C. Teddlie (Eds.), *Handbook of mixed methods in social and behavioral research* (pp. 595-615). Thousand Oaks, CA: Sage.

Sandelowski, M. (2001). Real qualitative researchers don't count: The use of numbers in qualitative research. *Research in Nursing & Health, 24*, 230-240.

Schwandt, T. A. (2001). Dictionary of qualitative inquiry (2nd ed.). Thousand Oaks, CA: Sage.

Shadish, W. R., Cook, T. D., & Campbell, D. T. (2001). *Experimental and quasi-experimental designs for generalized causal inference*. Boston: Houghton Mifflin.

Smith, M. L., & Glass, G. V. (1987). *Research and evaluation in education and the social sciences*. Englewood Cliffs, NJ: Prentice Hall.

Strauss, A., & Corbin, J. (1998). *Basics of qualitative research: Techniques and procedures for developing grounded theory.* Thousand Oaks, CA: Sage.

Tashakkori, A., & Teddlie, C. (1998). *Mixed methodology: Combining qualitative and quantitative approaches.* Applied Social Research Methods Series (Vol. 46). Thousand Oaks, CA: Sage.

Tashakkori, A., & Teddlie, C. (Eds.). (2003a). *Handbook of mixed methods in social and behavioral research.* Thousand Oaks, CA: Sage.

Tashakkori, A., & Teddlie, C. (2003b). The past and future of mixed methods research: From data triangulation to mixed model designs. In A. Tashakkori & C. Teddlie (Eds.), *Handbook of mixed methods in social and behavioral research* (pp. 671-701). Thousand Oaks, CA: Sage.

Twinn, S. (2003). Status of mixed methods research in Nursing. In A. Tashakkori & C. Teddlie (Eds.), *Handbook of mixed methods in social and behavioral research* (pp. 541-556). Thousand Oaks, CA: Sage.

Waszak, C., & Sines, M. C. (2003). Mixed methods in psychological research. In A. Tashakkori & C. Teddlie (Eds.), *Handbook of mixed methods in social and behavioral research* (pp. 557-576). Thousand Oaks, CA: Sage.

Wolcott, H. F. (1990). On seeking—and rejecting—validity in qualitative research. In E. W. Eisner & A. Peshkin (Eds.), *Qualitative inquiry in education: The continuing debate* (pp. 121-152). New York: Columbia University, Teachers College Press.

Wolf, S. M. (1994). Shifting paradigms in bioethics and health law: The rise of a new pragmatism. *American Journal of Law and Medicine, XX*(4), 395-415.

Figure 1.
The Research Process

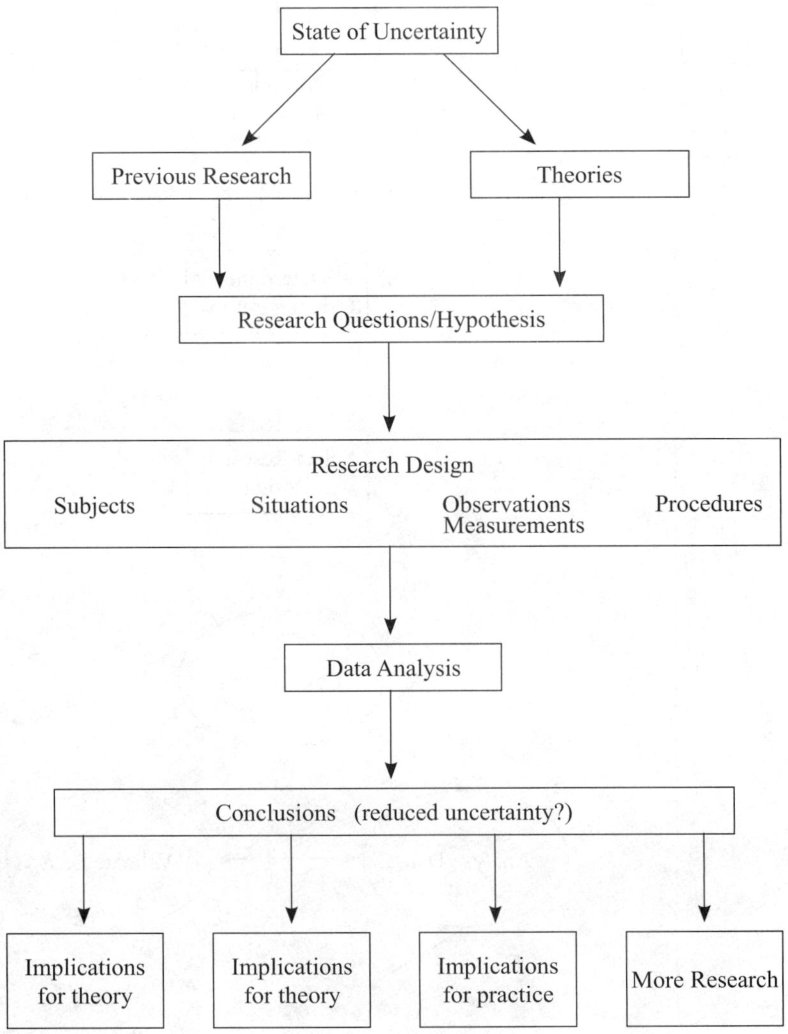

Figure 2.
Steps in the Mixed-Methods Research Process

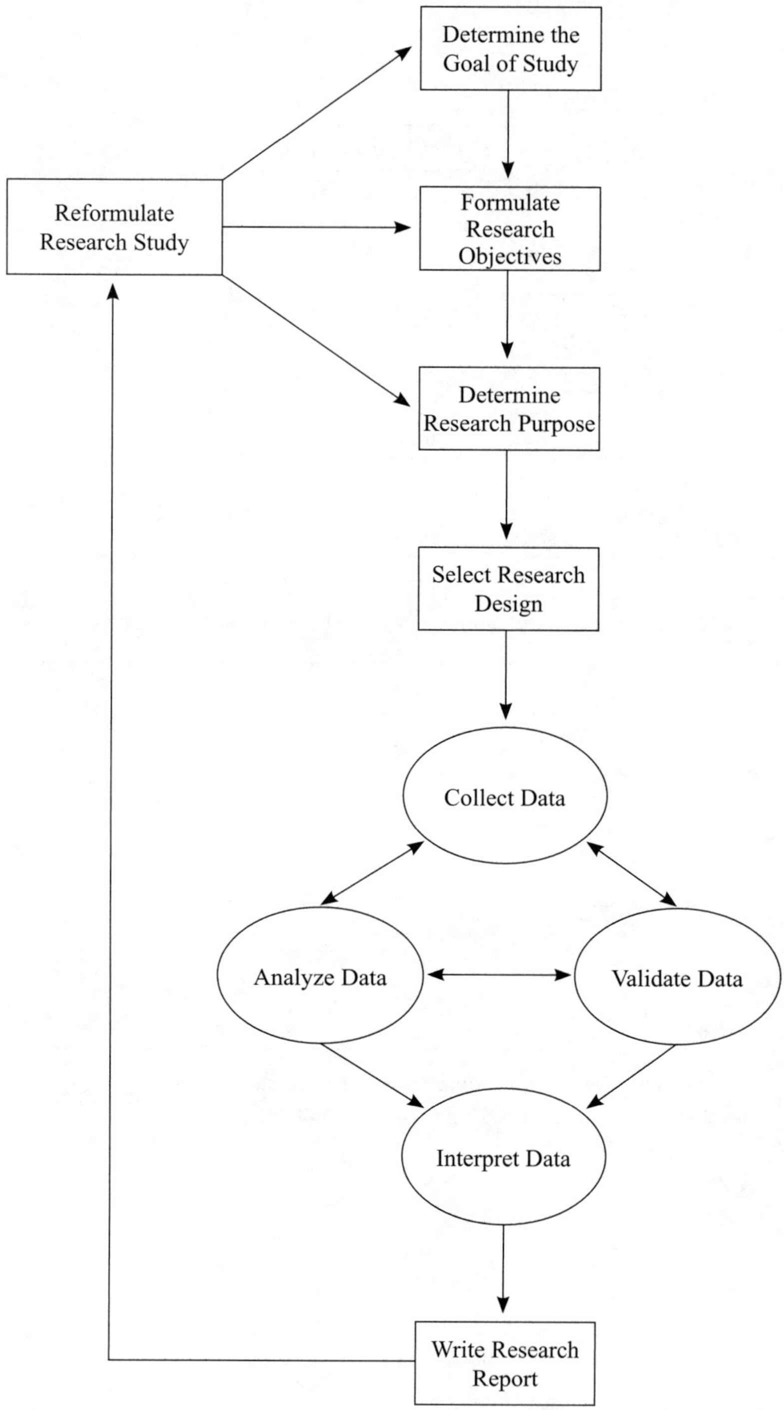

Figure 3.
Mixed-Method Design Matrix with Mixed-Method Research Designs Represented in the Four Cells

		Time Order Decision	
		Concurrent	Sequential
Paradigm Emphasis Decision	Equal Status	QUAN + QUAL	QUAN → QUAL QUAL → QUAN
	Dominant Status	QUAN + qual QUAL + quan	QUAN → qual quan → QUAL QUAL → quan qual → QUAN

Notation: "quan" stans for quantitative, "qual" stands for qualitative, "+" stands for concurrent, "→" stands for sequential, uppercase letters denote highest priority, and lowercase letters denote lowest priority.

Figure 4.
MonoMethod and Mixed-Method Designs

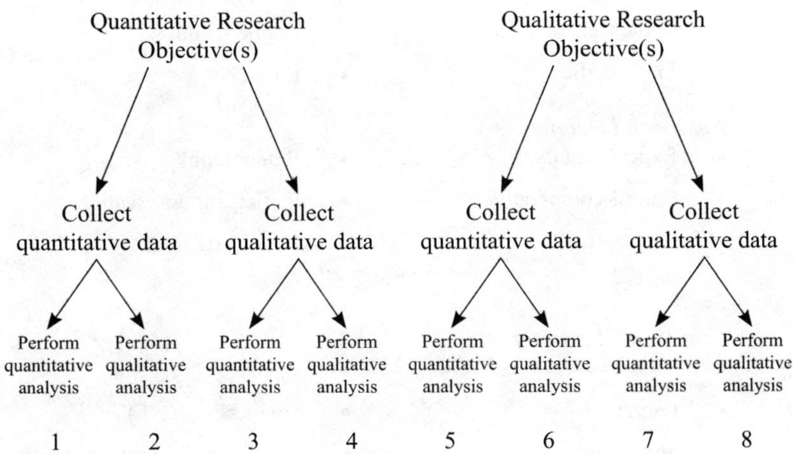

Note: Designs 1 and 8 on the outer edges are the monomethod designs. The mixed-model designs are designs 2, 3, 4, 5, 6, and 7.

Figure 5.
Continua Implied by the First Research Principle

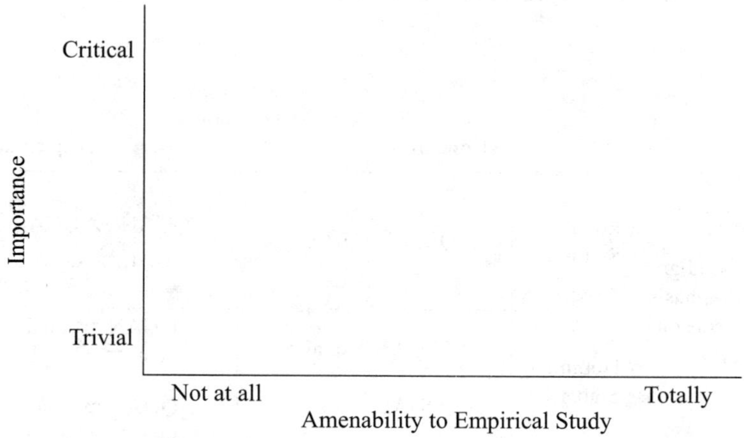

Table 1.
A Dualist View: Qualitative vs. Quantitative Inquiry

Quantitative	**Qualitative**
Nature of Inquiry	
• Context free	• Context bound
• Universal principles	• Interpretative
• Value free	• Explicit values
• Pre-specified	• Emergent
Research Designs	
• Experimental	• Ethnography
• Causal-comparative	• Participant observation
• Descriptive	• Naturalistic inquiry
• Survey	
Common Characteristics	
• Numbers/statistics	• Words
• Larger N	• Smaller N (depth)
• Structured	• Emergent – unfolds over time
• Detached	• Involved
• Explanation	• Understanding

Table 2.

Strengths and Weaknesses of Quantitative Research of Legal Issues

Strengths

- Can generalize research findings from sample to population when the data are based on large and random samples
- Can generalize a research finding when it has been replicated on many different samples, populations, and subpopulations
- It is useful for studying large numbers of individuals
- It is useful for studying behavior in a longitudinal manner
- Data can be collected relatively quickly via surveys and other standardized instruments
- Can test hypotheses and confirm/disconfirm theories that are constructed before data are collected
- It is useful for obtaining data that facilitate quantitative predictions whose accuracy can be assessed
- Enables the assessment of causal relationships that emerge in experimental studies.
- Potential confounding variables can be controlled for in a statistical manner.
- Numerical data can be used to assess the reliability and validity of findings
- Data analysis is relatively less time consuming via statistical software
- Data interpretation is relatively systematic (e.g., statistical significance, effect sizes)
- Findings can be synthesized relatively systematically (e.g., meta-analysis)
- It may have higher credibility with many people in power (e.g., judges, jury members, administrators, policymakers, stakeholders)

Weaknesses

- The researcher may misinterpret data due to the focus on theory or hypothesis *testing* rather than on theory or hypothesis *generation* (i.e., *confirmation bias*)
- Assumptions underlying most statistical tests (e.g., random sampling) typically are violated
- Use of statistical and practical significance indices is subject to misunderstanding, abuse, and misuse, for example, leading to overly simplistic dichotomous reject-do-not-reject hypothesis/theory decisions

Table 2 ***continued.***
Strengths and Weaknesses of Quantitative Research of Legal Issues

- Guidelines for interpreting measures of practical significance are generally inconsistent and arbitrary
- Statistical and practical significance indices are not always meaningful or useful for consumers of research
- Data can be analyzed appropriately only by researchers with adequate training.
- Can justify statistical techniques that cannot be undertaken via computer software (e.g., nonparametric multivariate analyses)
- Knowledge produced may be too abstract and general for direct application to specific local situations, contexts, and individuals

Table 3.
Strengths and Weaknesses of Qualitative Research of Legal Issues

Strengths

- Data often represent participants' own voices and meaning they attach to their experiences
- It is useful for studying a limited number of cases in depth
- It is useful for describing and interpreting complex phenomena
- Can facilitate cross-case comparisons and analysis
- Provides description and understanding of individual's personal experiences (i.e., the "emic" or insider's viewpoint)
- Can describe, in rich and thick detail, phenomena as they are situated and embedded in local contexts
- The researcher almost always identifies contextual and setting factors as they relate to the underlying phenomenon
- The researcher can study dynamic processes (i.e., documenting sequential patterns and change)
- The researcher can use techniques (e.g., grounded theory) to generate or expand theory about a phenomenon
- Can determine how participants interpret "constructs" (e.g., self-esteem)
- Data are usually collected in naturalistic settings
- Qualitative approaches are especially suited to needs at the micro-level and local level.

Table 3 *continued.*

Strengths and Weaknesses of Qualitative Research of Legal Issues

- Qualitative researchers are especially responsive to changes that occur during the conduct of an inquiry (especially during extended fieldwork) and may shift the focus of their studies as a result
- Qualitative data, which represent the words and categories of participants, lend themselves to exploring why and how phenomena occur
- You can use an important case to demonstrate vividly a phenomenon to the readers of a report (e.g., critical case sampling, politically important case sampling)
- Can be used to determine *idiographic* causation (i.e., determination of causes of a particular event)

Weaknesses

- Knowledge produced may not generalize to other people, contexts, locations, settings (i.e., findings may be unique to the relatively few people included in the research study)
- It is difficult to make predictions
- It is more difficult to test hypotheses and theories
- It may have lower credibility with some administrators and commissioners of programs due to the current emphasis at the Federal level on experimental research (i.e., Gold Standard)
- It typically takes more time to collect the data when compared to quantitative research
- Data analysis is often time consuming
- The results are more easily influenced by the researcher's personal biases and idiosyncrasies
- Data can be analyzed appropriately only by researchers with adequate training.
- Qualitative Computer Software is underutilized

6 Researching Legal Topics from a Policy Studies Perspective

Patricia F. First

"I believe in law. At the same time I believe in freedom. And I know that each of these things may destroy the other. But I know too that, without both, neither can long endure ... Law, freedom and justice—this trinity is the object of my faith."

-Supreme Court Justice Wiley Rutledge

Introduction

Policies are manifestations of the choices society has made about its future. A policy studies approach to researching legal topics is the broadest and most loosely defined of the research approaches addressed in this book. The essence of policy studies is the provision of timely information for society's decision makers. Policy studies and other social science research have been used in the briefs and rulings of significant legal decisions for decades. From *Brown v. Board of Education* in 1954 to *Gratz v. Bollinger* and *Grutter v. Bollinger* in 2003, social science research has influenced the outcome in landmark education cases. In the intervening decades, social science research has also influenced the crafting and evaluating of legislation, though perhaps not to the extent that policy researchers would prefer.

In order for a policy study to make a difference in society's choices, it is often necessary to release the information as the study progresses. Waiting for the final results may be important in other kinds of research, but in policy studies it is important to cut to the essentials of the questions and make the work timely and useful for policy makers. An assumption underlying this chapter is that good policy research, delivered in a timely manner in a usable format, can improve the decisions made for and by society. If it is good research and if it is properly used, policy research can contribute to maintaining the balance in Justice Rutledge's trinity of law, freedom, and justice.

Louis D. Brandeis argued that judges should attend to the available research because, he contended, judges must consciously consider the probable social results of their decisions (Gray, 1963). He prepared briefs filled with sociological evidence. Use of the "Brandeis brief" was popularized by Roscoe Pound in a series of articles showing the need for and relevance of sociological research on the ways the laws operated in practice (Cushman and Cushman, 1958). Nevertheless, disagreement about the proper relationship between the law and social science research continues to this day. This uncertain partnership between the disciplines of the law and the social sciences has created instances of use and misuse or research adding to the legal labyrinth of education. Nowhere is this more apparent than in the field of education finance (First and DeLuca, 2003; McUsic, 1999).

Decisions about financing the public schools are examples of policies as choices society makes about its future. When a state government chooses to decrease funding for K-12 education, the effects will influence its citizens far into the future. The passing of a law makes it state policy. The constitutionality of the law will be challenged in court, and those decisions will make more state policy. Obvious, subtle, and interrelated effects resulting from this policy will continue for generations. Policy studies are the scholarship about such choices; about the people, groups, and governments that make such choices; about the options considered and not considered; and about the impact of such choices, both immediately and long term.

Clearly, this is a broad category of research, and it can include, overlap, or duplicate other kinds of research. What makes "it" a policy study? The use to which it is put is the factor that makes it a policy study (Yudof, Kirp, Levin & Moran, 2000; Kahne, 1996; Anderson & Biddle, 1991). It is research "specifically directed at providing policymakers with the options and information they need to solve the problems we face today" (Majchrzak, 1984, p. 11). A policy study can be simple or complex, depending upon the questions asked. The purpose of a policy study may be the defining of questions for future research. When doing a policy study, the researcher may use any or all of the methods described in previous chapters. In fact, a researcher may do exactly the same things described in any of the other chapters, but as stated above, the use for which the study is intended will define it also as a policy study.

This chapter defines policy; outlines the values, paradigms, and disciplines in policy studies; examines the various forms of policy studies (e.g., policy analysis, policy research, and evaluation research); identifies the major activities in the policy research process; suggests approaches to cooperative policy research; and discusses criteria for determining a good policy study.

Policy Defined

Policy can be simply defined as a vision of where to go and guidelines for getting there. A policy statement can take many forms ranging from an act of the United States Congress, such as the No Child Left Behind Act of 2001, which sets national direction on education, to a local school guideline which describes what courses of action the school board approves in a given situation. Policy can also emerge from a series of decisions from one or more sets of decision makers, which is often how our national policy on an issue emerges (Weiss, 1991). We can look at decisions made and actions taken and, after the fact, discern the policy or the policy direction (Weiss, 1980).

Policy research can also take many forms and is subject to many descriptions. The following description is from Sandell (1977): [a] set of procedures for inventing, anticipating, exploring, comparing, and articulating the alternatives available for achieving certain objectives. It is a method of managing … collecting and organizing … information. It is an effort to ease the consternation that stems from seeking better ways to ordain the process of decision making (p. 48).

A working definition of "policy" may be helpful at this point. Figure 1 presents the working definition of policy and a policy statement used by the Illinois State Board of Education in its policy-development cycle. The crucial points to note are the references to policy as long term, involving leadership, and giving direction to subsequent decisions such as the allocation of resources. Note that in this working definition, it is also pointed out that policy statements may require the subsequent development of procedural statements such as guidelines, rules, and regulations. It is the confusion between policy and procedural statements that often creates chaos for both the decision maker and the researcher.

It is important that we understand that policy is wide, rather than narrow, long term, rather than short term and that it involves leadership. The leader is needed to paint the vision that becomes the policy (Keane, 2000; Gardner, 1995; Liswood, 1995). The policy researcher is needed to provide comprehensive information to the leader/decision maker.

Figure 1.
What is Policy? A Working Definition

In general, *policy making* involves decisions intended to have wide, rather than narrow, influences on people and operations and which are intended to have more than a short-range impact. In somewhat less general terms, *policy making* has the following three characteristics:

1. Policy making involves the strategic function of leadership and guidance.
2. Policy making shapes and clarifies substantive goals and major objectives.
3. Policy making gives direction to the development and operation of programs, influencing or determining the allocation of resources vis-à-vis competing demands.

A policy statement can be defined as having the following characteristics:

1. A clear intent to provide general direction (statement of position), rather than specific orders (statement of procedure);
2. Application to a well-defined population;
3. The (usual) absence of specific reference to time;
4. Addressing an area over which the policy-making body has authority or particular influence.

Statements of policy, by design and by definition, are intended to have relatively long-term effects. They may require the development of procedural statements (e.g., guidelines, rules, and regulations) that assist the respondent in the implementation of policy.

Source: Illinois state Board of Education. (n.d.). *The state board of education policies and procedures handbook*. Springfield, IL: Author.

It may be helpful here to briefly consider the related terms of policy-development processes and policy analysis. In its broadest sense, a policy-development process is an attempt at systematically anticipating and improving the future. Policy analysis is the process of identifying the issues inherent in, or related to, a policy statement. There are many definitions of these terms. "It must be noted that no one definition of policy should be glibly accepted" (Musial, 1986, p. 3). Musial goes on to point out that not all definitions are equal in their consequences for policy analysis: "Each definition calls for its own data, sources, and methods and each produces unique outcomes. Explicitly or tacitly, each different definition has an enormous impact on the processes and products of policy analysis" (p.3).

What constitutes a better definition is a matter of values, and the selection of a particular definition involves a value choice. If we value the fundamental principles of truth, goodness, and beauty, we may choose to define policy broadly as, for example, the effect of the curriculum on the child's life-long opportunity versus defining policy narrowly, such as policy regarding the choice of reading materials in a given year. If we value the great ideas of liberty, equality, and justice or Justice Rutledge's trinity of law, freedom, and justice, we would define school finance policy in relation to its effect upon those goals versus its effect on the budget in a particular school district. The budget and the reading selections may become intermediate indicators of progress toward policy attainment, or they may become incidental trivia.

No matter how we define policy, policy-development processes, or policy analysis, knowledge and its creators can enhance or influence public policy (Golan, 2004; Faigman, 2000). Analyses, planning, and forecasting can improve public decision making (First, 1996, 1986). This may be an unfashionable view, a bit too optimistic in the face of questionable decisions made during the decades of educational reform at the end of the twentieth century and the nationally driven high-stakes testing of the twenty-first century. Some writers call the belief—that more and better information leads to better decision making—a "myth" of policy analysis (Fischer & Forester, 1987). However, we can improve educational policymaking, although it may be necessary to proceed with small steps and incremental improvement, to "let go the finishing" (May, 1985, p.201) and be content with incompleteness. To better understand policy in this broad sense, let us step back, both in time and psychological distance, to examine a policy that we take for granted: compulsory schooling.

A Basic Policy Issue: Compulsory Education

We so take for granted that children must go to school, and it is easy to forget that this was once a controversial notion, one seen as infringing on parental rights and the primacy of the family unit. It is worth re-visiting this battle briefly for it illustrates the notion of policy as being broad and with long-term effects. Also, the tug-of-war between parental and state rights, which was at the heart of the compulsory schooling debate in the 1920s, is still an issue of the twenty-first century in the form of home schooling. All fifty states now permit home schooling under certain circumstances, but the procedures for the approval of home schools vary widely (Yudof, Kirp, Levin & Moran, 2000; Mawdsley, 1999). When states try to ensure adequate education for home schooled children with disabilities, as in the Vermont Home Study Law, the conflict between parental and state rights has multiple layers (*In re* S.M., 2003). Parental rights versus states' rights also form one of the polarities around which religious issues rage in the schools.

Pierce v. the Society of Sisters (1925) was the landmark Supreme Court decision that established the basic constitutional framework within which the states regulate schooling. The decision was called the *Pierce* Compromise because it gave the states unquestioned power to compel attendance at a school; however, it also established that the states cannot employ that power to eliminate all educational choices. As a result of *Pierce*, parents may choose public or private schools; and if private, they must choose between a secular or religious education for their children.

Far-reaching national policy emerges often from such Supreme Court decisions. In the specifics of this case, the state of Oregon had passed a law requiring children to attend public school. The issue at hand involved antipathy toward immigrants who often chose private schools as a route to preserving their religions and cultures. In the 1922 referendum campaign in Oregon, a Ku Klux Klansman was quoted as saying, "Somehow these mongrel hordes must be Americanized; failing that, deportation is the only remedy" (Yudof, Kirp, Levin & Moran, 2000, p. 12).

In settling this specific dispute within one state, the Supreme Court supported the states in requiring children to attend school and preserved for posterity choices and options within that requirement. But policy changes and grows. It accumulates incrementally; one policy may lead to more policy questions. The *Pierce* decision opened new areas of controversy, some litigated and continuously refined to this day. For instance, to what extent can the states regulate the private schools? How can the states regulate and still not interfere with the religious rights of these schools and the families who choose them? How far can a state go in regulating home schooling? This is a problem of great concern in the twenty-first century and raises again some basic questions about the state's responsibility to speak for the children, as critics of home schooling say that the very loose regulation in some of the states amounts to an abrogation of responsibility to the affected children.

The use of vouchers and the creation of charter schools pose other questions that are alive today because of the *Pierce* Compromise. Can or should state supported vouchers support religious schools? In *Zelman v. Simmons-Harris* (2002), the U.S. Supreme Court ruled that the Ohio voucher program did not violate the Establishment Clause, even though nearly all of the participating students attended religious schools.

Can or should public money support religiously affiliated charter schools? In 1997, the Supreme Court of Michigan ruled that the definition of public school includes charter schools and supporting the charters does not constitute parochiaid to religious schools (*Council of Organizations of Others for Education About Parochiaid v. Governor*). The growth of the charter schools movement is forcing the development of new legal relationships for schools (Green & Mead, 2003).

There are different kinds of interpretations to explain the phenomenon of compulsory education (Yudof, Kirp, Levin & Moran, 2000). For our purposes, it is an example of looking for the roots of some of the policy questions that are on the agenda today. Understanding the policy issues of the past can help us in our policymaking.

Why the Researcher Should Care About Policy

The researcher should care about policymaking and his or her policy-related roles because he or she has a unique contribution to make in the policy arena. Removed from the immediate scene, the school law researcher may be the only one with certain pieces of information needed to improve public policymaking. Educators at all levels and in all roles have an opportunity to set, or at least to influence, educational policymaking. In 1986, Gooler warned of the consequences of the noninvolvement of educators in policymaking: "It might be argued that educators have an obligation to help shape educational policy, for without engaging in this policymaking role with diligence, educators in effect proclaim that they are less than professionals in their own field. Not to be involved in policy setting is to abdicate leadership in education to others" (p. 37).Gooler's prediction seems to have materialized in 2005, much of the criticism of the No Child Left Behind Act and its state counterparts centers around these laws being the product of political, rather than educational, leadership.

Participating in the educational policy-development processes is important to the democratic notion of self-government. The ability of citizens to assert control over educational institutions through elections and other participatory means is the heart of democratic legitimacy (Yudof, Kirp, Levin & Moran, 2000). Regarding most educational policy, elections are seldom the means available, except at the local level where most school board members are elected. But administrators and other educators can impact the educational policy-development processes and thus help shape the goals of government by exerting influence, both individually and collectively through their professional associations, on policy being made by state legislatures, the U.S. Congress, and accreditation organizations. Superintendents of schools have direct responsibility to lead their boards in policymaking. In that role, they have an opportunity to examine their values and advocate for policy broadly defined to attain a greater value, such as equality, or narrowly defined to attain short-term goals such as keeping the district "safe" from suit (First, 2001).

The goals of government in the educational realm have varied through the decades from efficiency to equity to quality. Societal forces have determined which of these goals is paramount at any one time, and their rotation can most easily be seen in state policymaking. Underlying all of these goals has been the continuing theme of choice (Marshall, Mitchell, & Wirt, 1989). In the twenty-first century, choice has emerged as a major goal itself, and in debating the parental right to choose which school a child will attend, policy researchers and decision makers come face-to-face with questions of values as well as with the newly emerging legal relationships discussed by Green and Mead (2003).

Confronting Values, Paradigms, and Disciplines in Policy Studies

Values

We cannot claim that the uses to which policy studies are put are objective or value-free. Quite the opposite is true. During their use (or misuse) by an intended audience in the political world of governments and organizations, policy studies provide information to further someone's view of the better society. The belief that policy studies can contribute to the "good," to the better world, puts it in a long philosophical tradition back to and through Kant (Durant, 1926). Kant's great thesis was that the mind of man is an active organ that transforms the chaotic multiplicity of experience into the ordered unity of thought. Things can be better. It is up to people to make them better, and policy studies are one means of providing people with the orderly and systematic information to transform chaos into order.

Sometimes the same policy studies can be used to further conflicting arguments. In debates about charter school legislation, the same data on state educational mandates can be used by both sides. Competing values about how best to educate all children contribute to the debate about the high-stakes testing built into the No Child Left Behind Act (2001). But as Babbie (2001) stresses, science proceeds despite conflicting values and can even be improved by acknowledging them. "Science is not untouched by politics. An awareness of ideological considerations enriches the study and practice of social science methods" (Babbie, 2001, p. 485).

Values must be confronted, not ignored, in policy studies. Social values relate to the goals that a society seeks to achieve and that policy researchers should understand when systematically evaluating alternative public policies. Examples of value-laden policy options include direct public support for private and perhaps religiously affiliated schools; indirect public support for these schools via charter, voucher, or tuition tax credit; or no public support for private schools. Values related to the separation of church and state would not be the only values at work in consideration of these policy options. Values related to the potential side effect of resegregation of public schools via the voucher and charter mechanisms would also impact these policy decisions. Since polices are not value-free, the policy researcher must understand and address the values underlying a position or an issue. Problems for policy analysts in dealing with values have long been recognized.

> The key dilemma here is the extent to which policy analysts have an obligation to go beyond the purpose of merely describing the impact of one or more public policies and discussing the public policies that ought to be adopted for optimizing societal goals or subgoals. Another end or goal-oriented dilemma is the extent to which policy analysts can ethically pursue the values of groups such as political parties or interest groups and the values of individuals such as incumbent politicians, as well as what seems to be the values of society. Another concern for ends or effects is the extent to which policy analysts have an ethical and possible legal obligation to go out of their way to foresee foreseeable consequences, as contrasted to truly unforeseeable consequences (Fischer & Forester, 1987, p. 9).

The point is not to try to ignore values and play a losing game of value neutrality, but rather to acknowledge the values upon which the policy study is built. Values are expressed in the seeking and organizing of the information and in the strategies and research tools chosen. The best policy studies use multiple methods, including qualitative, quantitative, and traditional legal research, but multiple methods do not reduce the need to acknowledge the value base. Choice of method depends upon the intended use, the audience(s), and the timeline. The value of the timeliness in policy studies cannot be overstressed; an excellent policy study completed after the statute is passed or after a board has ruled is doomed to the storage closet. This is the fate of far too many doctoral dissertations. A study less excellent, but delivered when needed, has contributed to societal change. Of course the goal, or the "best" accomplishment is both excellence and timeliness in policy studies research.

Paradigms

"A paradigm is a world view, a general perspective, a way of breaking down the complexity of the real world" (Patton, 1978, p. 203). It became generally accepted that during the last decades of the twentieth century, our society partially moved through a paradigm shift from a positivist to a naturalist view of the world (Lincoln

& Guba, 1985), and this has brought some confusion to research, particularly applied research such as policy studies. We may find ourselves, both as private people and as researchers, operating in both paradigms, positivist and naturalist. Figure 2 displays Lincoln and Guba's (1985) contrasting axioms in the positivist and the naturalist paradigms. We may cling to the belief that reality is single and yet be faced with policy research that forces us to admit that realities are multiple; we may still believe that value-free inquiry is the ideal while being forced to inquire in a value-bound context. Robert Coles (1997) considers how fine the line is between fact and perception. In discussing documentaries, Coles shows how both prose and pictures are influenced by the observer's frame of reference: their social and educational background, personal morals, and political beliefs. As Babbie (2001) reminds us, "Reality is a tricky business" (p.18).

Figure 2
Contrasting Positivist and Naturalist Axioms

Axioms About	Positivist Paradigm	Naturalist Paradigm
The nature of reality	Reality is single, tangible, and fragmentable	Realities are multiple, constructed, and holistic.
The relationship of knower to the known	Knower and known are independent, a dualism.	Knower and known are interactive, inseparable.
The possibilities of generalization	Time- and context-free generalizations (nomothetic statements) are possible.	Only time- and context-bound working hypotheses (idiographic statements) are possible.
The possibilities of causal linkages	There are real causes, temporally precedent to or simultaneous with their effects.	All entities are in a state of mutual simultaneous shaping, so that it is impossible to distinguish couses from effects.
The role of values	Inquiry is value-free.	Inquiry is value-bound.

Source: *Naturalistic Inquiry* (p. 37), by Y. Lincoln and E. Guba, 1985, Newbury Park, CA: Sage. Copyright 1985 by Sage. Reprinted by permission of Sage.

It is important for the policy researcher to examine his or her paradigm base because operating within a familiar paradigm allows us to operate without long and anguished debate over every action and decision. Some of the social science paradigms from which we may view the world are macro and micro theory, early positivism, social Darwinism, conflict, symbolic interactionism, ethnomethodology, structural functionalism, feminism, and reconsidered rational objectivity (Babbie, 2001). Our immersion in any of those paradigms, or others, may mask assumptions that should be questioned. For example, our present world view (or paradigm) may allow us to believe that it is reasonable or even necessary for children to have a two- or three-month summer vacation from school. We may have assumptions about the desirability of more choice in education based on the paradigm from which we operate. But perhaps these and other assumptions needs to be questioned if we are to investigate the ways a school district can provide equal educational opportunity to all children. "Paradigms are deeply embedded in the socialization of adherents and practitioners: paradigms tell them what is important, legitimate, and reasonable. Paradigms are also normative, telling the practitioner what to do …" (Patton, 1978, p. 203). The policy researcher needs to pause, step back, and examine what the paradigm is telling the researcher to think and do.

Disciplines

As philosophers continue to call for a better world, policy studies that include legal analysis increasingly inform their thought and writing, which in turn, informs another round of policy studies. For example, in her 1992 philosophical exploration of the ideal in schooling, Jane Roland Martin asked, "What about attempting to change the real world?" (p. 161). The bibliography in Martin's book testifies to the legal research in policy studies that helped shape her thinking. These policy studies included analyses of women's rights, children's rights, and the meaning of justice. Her work is a description of what a good school for children can be, as well as a call for action for us to make it so.

Use of Martin's philosophical work to inform policy studies focusing on legal issues is an example of the interdisciplinary heart of policy studies. Policy studies come from and bear upon multiple disciplines, including the one we care most about here:

the law. Edward O. Wilson (1998) uses the term "consilience" as he calls for interdisciplinary research. Consilience, writes Wilson, is "literally a 'jumping together' of knowledge by the linking of facts and fact-based theory across disciplines to create a common groundwork of explanation." Wilson explains that the separation of domains and disciplines results in confusion that is detrimental to society.

Crow, Levine, and Nager (1992) describe the benefits and the problems of collaborative, interdisciplinary research done by an anthropologist, a psychologist, and a sociologist. The benefits they list include coming closer to tapping the complexity of the subject (career change), pushing to attain clarity of meaning across the disciplines by using more precise language, and yielding unanticipated data because of the multiple perspectives provided by the methodologies of the disciplines. These are three benefits that add richness and depth to policy study.

Yet the disciplines clash, and there is the suspicion that interdisciplinary work may lack rigor. The separation of domains and disciplines results in confusion that is detrimental to society, but there is still distrust and misunderstanding among the disciplines and misuse of research across disciplines. Roadblocks to interdisciplinary work exist in the law in its dependence on legal precedent. And roadblocks to interdisciplinary work exist in education in the distrust of education research by educators, the arguing among educators in different roles (teachers, administrators, specialists, etc.) and the failure of educators to accept the necessity of providing research in a usable form and in a timely manner.

As statutes are crafted and court cases decided, we would hope that those with the power to craft policy, those with the power to transform chaos into order, would look to the great minds in many disciplines for a vision of what can be: the stuff of which our dreams of a better society are made. In today's proof-conscious atmosphere, the dream side of policy studies is often ignored; but to continue to ignore it dooms us to repetition of the tried, whether or not the tried has proved to be the true. Thus, states resist loosening schooling's dependence upon property taxes, fail to equalize opportunity for excellence in education, and in countless other ways, cling to the old.

The Forms of Policy Studies

Policy Analysis

As a policy analysis, or study of the policymaking process, we could investigate the incidents and cases that led to a particular court decision, a state statute or a school board policy. We could study the policymaking processes used by the decision-making bodies dealing with the topic and the environment impacting those processes. This could be traditional legal research if applied to a court case, but it is also a policy analysis when applied to other items, such as a state statute or school board policy. If we were analyzing *Elk Grove Unified School District v. Newdow* (2003), we could apply traditional legal research to the case and add a policy analysis of the political pressures and religious lobbying around the issues in the case. This could be done, for example, by conducting interviews with legislators, lobbyists, and other political leaders who speak out on associated topics; examining the legislative record and pertinent statutes; analyzing newspaper accounts of the case and similar controversies in selected cities; and adding other interviews with administrators responsible for implementing the resultant law and policy. The result could be a rich portrait of the nation's law, policy, and mood about prayer in public schools. Taking another avenue, we could analyze the similarities and differences in the state laws concerning recitation of the Pledge of Allegiance, which came to the public's attention during the extensive press coverage of the *Newdow* case.

Policy Research Before Decision Making

As policy research before decision making, we could gather all the information on the topic and filter it down to a set of options and their foreseeable consequences for a policymaking group such as a legislature or a university senate. This could be done after a court case or as testimony in a case such as *DeRolph v. State* (2002) where extensive social science research made little difference to a court and a legislature considering a state's school funding system (First and DeLuca, 2003). In cases concerning cyberspace and information technology, policy research done before decision making by state legislatures or school boards may ground those policies in a sounder knowledge base (First and Hart, 2002). Social science research before decision making was used by the U.S. Supreme Court in the University of Michigan Law School affirmative action case, *Grutter v. Bollinger* (2003): "… numerous studies show that student body diversity promotes learning outcomes and 'better prepares students for an increasingly diverse workforce & society, & better prepares them as professionals.'"

Policy Research After Decision Making

As policy research after decision making, we can ask what difference(s) the decision made. The difference desired may have nothing to do with the decision's impact on the intended audience or secondary audiences. The impact on children is often a side effect of policy decisions when children's rights are not specifically taken into account. Policy research done after decision making is often called an impact study. Impact studies can be snapshots (what difference has the decision made at this point in time?) or longitudinal efforts (what difference is the decision making over an extended period of time?). The major question is what is the effect of this court decision/statute/school board policy on children and families, or on a layer of government such as school boards? The researcher asks if the decision is doing what it is intended to do, if there are side effects, favorable or otherwise, and if there are blocks to implementation.

This kind of policy research is being conducted extensively in the aftermath of the No Child Left Behind Act of 2001 (Duran, 2005; Ryan, 2004). Ideally, results of impact studies are fed back into the policymaking process for the making of further policies and/or the modification of the policy being studied. Odden (1991) has edited a collection of influential policy research done after earlier major federal policy initiatives. Heubert's (1999) edited volume of six law-driven school reforms is another source of policy research that has made a difference after decision making.

Another specialty within policy research after decision making is called evaluation research. Programs flow from policies, and thus program evaluation is a form of policy research and another kind of impact study. It is important to note that all of these terms are used quite interchangeably. Much of the discussion of methodology and criteria in policy studies comes from the evaluation literature. Therefore, whether evaluation is a subset of policy studies or whether policy studies are a subset of the evaluation world, the issue can provide a lively discussion for the researchers involved. The more important point is that the study be done in the spirit, and based on the values, of improving society (Sirotnik, 1990).

Impact studies are now underway in the aftermath of the University of Michigan affirmative action cases (*Gratz v. Bollinger,* 2003; *Grutter v. Bollinger,* 2003; Stohr, 2004). Also, studies to gauge the impact on the schools will now begin in the aftermath of the Supreme Court decisions on age discrimination and Title IX protection for whistle blowers (*Smith v. City of Jackson, Mississippi,* 2005; *Jackson v. Birmingham Board of Education*, 2005).

The issue of search and seizure in the public schools has provided fertile ground for impact studies and evaluation research. Longer term impact studies have been taking place for years in the aftermath of *T.L.O. v. New Jersey* (1995) as some schools and states resisted and others adapted to the decision. In fact, search and seizure is a particularly interesting topic for a broadly based interdisciplinary policy study. Ehrensal (2003) has written of the social construction of children after *T.L.O.*, and Sughrue (2003) has written of zero tolerance for children policies after the Gun-Free Schools Act of 1994.

Exploratory Policy Studies

Finally, there is a wide category of work we can call exploratory policy studies. Here we watch and document the development of an interest area, track new movements, and trace what is happening in anticipation of the statutes, cases, and policies to come. The topics of school choice and full-service or integrated services schools were in this exploratory category for a long while (Gerry, 1999). The law of cyberspace is there now (First and Hart, 2002). Analysis of the emerging and/or underlying values in new directions in federal policy would fall in this category, as would philosophical studies of a curricular question as basic as "What makes an educated person?" In the academic setting, exploratory policy studies are useful for establishing the theoretical base for one's policy work. For example, such studies have led to the theoretical base used in my work and that of my students: a bottom-line value of justice and care for all children. It would make an interesting exploratory policy study to juxtapose the issues of prayer, vouchers, and charters and analyze where choices we are making now are leading our schools for the future.

Traditional Research Put to Policy Use

Sometimes research not originally intended as policy research is used after the fact to inform policy decisions. Three particularly interesting examples of social science research used in this way are found in *Brown v. Board of Education of Topeka* (1954), *Abbott v. Burke* (1990), and *Lee v. Weisman* (1992). In *Brown* the famous footnote 11 cites, seven studies supportive of the court's view about children in grade and high schools that "to separate them from others of similar age and qualifications solely because of their race generates a feeling of inferiority as to their status in the community that may affect their hearts and minds in a way unlikely ever to be undone … Whatever may have been the extent of psychological knowledge at the time of *Plessy v. Ferguson*, this finding is amply supported by modern authority." There has been much controversy over the extent to which the *Brown* decision relied upon the social science evidence rather than principles of law and over the appropriateness of the use of such evidence. Despite the controversy, this is an important example of research used in a policy-oriented way in a legal situation that shifted the course of our societal development.

In the 1990 case, *Abbott v. Burke*, in which a New Jersey court ruled that state's school funding system unconstitutional, the use of social science research to inform policy decisions made in the courts is clearly in evidence, and its use was much less controversial, though arguments over the quality of the research remain. The *Abbott* court made ample use of policy research, dealing with the information at hand while admitting, "The inconclusiveness of the research is conceded." The research used included educational theory, methodology in urban education, work on dropouts and alternative educational settings, social and home conditions of children, and educational finance research from many perspectives.

Abbott offers a clear example of an assumption underlying the work of the policy researcher: it is better for the policymaker to have the benefit of the best information available at the time of decision making, even if the state of the research is "inconclusive." The alternative is public policy decision making by groping in the dark. The variety of research presented to the *Abbott* court contributed heavily to a decision that should over time bring improvements to the education of New Jersey's disadvantaged children. The court wrote, "Obviously, we are not more able to identify what these disadvantaged students need in concrete educational terms than are the experts. What they don't need is more disadvantage, in the form of a school district that does not even approach the funding level that supports advantaged students. They need more, and the law entitles them to more." Longitudinal impact studies (policy research after decision making) will show whether or not all children get the "more" the court said they are entitled to.

In 1992, in *Lee v. Weisman*, the Supreme Court supported its notion of student impressionability by citing to psychological authority. The Court was considering whether or not opening graduation exercises with prayer in a middle school violated the Establishment Clause of the Constitution. The Court used the results of psychological research on the impressionability of students of middle-school age as part of its determination about the presence of governmental coercion if prayers are included in graduation. This is an example of traditional research later used as policy research. The Court expressed concern for impressionable students who might perceive the efforts of school officials to facilitate prayer as coercing participation in a religious ritual, which they might otherwise reject.

Decision Points/Policy Processes

Sometimes it is difficult to determine which of the forms of policy research to use and where in the policymaking process to apply the research. Any time a policy-level decision is made, some multi-stepped process has taken place. It may be formal and complex, as in the Illinois State Board of Education example in Figure 3,or it may be simple, informal, and perhaps barely acknowledged or known by the participants. In either case, it may be institutionalized and perhaps literally diagrammed as in the Illinois example, or it may be just "known" or understood by the participants. It is very helpful to the policy researcher (and sometimes crucial to the study) to make a visual of the policymaking process under consideration. Any of the forms of policy research may then be appropriately applied at any of the decision points in the process, depending upon the purpose(s) of the study. Note in the diagram of the Illinois process the variety of sources from which an issue may emerge before serious state policy development begins.

Figure 3
Policy Making Process

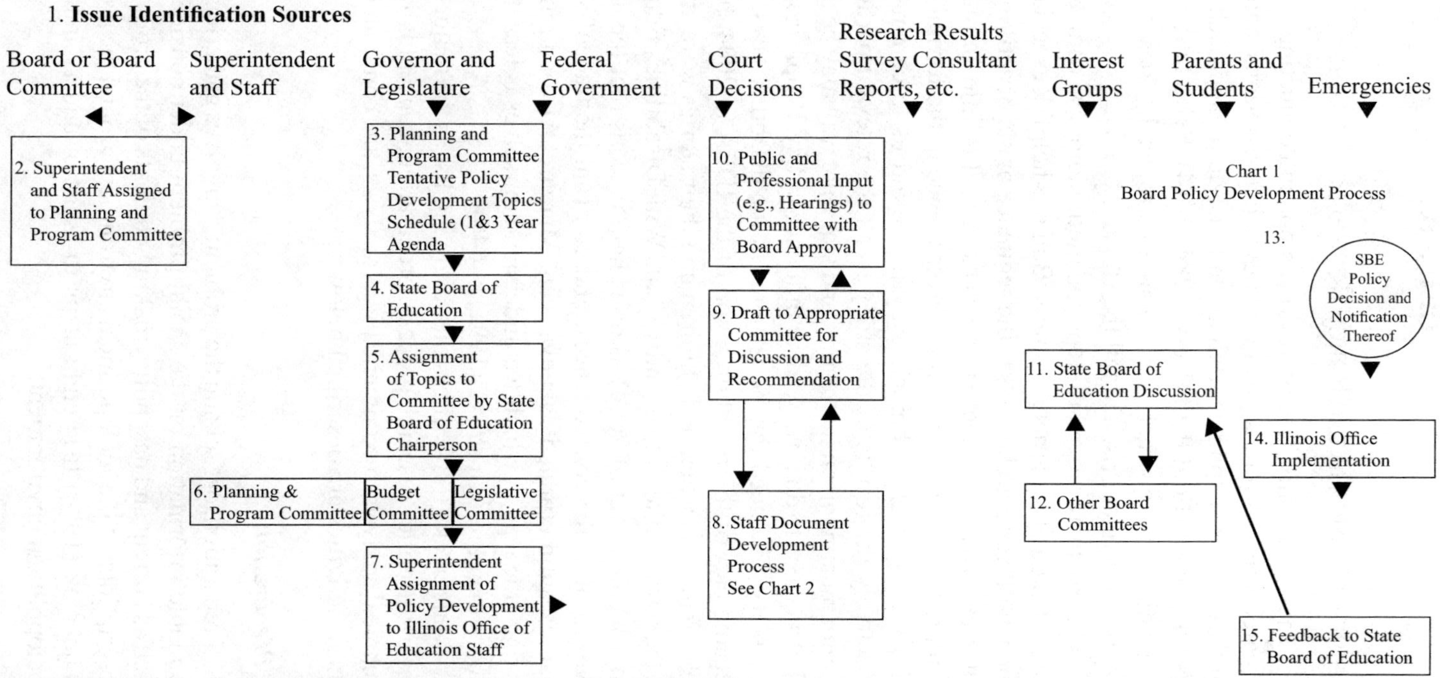

Source: Illinois State Board of Education (n.d.). *The State Board of Education Policies and Procedures Handbook.* Springfield IL: Author.

How to Do It:

Major Activities in the Policy Research process

There are many lists of various steps in conducting a policy research study. A fun list, which is nevertheless serious, and beautifully conveys a "plunge in there and just do it" approach is The Way of the Six-Fold Path (Dery, 1984, p. 14): Seize the problem, hustle the data, construct the alternatives, project the consequences, confront the tradeoffs, and tell the story.

Clearly there are many steps and methodological choices to be made at each of these action points. But, it is helpful, especially for a new policy researcher, to see the sequence of major activities laid out in everyday language. The words used in this little formula give us hints for success as much as the sequence in the formula does. "Story" may seem a flippant way to remind us to communicate effectively the results of the study to all the relevant parties, but communicating in an interesting and storylike way may be exactly what we need to do if we wish to influence policy. People can relate to a story. The need for the changes in the disability laws, which became part of the reauthorization of the IDEA in 2004, became more real to us when real children and their stories were attached to the various alternative (Individuals With Disabilities Education Improvement Act of 2004). Stories help us construct the alternatives, project the consequences, and confront the tradeoffs better than the uninterpreted data ever can. Margaret Atwood reminded us that "the way in which we understand ourselves is less through theory than through story" (1991, p. 648).

Majchrzak (1984) offers the following list as the major activities in the policy research process: preparation; conceptualization; technical analysis, recommendations analysis; and communication. These activities are described below:

1. Preparation

Preparation, or "seizing the problem," involves gathering all the available information on the social problem under consideration, such as current and past policymaking contexts of the problem and descriptions of the sociopolitical environment around the problem. Majchrzak (1984) lists eight steps to assist in understanding the sociopolitical environment:

a. Select the social problem;

b. Identify key policy issues;

c. Analyze legislative history of policy issues;

d. Trace progress of previous research and change efforts;

e. Obtain organizational charts of decision-making bodies;

f. Draw model of policymaking process;

g. Interview stakeholders; and

h. Synthesize the information.

2. Conceptualization

Conceptualization involves identifying the questions to be answered and the methods to be used to find the answer. Too often, beginning researchers attempt to jump to the conceptualization stage without completing a thorough preparatory stage. In the preparatory stage the researcher immerses himself or herself in the problem area in order to know what questions are worth asking, what questions are answerable, and what questions answered can possibly make a difference in the future. Defining the problem and wording the questions can be the most crucial step in the policy research process (Dery, 1984). Bernard Berelson (1976) offered five criteria of research questions most likely to advance public policy. He stated that the research question should:

a. Address an important aspect of the social problem;

b. Be do-able, that is, feasible given expected study constraints;

c. Be timely by providing information that will be useful for current and future decision making;

d. Provide a synthesis of diverse viewpoints so that the results represent an integration to the field, rather than simply an addition; and, last but not least,

e. Exhibit policy responsiveness by addressing issues in a manner that will help policymakers act on the social problem.

3. Technical Analysis

During technical analysis, you are "hustling the data." You collect any further needed data, and then you do with it what is necessary to answer your questions. This is the stage in policy research most like traditional research processes, and it is here that you may use some or all of the methods described in other chapters in this book. Majchrzak (1984) divides the technical analysis into four major areas: operationalize the variables, i.e., define the variables in terms of specific measurable indicators; design the study methodology; conduct the analysis; and develop conclusions and tentative recommendations.

4. Recommendations Analysis

In this step, you are constructing the alternatives and projecting the consequences. Here the analyst develops a set of conclusions and policy recommendations. Depending upon the uses and audience for the study, the analyst may also need to draft an implementation plan for the policy recommendation. For example, if an analyst for a state board of education recommends a state initiative to include all-day kindergarten in the curriculum of the public schools, it is highly likely that the state board would expect a detailed implementation plan as part of the policy study. Some researchers feel strongly about the inclusion of an implementation plan in a policy study: "Merely saying that something should be done-with-out saying how-is an abdication of responsibility" for which social scientists are frequently guilty (Wildavsky, 1979, p. 126).

5. Communication

As you communicate, you are confronting the tradeoffs and telling the story. Method and timing of communication will vary depending upon the use(s) and audience(s) for a particular study. But, in general, Majchrzak (1984) suggests four techniques for the effective communication of the results of a policy research study. The first is to build credibility with the potential users by communicating throughout the study with progress reports and the acceptance of feedback, rather than once at the end. Second, communicate with different potential users of the study, and choose to emphasize the information and progress each would be most interested in. If your policy study is connected with your dissertation research, the high interest items may be very different for your professor and your school board. Third, make the presentation appropriate to the audience. Different versions, an executive summary being just one common example, may need to be prepared. The dissertation format required at your university is almost never suitable for putting your findings in the hands of policy makers who may use it or of book or journal editors who may publish parts of it. Failure to package the results of dissertation research in useable formats is why so much of it sits on the shelf. And last, remember that oral communication may be more effective than written communication, so plan appropriate verbal presentations to accompany the delivery of your carefully packaged policy study.

Working on a Big Scale: Cooperative Research

I have been writing about how to do research that "makes a difference." An idealist would hope that this research translates into action that in turn translates into making the world a little better place. Since our field is education and our specialty under discussion is education law, the portion of the world our research may affect is schools—making them better places for the children who must attend them. A basic belief underlying this chapter is that research can make a difference by having a positive effect on the quality of educational policy decisions at all levels of the educational governance system. Despite all I have read to the contrary, I rather stubbornly assume that good information, easily accessed and delivered in a timely manner can make a difference in sound decision making. Since today's social problems require multiple viewpoints, interdisciplinary policy-oriented research, and the voices of many researchers, cooperative research may be the key to the kind of research that does, in fact, make a difference.

Valuing collaboration and a team approach to research grows out of my past professional experience. I was a state education policy analyst early in my career, working as a member of multidisciplinary teams. Standard operating procedure engaged many minds and voices collaboratively. One just didn't work in isolation. Many of the graduate students using this book may have learned the value of a collaborative approach as a practitioner, perhaps running a school through administrative and instructional teams. The skills acquired in these group endeavors can be easily and meaningfully applied to policy research.

The benefits of collaborative research on educational policy issues could be substantial for the researchers and their organizations, but more importantly, for the real clients of all our efforts, the consumers of information about educational law and, ultimately, the school children whose experience is affected by decisions based on that information. Suggested here are ways to foster collaborative policy research so that such cooperation will strengthen and broaden the research an individual may be doing on his or her own, and so that educational organizations can nurture more research that will provide meaningful contributions to the field.

There are several strategies by which this goal can be accomplished. One is for educational policy researchers to do more of what they are doing anyway but to coordinate with each other and perform their research in an organized way so that there is a national snapshot, rather than a regional or state snapshot, of an educational law problem or perhaps a school district snapshot rather than one for a single building. An example of such a snapshot would be to ascertain what members of some targeted group (such as administrators, school board members, teachers, or teachers in training) actually know about a certain area of the law. This is a popular school law dissertation approach, often with interesting results but with limited impact. But if done nationally, via a cooperative network and coupled with a supportable vision of what the group should know, such research could influence curriculum in training programs for the group studied. If done in a school district, such research could assist administrators in planning meaningful professional development activities.

A second strategy involves the planning of impact studies after a major education law event. The impact could be studied immediately (the first stages of implementation or resistance) and/or over time. Such major events would include Supreme Court decisions, federal statutes, and studies of how state statutes have developed under the influence of a strong national movement such as the implementation of the No Child Left Behind Act. A study of how states and districts struggled in the first year after the passage of NCLB over such issues as the meaning of "highly qualified" teacher would provide a portrait of resistance and political gamesmanship.

There is a huge need for longitudinal impact studies in school law. Decades after *T.L.O.* (1985) do we know, beyond anecdotal evidence and extreme examples, if school administrators are properly searching students? Can we be sure they are even well educated in the area of search and seizure? Impact studies conducted by a network of educational policy researchers could provide valuable information for the refinement of existing policy and for future policy making. Impact studies of this type could be built on the existing literature on compliance, implementation, and impact, which would provide rich follow-up to the legal analysis of the court decisions themselves (Kelly, 2001; Wong, 1996; Fuhrman, 1993; Anderson & Biddle, 1991; Rebell & Block, 1982).

A third strategy for cooperative research incorporates the examination of both court cases and statutes in selected states vis-à-vis some topic on which there is as yet no national consensus. An example is the proliferation of proposed state and national statutes on vouchers in the aftermath of the Cleveland, Ohio, voucher case (Zelman v. Simmons-Harris, 2002). An interesting addition to this kind of study would be to relate the findings to some of the existing politics of education literature, such as that on state policy cultures (Spring, 1998; Marshall, Mitchell, & Wirt, 1989). Tying legal knowledge to knowledge from other disciplines about the same topics would produce strengthened interdisciplinary reports and better illuminate what is taking place in educational institutions. Bateson (1990) provides us with another reason to stress the interdisciplinary: "It also seems probable that the most creative thinking occurs at the meeting place of the disciplines. At the center of any tradition, it is easy to become blind to alternatives. At the edges, where lines are blurred, it is easier to imagine that the world might be different." (p.73). Working cooperatively on education policy studies could lead policy researchers to "the meeting place of the disciplines."

Conclusion

We have seen that policy studies research is a broad category of research that may both overlap, and be used in conjunction with, other methods; that the richest policy studies are those that use multiple methods and are grounded in interdisciplinary points of view; and that what makes "it" policy studies is the use to which it is put by policy-level decision makers in solving today's societal problems. We are left then with another question: How do we know a study is a good policy study? Given the acknowledgement of the often tight timelines and other constraints, often political, involved in real world policymaking, are there criteria that help the researcher know when a good job has been done?

Lincoln and Guba (1985) and Guba and Lincoln (1989) offer criteria useful for the policy analyst in determining the trustworthiness of the study. These are credibility, transferability, dependability, and confirmability. Credibility is concerned with the truth of the findings for particular subjects in a particular context and would replace the concern with internal validity found in traditional research methods. Credibility can be corroborated by the use of such methods as crosschecking and triangulation (Worthen, Sanders & Fitzpatrick, 1996).

To determine the transferability or applicability of a policy study to another context, the researcher would assess the fit of the findings to that problem or that setting. The more complete or thick the description in the original study, the more likely that a potential fit can be assessed. Concern with applicability replaces the concern with external validity found in traditional research studies.

The dependability or the consistency of the study replaces concern for traditional reliability. An audit trail is used to determine this kind of dependability, i.e., if a second policy researcher or policy research team reviewed the documentation and the underlying reasoning, would agreement on the findings be reached?

Confirmability means neutrality or objectivity. Simply put, the data should be factual and confirmable, and the policy researcher should require that each piece of information is confirmable at each step in the research process. In the often highly charged political atmosphere in which the results of policy studies are used, confirmability is a basic must and the place where faults in a policy study can become most readily apparent.

All four criteria are even more important for the policy researcher in the aftermath of the No Child Left Behind Act (2001). The federal government is promoting scientifically based research for use in the public schools. Criticism of education research has led to calls for randomized trials in education like those conducted in medicine and agriculture. In the political atmosphere of 2005, policy researchers must be able to clearly demonstrate the quality and trustworthiness of their work. When excellence in the work can be demonstrated, policy studies can strengthen the relationship between social science and public policy (Anderson, 2003).

If the policy researcher attends to these four criteria, treated in detail in Worthen, Sanders, & Fitzpatrick (1996), and if the policy study is delivered when and where it is needed for decision making leading to the "good" society, the researcher can be proudly confident that it is a good policy research study. He or she can have the satisfaction of knowing that the work is likely to make a positive difference in the ongoing quest for the "good" society, one based upon Justice Rutledge's trinity of law, freedom, and justice.

References

Abbott v. Burke, 575 A.2d 359 (N.J. 1990).

Anderson, L. (2003). *Pursuing truth, exercising power: Social science and public policy in the twenty-first century (University seminars/ Leonard Hastings Schoff memorial lectures).* New York: Columbia University Press.

Anderson D. S. & Biddle, B. J. (1991). *Knowledge for Policy: Improving Education Through Research.* London: The Falmer Press.

Atwood, M. (1991, Fall). Northrop Frye remembered. *Michigan Quarterly Review*, 647-649.

Babbie, E. (2001). *The practice of social research, 9th Ed.* Belmont, CA: Wadsworth.

Bateson, M. C. (1989). *Composing a life.* New York: Plume.

Berelson, B. (1976). Social science research in population: A review. *Population and Development Review*, 2(2), 219-266.

Brown v. Board of Education of Topeka, 347 U.S. 483, 74 S. Ct. 686 (1954).

Coles, R. (1997). *Doing documentary Work.* Oxford: Oxford University Press.

Council of Organizations of Others for Education About Parochiaid v. Governor (1997)

Crow, G.M., Levine, L., & Nager, N. (1992, Winter). Are three heads better than one? Reflections on doing collaborative interdisciplinary research. *American Educational Research Journal,* 29(4), 737-753.

Cushman, R. E. & Cushman, R. F. (1958). *Cases in Constitutional law.* New York.

Dery, D. (1984). *Problem definition in policy analysis*. Lawrence, KS: University Press of Kansas.

Durant, W. (1926). *The story of philosophy*. New York: Simon and Schuster.

Ehrensal, P. (2003). Constructing children in schools: Policies and the lessons they teach. *Journal of Curriculum Theorizing, 19, (2),* 117 –134.

Elk Grove Unified School District v. Newdow (2004)

Faigman, D. L. (2004). *Laboratory of justice: The Supreme Court's 200-year struggle to integrate science and the law.* New York: Times Books.

Faigman, D. L. (2000). *Legal alchemy: The use and misuse of science in the law.* New York: W.H. Freeman.

First, P.F. (1986, May). *The role of the policy analyst. Thresholds in Education, XII* (2), 40-42.

First, P.F. (1992). *Educational policy for school administrators*. Boston: Allyn & Bacon.

First, P.F. (1996). Researching legal topics from a policy studies perspective. In Schimmel, D., Ed., *Research that makes a difference: Complementary methods for examining legal issues in education*. Topeka, KS: National Organization on Legal Problems of Education.

First, P. (2001). The new superintendency as guardian of justice and care. In *The New Superintendency*, C. Cryss Brunner & Lars G. Bjork, Eds., Oxford, England: Elsevier Press, 249-266.

First, P. & Hart, Y. (2002). Access to cyberspace: The new issue in educational justice. *The Journal of Law and Education*, 31, (4), 385-411.

First, P. & DeLuca, B. (2003). The eaning of educational adequacy: The confusionof DeRolph. *The Journal of Law and Education, 32, (2),* 185 -215.

Fischer, F., & Forester, J. (Eds.). (1987). *Confronting values in policy analysis: The politics of criteria.* Beverly Hills, CA: Sage.

Fuhrman, S. H., Ed. (1993).*Designing coherent education policy: Improving the system.*San Francisco: Jossey-Bass.

Gardner, H. (1995). *Leading minds: An anatomy of leadership.* New York: BasicBooks.

Gerry, M. (1999). Service integration and beyond: Implications for lawyers and their training. In Heubert, J.P., Ed. *Law and school reform: six strategies for promoting educational equity.* New Haven, CT: Yale University Press, 244–305.

Golan, T. (2004). *Laws of man and laws of nature: The history of scientific expert testimony in England and America.* Cambridge: Harvard University Press.

Gooler, D.D. (1986, May). Educating educators for their policy making roles. *Thresholds in Education, XII*(2), 37-40.

Gratz v. Bollinger, 123 S.Ct. 2411, (2003)

Gray, J.C. (1963) *The nature and sources of the law, 2nd Ed.* Boston.

Green, P.C. & Mead, J.F. (2003). *Charter schools and the law: Establishing new legal relationships.* New York: Christopher-Gordon.

Grutter v. Bollinger, 123 S. Ct. 2325 (2003)

Guba, E.G., & Lincoln, Y.S. (1989). *Fourth generation evaluation.* Beverly Hills, CA: Sage.

Gun Free Schools Act of 1994, 20 U.S.C. §§ 8921-8922 (1995). Reauthorized under The No Child Left Behind Act, 20 U.S.C. § 7151 (West 2001).

Heubert, J.P. (1999). *Law and School Reform: Six Strategies for Promoting Educational Equity.* New Haven: Yale University Press.

Illinois State Board of Education. (n.d.). *The state board of education policies and procedures handbook.* Springfield, IL: Author.

Individuals With Disabilities Education Improvement Act of 2004, H.R. 1350.

Jackson v. Birmingham Board of Education (S. Ct. Case No. 02-1672, March 29, 2005)

Kahne, J. (1996). *Reframing Educational Policy: Democracy, Community, and the Individual.* New York: Teacher's College Press.

Kelly, A. (2001). *Benchmarking for school improvement: A practical guide for comparing and improving effectiveness.* London: RoutledgeFalmer.

Lee v. Weisman, 112 S. Ct. 2649, 2682 (1992).

Lincoln, Y.S., & Guba, E.G. (1985). *Naturalistic inquiry*. Beverly Hills, CA: Sage.

Liswood, L.A. (1995). *Women world leaders: Fifteen great politcians tell their stories.*New York: Harper Collins.

Majchrzak, A. (1984). *Methods for policy research*. Beverly Hills, CA: Sage.

Marshall, C., Mitchell, D., & Wirt, F. (1989). *Culture and education policy in the American states*. Briston, PA: The Falmer Press.

Martin, J.R. (1992). *The schoolhome*. Cambridge, MA: Harvard University Press.

May, R. (1985). *My quest for beauty*. San Francisco: Saybrook.

McUsic, M. (1999). The law's role in the distribution of education: The promises and pitfalls of school finance litigation. In Heubert, J. P., Ed., *Law and school reform:Six strategies for promoting educational equity.* New Haven: Yale University Press, 39 – 87.

Musial, D. (1986, May). First principles and policy development: A perspective from educational foundations. *Thresholds in Education, XII*(2), 2-4.

New Jersey v. T.L.O., 469 U.S. 325 (1985).

No Child Left Behind Act of 2001, Pub. L. 107-110, 115 Stat.1425.

Odden, A.R. (ed.). (1991). *Education policy implementation.* New York: State University of New York Press.

Patton, M.Q. (1978). *Utilization-focused evaluation.* Beverly Hills, CA: Sage.*Pierce v. Society of Sisters of the Holy Names of Jesus and Mary*, 268 U.S. 510 (1925).

Plessy v. Ferguson, 163 U.S. 537 (1896).

Rebell, M. A. & Block, A. R. (1982). *Educational policy making and the courts: An empirical study of judicial activism.* Chicago: University of Chicago Press.

Rutledge, W. (1947). *A Declaration of Legal Faith.* Lawrence: University of Kansas Press, p. 6. In O'Connor, S.D. (2003). *The Majesty of the Law: Reflections of a Supreme Court Justice.* New York: Random House.

Ryan, J. E. (2004). The perverse incentives of the No Child Left Behind Act. *New York University Law Review,79, (3),* 932 – 989.

Sandell, S. (1977, March). Does your board need its own policy analyst? *The American School Board Journal,* 48-49.

Sirotnik, K.A. (Ed.). (1990, Spring). Evaluation and social justice: Issues in public education. *New Directions for Program Evaluation*, 45.

Smith v. City of Jackson, Mississippi (S. Ct. Case No. 03-1160, March 30, 2005)

Spring, J. (1998). *Conflict of interests: The politics of American education, 3rd Ed.* Boston: McGraw Hill.

Sughrue, J. A. (2003). Zero tolerance for children: Two wrongs do not make a right. *Educational Administration Quarterl, 39, (2),* 238-258.

Weiss, C. H. (1980). *Social science research and decision-making.* New York: Columbia University Press.

Weiss, C. H.,Wagner, P., Wittrock, B., Wollmann, H., Eds. (1991). *Social sciences and modern states: National experiences and theoretical crossroads (Advances in political science).* Cambridge: Cambridge University Press.

Wildavsky, A.B. (1979). *Speaking truth to power: The art and craft of policy analysis* Boston: Little, Brown.

Wilson, E.O. (1998). *Consilience: The unity of knowledge.* N.Y.: Random House.

Wong, K.`K. (1996). *Advances in educational policy: Rethinking school reform in Chicago.* Greenwich, CT: JAI Press.

Worthen, B.R., Sanders, J.R. & Fitzpatrick, J.L. (1996). *Program evaluation: Alternative approaches and practical guidelines* (2nd ed.) Boston: Allyn & Bacon.

Yudof, M.G., Kirp, D.L., Levin, B. & Moran, R.F. (2000). *Educational policy and the law* (4th ed.). St. Paul, MN: West.

Zelman v. Simmons-Harris, 536 U.S. 639 (2002)

7 Conducting Legal Research Using Technological Tools

Dennis W. Van Berkum,
Kermit Buckner, & Kenneth E. Lane

Introduction

Vast technological changes over the last two decades have greatly improved the educator's ability to compile legal precedents and issues and apply them to everyday administrative concerns. While traditional research on legal issues has generally been conducted in one of three basic settings—law libraries at universities, county law libraries, or attorney offices—using the Internet is becoming the first option in conducting research.

In 1992, Levinkind wrote:

> Legal research is rapidly becoming automated.... However, book lovers take heart—it doesn't appear that silicon chips will take the place of well-stocked libraries. [T]he computer-assisted legal research now available can profitably be used only by persons already skilled in legal analysis and research. Currently, only law schools and large law firms use such a system to any great degree. And they use them to supplement, and not replace, written materials.... The other major factors affecting the use of computer-assisted legal research systems are their restricted availability and their cost (p. 2).

Only one year later, in 1993, the World Wide Web was created, and we were off to a world of expanded bases for the acquisition of knowledge. For example, Blackman (1998) notes that patterns are surfacing about Internet sources. Nearly every company worth its salt has a website. The same holds true for colleges, universities, and trade organizations. Anything you subscribe to for a fee will eventually be available online in full text. For the most part, entire books (such as almanacs, dictionaries, encyclopedias, and so forth) have not yet made it online to the extent that subscription-based periodicals have.

WestLaw (1999) illustrates the impact of this expanded information base and the continually changing needs of legal researchers:

> The legal and information industries are going through some dramatic changes. Anticipating these changes, and recognizing the issues they raise for legal and business professionals, West Online has set in motion plans for the future that will enable us to adapt to the customer's evolving needs.
>
> Today, for example, there is an increased emphasis on specialization. Customers are demanding information tailored to their own specialties and jurisdictions. And, with the globalization of economies, the need for legal information internationally is critical for attorneys and business professionals alike.
>
> Complicating matters is the fact that traditional boundaries of information needs are changing. Law firms can no longer operate using only "legal" information, while businesses need access to more and more legal information in order to operate within the law and to maintain a diverse and changing labor force.
>
> These professionals may need business news and information one day, public records the next, and regulatory, tax or topical information the next. The need to put all of that information into the context of their situation requires tools that will enable them to cut through the myriad of content types and zero in on pertinent information.
>
> Finally, domestic and international law is becoming more voluminous and complex, driving professionals' demand for easier ways to find and apply the law to any given situation. The ideal research products will point users to the right information and allow them to filter and make sense out of vast legal and non-legal content in the easiest, most cost- and time-efficient manners.

Indeed, legal research involves finding statutes, regulations, law cases, law reviews, and legal interpretations to enable us to intelligently discuss how to apply legal concepts to our job settings and everyday lives. Yell (1998) addresses this concept well, stating, "[b]y accessing the law through legal research, educators will have a better understanding of the principles of law, the facts giving rise to these principles, and the application of those facts to situations they may encounter" (p. 9).

Conducting Legal Research

While there are an array of available starting points from which to begin legal research on a given topic, Louis-Jacques (2004) suggests checking local resources first. The local library and its Internet resources may save you time and money. Therefore, try to develop an approach to using the Internet. Get to know a few sites and search engines well. However, never rely on Internet sources totally, as there may be gaps in the Internet.

Further, Ballard, Spahr, Andrews, & Ingersoll (1999) concur, offering that when conducting research, you should master a mix of research tools and techniques to be successful. This can only be accomplished if you master five basic components of good research:

1. An understanding of what to look for;
2. An appreciation of why the research is needed;
3. Know where the research can be found, while considering appropriateness and accessibility;
4. Know how it can be retrieved; and
5. Know what to do with the research so it can contribute to a body of knowledge.

Evaluating Authority and Quality of Content

Farmer (2004) identified authority and content to be two of the most important factors when searching the Internet for legal information. He suggests to search the legal authority for information, usually known as the primary sources of law, before moving into other sources. Look for the top level of the domain to check the authority of the site. Secondary legal authority is found in law articles and law periodicals. You must consider the content of the website you are visiting and how current the posting is before using the information available. Be sure and careful in your research.

Conducting legal research on the Internet is comparable to shopping online: you search a variety of sites until you find exactly what you want. It can be trial and error. Further, the Internet is a powerful tool for researching legal issues due to its convenience, large array of information, up-to-date information, and more importantly, the amount of valuable time it saves. Skepticism is crucial when choosing any information from a source. It is advisable that you check and recheck any information before holding it to be true.

Keep in mind the following suggestions if you will be using an online source as part of your search:

1. Have a specific and narrowly defined legal issue or factual situation.
2. Make sure the issues can be expressed in a limited and clearly defined way.
3. Combine search terms that are not too common (such as crime, court, trial).
4. Make sure the issue is not one of procedure.
5. Recognize that an issue may be new or developing (legal information is forever changing).

The knowledge of how to conduct legal research and where to go for information, whether it is the law library or Internet sources, gives you an immense advantage as a teacher or an administrator. You can find current information quickly to enable you to address immediate issues in the educational setting. This ability will be of tremendous value to you as you provide leadership to your faculty, students, and community. To quote the old admonition, "knowledge is power!" Never underestimate its value!

Using the Internet for Legal Research

Planning

To begin researching a legal issue, you should recognize that primary legal documents and law-related commentaries are plentiful in both the physical and virtual law libraries. You can find United States federal statutes, pending legislation and regulations, current federal appellate cases, state court opinions, legal opinions, and other information. Levinkind (1992) offers that regardless of the format you are going to use to conduct the search, a few basic planning tips should be considered:

1. Learn the system first.
2. Plan your search for both written and computer based materials.
3. Chose your database wisely.

There are also questions to be asked regarding any legal information so as to ensure its quality and accuracy, whether in the library or on the Internet. These questions include:

1. Where does all this wonderful information reside?
2. Do conventional online searching methods work at popular web search sites?
3. What other strategies should researchers apply?
4. Can researchers trust information they find?
5. Who is responsible for providing it?
6. Is it complete or otherwise accurate?
7. Is it authentic, timely, and up-to-date? Objective?
8. What evaluation skills should Internet researchers possess?
9. How do researchers cite to legal documents and commentary they locate on Internet?
10. How do researchers determine when to scout around the web for information or when to rely on traditional resources?

Basic Requirements and Steps

In order to use the World Wide Web, you must have a computer with a Macintosh or Windows platform capable of running Foxfire Mozilla (www.mozilla.org); Netscape Navigator (www.netscape.com); or Internet Explorer (www.microsoft.com/windows/ie/default.mspx) with, preferably, a 56k modem, a minimum of 16 mg of RAM (internal memory), and a 100 MHz processor.

At this point, you type the address of the site you wish to access in the address bar at the top of the website. You may have to enter http:// in front of the address depending upon your browser's idiosyncrasies. You must then sort through the information to locate what you are seeking. The computer does not read your mind, so you must search just like you would use the card index in a physical library.

Blackman (1998) suggests that the professional researcher "maintain navigational reference points" (p. 18). These points include the types of sources, the economics of the sources, and the validity of the sources to insure appropriateness of the citations.

A useful tool called a bookmark allows users to keep a record of where they have been on the Internet. Bookmarks are essentially address books or directories of the Internet addresses of sites where you can return by merely selecting the bookmark. In conducting Internet research, you will likely find many sites to bookmark. If you forget to make a bookmark of a useful website and later decide you want to return to that site, the most popular browsers maintain a list of all sites visited during the current session on the Internet. Unfortunately, when the session ends, the list will be erased. It is, therefore, important to use the bookmark feature as you conduct your research.

Fee and No-Fee Searches

There are two main roads to obtaining information from the Internet: free sites and sites that charge a fee. Free sites, obviously, do not charge per visit. These sites contain an enormous amount of helpful information; however, they may not provide a comparable amount of information, legal cases, or specificity as does Westlaw or Lexis. Many of these sites are provided through the state and/or federal government (ex: californiacourts.com or supremecourt.com).

Two well-known sources for legal research on the Internet are LexisNexis and Westlaw. However, both require a subscription to use their services. Their addresses are: (1) LexisNexis: www.lexis.com and (2) Westlaw: www.westlaw.com. These sites charge a fee that is determined by charging the user with a daily/weekly/monthly fee, by-the-hour fee, or even by-the-minute fee. Because there are multitudes of databases to explore, it is a good idea to browse through a number of these to find what meets your needs.

There are also numerous free websites for conducting research. It must be noted that these websites are only as valuable and useful if the site is consistently and frequently maintained by someone with legal experience. As an example, the following sites are taken from the homepage for Dr. Kenneth E. Lane, Professor of Educational Administration, California State University, San Bernardino (2004) and updated in December of 2004 for this chapter. The sites include:

ACLU Students
- www.aclu.org/students/students.html

California Code
- www.leginfo.ca.gov/calaw.html

California Courts
- www.courtinfo.ca.gov

California Department of Education
- http://www.cde.ca.gov/index.asp

California Education Law Report
- www.mcn.org/a/celr

California Case Law (LOIS Law Library)
- www.pita.com

Cecil Greek's Searchable Law Databases
- www.criminology.fsu.edu/cjlinks/law.html

Chief State School Officers Council
- www.ccsso.org

Council of School Attorneys
- www.nsba.org/cosa

50 States Statutes and Legislation
- www.prairienet.org/~scruffy/f.htm

FindLaw California
- california.findlaw.com

FindLaw - Law Crawler
- lawcrawler.findlaw.com

John Burton's Cyberspace Bookmarks
- fusd.net/burton/index.html

LawLinks: The Internet Legal Resource Center
- lawlinks.com

Legal Search Engines and Tools
- www.lawguru.com

Library of Congress
- lcweb.loc.gov

The National Law Journal
- http://www.law.com/jsp/nlj/index.jsp

Orange County Law Library
- www.oc.ca.gov/lawlib

Special Education: Section 504
- http://www.chadd.org/fs/fs4.htm

Supreme Court Decisions: full text; searchable by subject; 1990-present
- supct.law.cornell.edu/supct

Supreme Court Decisions: full text; searchable by subject; 1937-1975
- www.fedworld.gov/supcourt/index.htm

U.S. Court of Appeals, First Circuit Cases
- www.law.emory.edu/1circuit

U.S. Court of Appeals, Second Circuit Cases
- http://www.findlaw.com/casecode/courts/2nd.html

U.S. Court of Appeals, Third Circuit Cases
- http://www.findlaw.com/casecode/courts/3rd.html

U.S. Court of Appeals, Fourth Circuit Cases
- www.law.emory.edu/4circuit

U.S. Court of Appeals, Fifth Circuit Cases
- www.law.utexas.edu/us5th/us5th.html

U.S. Court of Appeals, Sixth Circuit Cases
- www.law.emory.edu/6circuit

U.S. Court of Appeals, Seventh Circuit Cases
- http://www.findlaw.com/casecode/courts/7th.html

U.S. Court of Appeals, Eighth Circuit Cases
- http://www.ca8.uscourts.gov/index.html

U.S. Court of Appeals, Ninth Circuit Cases
- http://www.findlaw.com/casecode/courts/9th.html

U.S. Court of Appeals, Tenth Circuit Cases
- www.law.emory.edu/10circuit

U.S. Court of Appeals, Eleventh Circuit Cases
- www.law.emory.edu/11circuit

U.S. Court of Appeals, D. C. Circuit Cases
- http://www.ll.georgetown.edu /federal/judicial/cafed.cfm

U.S. Department of Education
- www.ed.gov

U.S. Code
- http://www.law.cornell.edu/uscode/

U.S. House of Representatives Internet Law Library
- www.access.gpo.gov/nara/cfr/cfr-table-search.html

U.S. Tax Code
- www.fourmilab.ch/ustax/ustax.html

It is important to note that websites sometimes change their addresses without notice. Therefore, additional searches may be needed.

Tips for Conducting a Law Search

The Virtual Paper website provides these tips in using your browser to search for information:

> Researchers depending primarily on popular search engines to locate information likely will miss mounds of valuable resources. Why? Because search engines do not, arguably cannot, collect and index all data available on the Web. One recent updated analysis of the authors' earlier article appearing in Science Magazine, found that the Web houses an estimated 800 million pages, or 6 terabytes of text excluding coding. Yet search engines index a mere 16%, at best. … Clearly researchers must develop other strategies for discovering information.
>
> Consider how to research the issue in question without a computer, and then transfer the technique to the Internet. When seeking resources in a physical library, patrons typically check the card catalog, ask a librarian, or browse the shelves. Apply these techniques to the Web. Examples of catalogs include FindLaw and CataLaw. Look for discussion groups frequented by librarians using tools like DejaNews, Lizst, or CataList. Visit known and trusted sites to browse for related resources.

> To find federal government Websites, use Google: U.S. Government Search or Louisiana State University's U.S. Government Agencies Directory. To locate a state or locate government site, try State and Local Government on the Net. Know your source of information. Don't rely on information until you ascertain its objectivity, accuracy, timeliness, and authenticity.
>
> Skepticism is a virtue on the Web. Use the checklist available on The Virtual Chase to determine the quality of information you discover. When you find a reliable resource, don't let it go. Record reliable resources. Do this with bookmarks, bookmark utilities a contacts list, card file, or your own hyperlinked Web page.

To derive the maximum benefit from the use of the Internet, it is important to focus on those sites that are beneficial, not just interesting. It is important to know when to stop viewing information on a site that is not useful in order to better use your time. Yell (1998) states that, "… it is important to realize that the Internet is not a panacea, nor is it a substitute for the law library. It is, however, an extremely valuable tool for the legal researcher." (p.23)

Ballard, Spar, Andrews, & Ingersoll (2004) offer a set of criteria to evaluate the quality of information on the Internet. They suggest to:

1. Consider the scope of the coverage. Does the scope of coverage consider time periods, jurisdiction, and related topics?
2. Consider the authority of the source. Is the source the official provider for the subject?
3. Consider the objectivity of the writer. Is there a balance presented in the argument?
4. Consider the "accuracy" of the writing. Is the information factually, irrefutable, and complete?
5. Consider the "timeliness of the writings. Look closely to the publication and revision dates. Do the dates reflect content or aesthetic changes only?

Blackman (1998) created a checklist to decide when to use the Internet:

1. What sources are needed to locate the date or information you need?
2. What is the likelihood of finding the source on the Internet?
3. How immediately can the resources be accessed elsewhere, if at all?
4. What will it cost?
5. Will I likely need to use these resources again? (p. 34)
6. Keep in mind that sources you use today may not be there tomorrow.

Researching Legal Databases on the Internet

The purpose of the following two charts is to present a visual illustration to conduct a search on the websites *Findlaw* and *WestLaw*. The charts will guide you through the maze of the vast amount of information available to the user. The goal in this search will be to find some general information on the topic of search and seizure, retrieve the initial information on search and seizure, and find more specific and useful information (i.e., legal cases). While it may seem to be overwhelming at times, keep in mind that by maintaining your original purpose/goal of the search, it will help in staying on track. It is quite easy to find yourself traveling down another path due to curiosity (a condition commonly referred to as "bird walking").

Figure 1.
Legal Research Flowchart

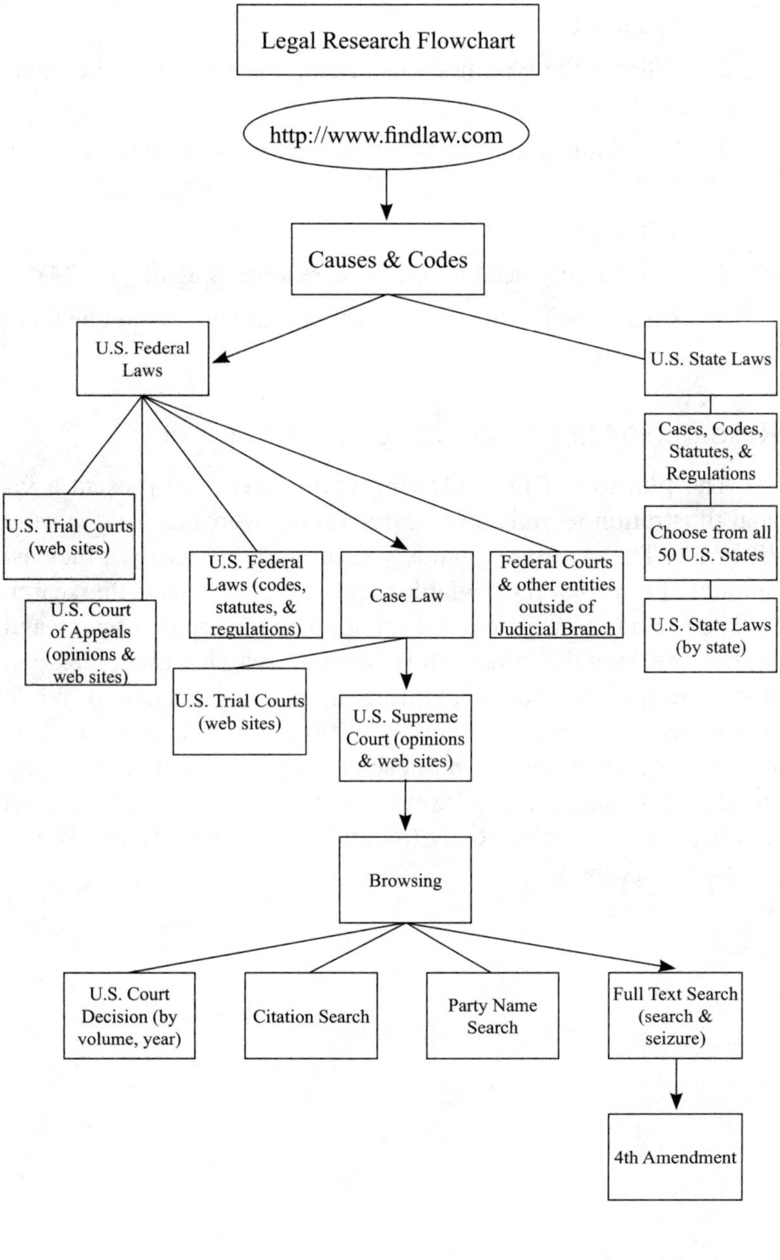

Figure 1 ***continued***.
Legal Research Flowchart

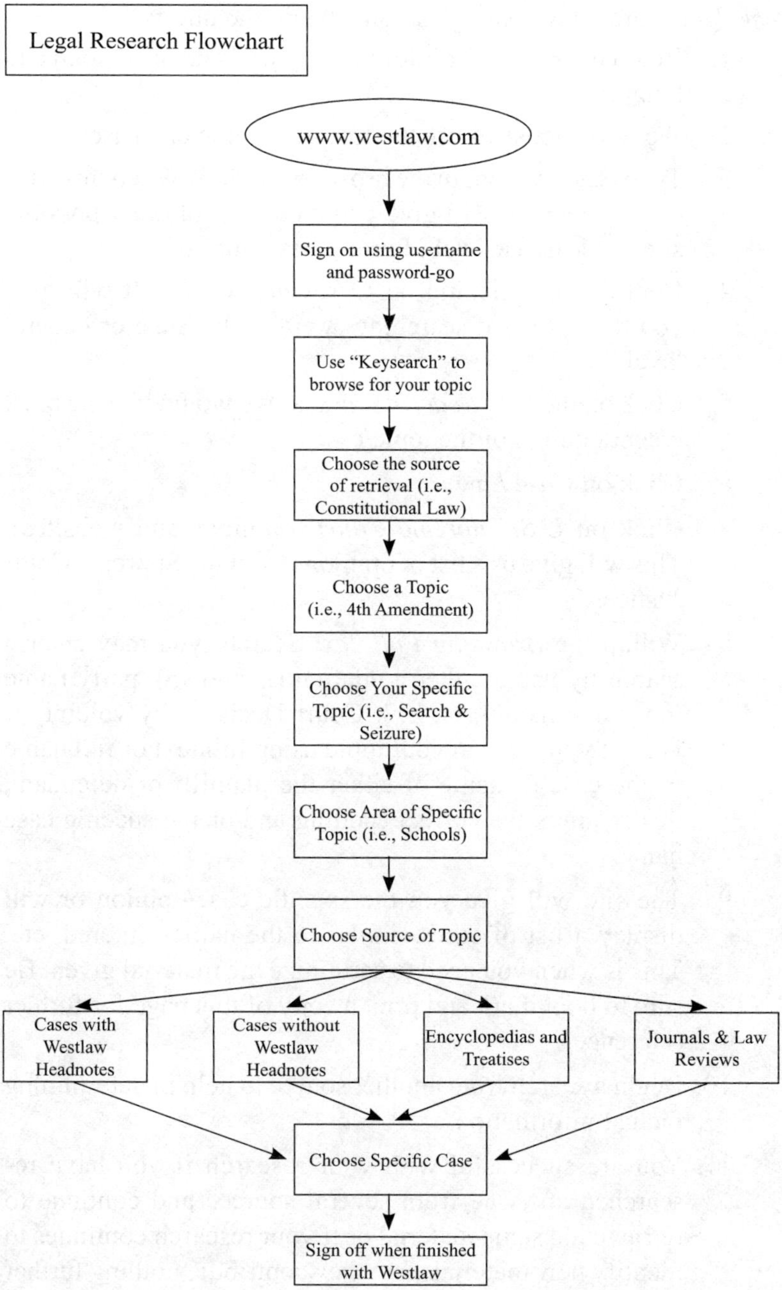

To begin our query on Search and Seizure (S&S), you must have access to the Internet/World Wide Web. Any popular search engine will work as long as it has a browser window. *Google*, *Yahoo*, and *Ask Jeeves* are a few examples. Let's begin the quest:

1. Begin the search for information by typing in "Search and Seizure."
2. We will choose to use the free accessible database.
3. Type: findlaw.com in the browser window. When this window appears, it will give you a number of other possible sites to search as well. Ignore these, for now.
4. Continue by clicking on *Cases and Codes*. It will give you the option of searching at either the State or Federal level.
5. Click on the *U.S. Federal Laws*, as we would like the most recent citation of the topic/case.
6. Click on *Case Law*.
7. Click on *U.S. Supreme Court* (opinions and websites). This will give us a list of opinions from the Supreme Court Justices.
8. Within the *Browsing-Full Text* Search; you may enter a search by using either a citation (if known), party name (only one name), or U.S. Court Decision by volume or year. If you enter in your topic using full text or full name of the case or name of either the plaintiff or defendant, this requires the correct spelling and/or the specific case name.
9. The site will give you the specific case/opinion or will display a list of cases similar to the names entered, etc. This is when you need to scrutinize the material given. Be sure to bookmark and print a copy of this page for further reference.
10. Begin a search from another source to help in determining factual information.
11. You are successful with your research if you have researched an issue from several sources and continue to retrieve the same material or if your research continues to identify new materials, but they contribute nothing further to the theories of the case (Harvard Law School, April, 2004).

Searching with Non-Legal Search Engines and Additional Sources

While "Westlaw" and "Findlaw" provide access to the law, they do not assist in the collection of factual information. Tertiary sources come from other ideas that you may have.

Tertiary sources are any other sites that provide insight into a particular legal issue and/or background to the issues. These sites include newsprint, various newsletters, state associations, and national associations. Newsprint informs the general public and cites facts, or fiction, of a particular issue. Newsletters are commonly produced by national and regional associations to present the viewpoint of the association. In addition, you may obtain legal information from several national associations' websites such as the American Association of School Administrators, the Council of Exceptional Children, the National Association of Elementary School Principals, the National Association of Secondary School Principals, and the American Association of School Boards. For instance, the National Association of School Boards publishes a weekly email entitled "Legal Clips," which presents a one to two-paragraph summary and Internet URL for current educational law cases before the various court systems in the U.S. Subscribing can easily be conducted through the organization's website.

Another means to research legal information is to use one of many different search engines. Many search engines can be used to supplement legal search engines. For example, Google and Alta-Vista are two common search engines. Searching in these formats allows you to investigate additional issues related to a legal issue, resulting in a deeper understanding.

Before you begin your query, Goodman (2003) offers some "Tips for Searchers."

1. Think about your topic before you start your query and identify some words or phrases that relate to your legal search.
2. No search engine is the same. Each search engine has an individual database. Therefore, you may want to consider several engines to use in your search. For example: Google receives high consumer marks because it uses "link popularity" to rank search results. Alta Vista is consistently ranked highly because of its advanced search capabilities and a very large database.

3. Take advantage of the search engine "help" screens. The screens will actually help you choose the right search technique.

Google Searching

Google offers different options to customize your search: do "exact phrase" searches; eliminate words for your search result; limit your search by date, file format; and more.

1. Exact phrase searches require that all words be in a specific order.
2. An all-word search is the same as doing a "Boolean" search which is the logical use of three major connectors between words in the search:
    - And
    - Or
    - Not
3. A limited format search is used for formats such as Microsoft Word,© Microsoft PowerPoint,© Rich, Text Format, etc.
4. Searches can also be limited by date of publication or last update.
5. A good research engine will also allow you to access other search engines.
6. Google ignores common words and characteristics, such as "where" and "how" as well as certain single digits and single letters, because they slow down your search without improving your results.
7. If a common word is essential to getting the results you want, you can include it by putting a "+" sign in front of it.

To run a search on "Google Advanced" connect to google.com. Then, click on the "advanced search" link. Advanced searching in Alta Vista is similar to searching on Google.Alta Vista allows you to:

1. Search for an exact phrase.
2. Require or exclude words form your search.
3. Rank pages according to words you select.

To build a query in Alta Vista, several choices are available. Using the search and seizure topic from earlier discussions, you can select "all these words" and place "search seizure" in the area provided. The "and" is not needed. The query would look for all sites related to the combination of the two words. If you select an advanced search using the exact phrase "search and seizure," the query becomes more select, and only the phrase cited would be found. One can also exclude a word or phrase for the query. This action is commonly conducted when one is tying to eliminate a specific location or region. Alta Vista also offers a means to limit searches by date, time, and location.

Another consideration in conducting Internet searches is whether or not to use "Boolean" connectors. Items such as "and," "or," "not," and "near" may be considered. A final consideration is to sort your search resulting in an ordered presentation of your query.

Legal Research Activity

There may be occasions when you, as a school leader, will want more information about some legal matter. In an endeavor to facilitate legal research through the use of technology, it may be helpful to conduct a practice session to prepare for a real activity. Therefore, the following activities should better prepare you for legal research via technology.

This activity is designed to give you practice in doing legal research on the Internet using findlaw.com and other websites. Your primary resource for this task will be findlaw.com, but you will find that legal information is available at a variety of sites, and part of the value of this task will be the exploration you will do.

To get you started, consider this example of how you can use findlaw.com to find a North Carolina (NC) statute. Let's say that you are a personnel director and you need to know if advocating the overthrow of the U.S. government is grounds for the dismissal of a teacher. You can find the answer to this question by locating and reading the North Carolina General Statutes that address teacher dismissal. All North Carolina statutes that address education are coded 115C. You can access these statutes online using findlaw.com. First, enter findlaw.com through your Internet provider. You will see *Legal Professionals* and under that *U.S. Laws: Cases & Codes ...* Click on *U.S. Laws: Cases & Codes....* This is the area in which you will be able to locate U.S. Supreme Court, Federal Court, and State Court cases as well as state and federal laws. This assignment will allow you to explore several of these areas. If you are looking for a federal law (for example IDEA), you can find it under *U.S. Code*. If you are looking for a U.S. Supreme Court decision, you can find it under *Case Law* and *U.S. Supreme Court....* The Federal Appeals court cases are next and so forth. A little further down are the U.S. State Laws. If you go there and click on *North Carolina*, you will find the NC legal materials. We want to find the statute that deals with teacher dismissal. So we click on *North Carolina General Statutes*. Under *Access the NC General Statutes*, we need to enter 115C to find the educational statutes. When you find the 115C statutes, you get all of them, and you must then find the specific section you need. The *Index of 115C Statutes* at the end of this section may help you find the section you need. By the way, you will find the information about teacher dismissal at 115C-325(e)1.h.

Your task is to find out something about each of the following and briefly describe what you found:

1. You are reading the newspaper and you see that the United States Supreme Court handed down a decision in a case titled *Zelman v. Simmons-Harris* in June, 2002. What was this case about?

2. You are reading in your text and you see a footnote reference (393 U.S. 503) to a case, and you want to know more about that case. What was this case name (___ v. ___) and what does it involve?

3. You just checked one of the association websites, and you see that an article talks about a Fourth Circuit Court of Appeals decision that you want to know more about. The case was *Sellers v. School Board of the City of Manassas No. 97-1762*. What is this case about?

4. You are talking with a friend and he tells you that the Fourth Circuit Court of Appeals handed down a decision that will impact all North Carolina schools, but he does not remember much about it. He says that he thinks it involved the Charlotte-Mecklenburg Board of Education and someone named Terry Belk. He also tells you that the case was decided in November of 2000. What was this case about?

5. You are about to go into your first interview for a principalship, and your mentor tells you to be sure to check NCGS 115C-288 before your interview. What does that statute address?
6. You are reading in your text and you see a reference to 42 USC 1983. What is that a reference to, and what does 42 USC 1983 address?

Research Topic

You should choose a research topic that interests you and one that will allow you to look at a legal issue related to district administration in depth. The purpose of this assignment is to allow you to do in-depth research in a specific area of education law. You may choose any topic that you like, but you must approach the topic from a school district perspective. You may have written research papers that focused on the principalship. This research will be similar except that it will focus on central office leadership. There are many acceptable topics for this research including the following:

1. No Child Left Behind Legislation for the School Board– This paper might present the basic elements of NCLB for presentation to a local school board.
2. Tort Liability for School Personnel – This paper would present tort liability for school personnel as in a general meeting of all school personnel.
3. Action Plans for Principals – This paper would present information about NCGS 115C-333 for principals and provide guidance in how to initiate and write a legal action plan.

These are just three topics that would be acceptable as research topics. There are hundreds more. As you can see from the three topics listed, the purpose of this research is to share it with an audience. You might even pick a topic that you feel needs to be addressed in your district. When you decide on a topic, also decide on the audience who will receive your research. Your findings should be presented clearly and concisely. You will be presenting this information as a paper, but you might imagine the paper as the handout you will present as a part of a workshop you are conducting on this topic. You should use references as needed and follow APA style when you do.

How long should the legal research paper be? That is always a hard question to answer. It is more important to be clear and concise than to have a report be a certain length, but the topic you choose will be the main determinate of the length of your paper.

Issue Paper Outline

Section One. In this section, you will describe a situation you have witnessed, know about, or made up in which the legal topic for the paper is at issue. For example, with the tort issue paper, the situation could involve negligence, supervision, harassment, or malpractice. This part of the paper should be no more than a page in length but should state what happened and should stop prior to any administrative decision or action.

Section Two. In this section, you should use the text, *North Carolina Public School Law*, your local School Board Policy, and any other appropriate sources to do a legal analysis of the situation. This analysis should be aimed at clarifying the law an administrator should know prior to taking action. For example, when writing your tort paper, you should use the tort criteria from the chapter to analyze your situation. You would say, "In Hudgins and Vacca, the authors identify the following questions to be resolved in tort claims:

1. Did the sued party have a duty of care under the law to avoid the injury suffered by the claimant?
2. If so, was that duty actually breached?
3. If a breach of legal duty occurred, was it the proximate cause of the injury?
4. If so, is the sued party shielded from liability by privilege or immunity conferred by law?"

You would then analyze your situation by considering each of these questions and how they apply to your situation. *North Carolina General Statutes*, school district policy, or school policies (for example, the school safety plan, etc.) will be a part of any legal analysis when appropriate. This section should be about a page in length.

Section Three. This is a very important section. In this section, you should use the list of leadership skills and the *Interstate School Leaders Licensure Consortium Standards* to explain which skills and standards will come into play in the resolution of your situation. This is also the section in which you address "selling" your decision. This section should be about a page in length.

Section Four. This is the section in which you tell what actually happened, if the situation is a real one, or what you think would happen if a school leader acts as you suggest in Section Three. This section need not be more that a few sentences.

Conclusion

While it is important to understand how to use technology to facilitate legal research, it is more important to be able to present and apply that research in a manner in which the audience can readily understand the issues, possible decisions, and the consequences of each decision. If the audience does not or cannot understand the research, the likelihood is that the issue will become much more of a litigious manner resulting in both a loss of time and financial resources for all parties.

References

Alexander, K. & Alexander, D. (2005). American Public School Law. St. Paul, MN: West Publishing Company.

Blackman, J. D. (1998). The Internet Fact Finder for Lawyers. Chicago, ILL: American Bar Association.

Ballard Spahr Andrews & Ingersoll, LLP. (1999). The Virtual Chase: A Research Site for Legal Professionals. [Available Online]: http://www.virtualchase.com/

Chapman, B. (October 17, 1997). Using the World Wide Web to Conduct Legal Research. [Available Online]: http://centum.utulsa.edu/~chapmanbj/www/lecture.htm

Elias, S. & Levinkind, S. (1992). Legal Research: How to Find and Understand the Law. Berkeley, CA: Nolo Press.

Harvard Law School (April, 2004). "Research Methodology."

Harvard Library Services. [Available Online]: http://www.lawharvard.edu/library.

Lane, K. E. (2004). Personal homepage. [Available Online]: dcr.csusb.edu/soe/klane/.

West Group. (1999). WestLaw White Paper. [Available Online]: http://www.westlaw.com/

Yell, M. L. (1998). The Law and Special Education. Upper Saddle River, NJ: Prentice Hall.

8 Language and Writing in School Law

Jennifer A. Sughrue,
David H. Goldenberg, & Steve Permuth

Introduction

Lessons taught from the Tower of Babel, to fundamentals of good speaking and listening, to meetings in which one is sure that the language being used is "foreign" suggest the critical importance of the oral and written word in effective communication. It is of particular importance to an arena as complex as law is that the communication is clear and cogent. Of added nature is the fact that the complexities of laws, as shared throughout this text, can and should be construed within the rich parameters of research, which in many ways also has complexities of language and substance to deal with.

Good legal writing and presentations have many of the same characteristics as other forms of speaking and scholarly writing. The thesis should be introduced early, then adequately argued free of bias or opinion, and sufficiently supported with evidence. Perhaps most importantly, the writer must write for the reader. A good thesis can be lost if the reader can not follow the analysis, is not provided with convincing arguments, or is overwhelmed with obscure or misused terminology.

As in professions such as medicine and psychology, law has a rich lexicon and requires careful phrasing for accurate articulation of legal principles and arguments. It is common knowledge that there are numerous Latin words and expressions that carry specialized meaning in the law, but it is less well understood how to use those words and expressions in developing papers for education law courses. Coherent legal writing depends on the utilization of appropriate terminology, the clear development of legal arguments, and the proper sequencing of legal principles.

This chapter focuses on the key elements of good legal writing for graduate students in education. First, it will explore the language of law. Second, the authors will share an explanation of why sequencing points of law is important and of how to build an analysis of those points. Finally, the chapter will offer strategies that will help students acquire competency in legal writing.

The Language of Law

> Costello: Well then, who's on first?
>
> Abbott: Yes.
>
> Costello: I mean the fellow's name.
>
> Abbott: Who.
>
> Costello: The guy on first.
>
> Abbott: Who.
>
> Costello: The first baseman.
>
> Abbott: Who is on first!
>
> Costello: I'm asking YOU who's on first.
>
> Abbott: That's the man's name.
>
> Costello: That's who's name?
>
> Abbott: Yes. (Abbott & Costello, undated)

For educators, the language of law oftentimes seems like the legendary exchange between Abbott and Costello. One is listening as closely as possible, but the words and meaning somehow have become confusing. It is the intent of this section to de-mystify case law by addressing three aspects of legal language. First there will be a brief explanation of the origins of American common law. Secondly, the importance of comprehending and heeding the precise meaning of legal terminology will be addressed. The last subsection will explore how to use the power of language to explain and to convince in the context of educational law.

Origins of American Common Law

Modern day American legal terminology did not simply spring forward from the Founding Fathers. It has been said that Sir William Blackstone (1723-1780), author of the *Commentaries on the Laws of England*, had the greatest influence on the framers of the republic. Blackstone was Professor of English Law at Oxford University, and whose writings were known and held by most of the influential American colonists. Blackstone, not Jefferson, is credited with having coined the phrase *pursuit of happiness* that so influenced the writing of the Declaration of Independence and our thinking to this day. Blackstone's dedication to chronicling common law provides those interested in the origins of law with an invaluable resource, but the study of legal language begins more appropriately in Greek and Roman times.

From ancient Rome, Cicero's dialogue *De Legibus* [Laws] sought the origins of justice.

> Well, then, the most learned men have determined to begin with Law, and it would seem that they are right, if, according to their definition, Law is the highest reason, implanted by Nature, which commands what ought to be done and forbids the opposite. This reason, when firmly fixed and fully developed in the human mind, is Law. And so they believe that Law is intelligence, whose natural function it is to command right conduct and forbid wrongdoing (p. 317).

Cicero's oratories are lasting legacies. In the case of *The Five Knights*, heard before the British Privy Council in 1627, the lawyer serving in defense of the Knights, stated,

> The statute of Magna Charta, that statute which if it were fully executed as it ought to be, every man would enjoy his liberty better than doth … out of the very body of this Act of Parliament, besides the explanation of other statutes, it appears, *nullus liber homo capiatur vel imprisonetur nisi per legem terrae* (p. 34).

The translation of the Latin is: *No man's liberty shall be taken away except by the law of the land.*

This meshing of the oratories of Greek and Latin root words and phrases along with the Queen's English makes for a rich history but also one that, when not fully understood, can seem garbled or confusing. The purpose of the following subsection, therefore, is to help the reader become better familiar with the terminology and with the necessity of being precise in legal writing.

Precision in Language

Learning and writing the language of law are not unlike learning and writing a foreign language. There is an extensive use of

Latin terminology, but the challenges go well beyond learning the meaning of a few key words and phrases. Even the most common of words take on significance when codified or adjudicated.

Consider the U.S. Supreme Court's decision in *Plyler v. Doe* (1982). The Texas state legislature amended the education code to deny funds to public school districts for the education of illegal immigrant children. In arguing its case, the appellant school district and state asserted that "undocumented aliens are not 'persons within the jurisdiction' of the State of Texas" (p. 2392) and, therefore, did not enjoy equal protection under Texas law. In parsing the appellants' claim, Justice Brennan focused on the meaning of "persons" in the context of the Fifth and Fourteenth Amendments.

> Whatever his status under the immigration laws, an alien is surely a "person" in any ordinary sense of that term. Aliens, even aliens whose presence in this country is unlawful, have long been recognized as "persons" guaranteed due process of law (p. 2391).

Likewise Justice Brennan took issue with the state's application of the phrase "within the jurisdiction" to deny undocumented aliens equal protection under the law.

> To permit a State to employ the phrase "within its jurisdiction" in order to identify subclasses of persons whom it would define as beyond its jurisdiction, thereby relieving itself of the obligation to assure that its laws are designed and applied equally to those persons, would undermine the principal purpose for which the Equal Protection Clause was incorporated in the Fourteenth Amendment. The Equal Protection Clause was intended to work nothing less than the abolition of all caste-based and invidious class-based legislation. That objective is fundamentally at odds with the power the State asserts here to classify persons subject to its laws as nonetheless excepted from its protection (p. 2391).

Equal attention must be paid when reading or using other common words and phrases, like *shall* or *will* and, conversely, *may* or *is authorized. Shall* and *will* necessitate government or individual action, while *may* or *is authorized* provides latitude or discretion. These distinctions are important in understanding the application of constitutional, statutory, and case law.

There are several legal terms that signify subtle differences in meaning. Take, for example, words like *malfeasance*, *misfeasance*, and *nonfeasance*. They have the same root, but denote different offenses. For instance, a school board that has done something unlawful in the performance of its duties is guilty of malfeasance. Misfeasance refers to someone or entity that has the legal authority to perform some duty, but does so inappropriately or improperly. Not performing one's duty is called nonfeasance.

Perhaps the most frustrating aspect of legal terminology is that the English language allows for multiple meanings of words. A common usage of a term in everyday language may have no relevance whatsoever in court proceedings and documents. Harder still are the subtle nuances associated with differences between common usages of words and their inclusion in legal proceedings. The following table provides readers with some examples.

Table 1
Terms that Have Common and Legal Applications

Term	Common Usage	Legal Usage
Brief	A measure of time, usually short in duration.	A written summary of ideas or position; it is sometimes published as an opinion designed to help study a case being heard.
Common law	The system of laws originated and developed in England and based on doctrines implicit in court decisions rather than on codified written laws.	A body of law that is based on custom and general principles and embodied in case law that serves as precedent.
Comity	An atmosphere of social harmony.	The informal and voluntary recognition by courts of one jurisdiction of the laws and judicial decisions of another.
Depose	To remove from office or power.	To testify to under oath or by sworn affidavit.

Term	Common Usage	Legal Usage
Face	(a) To overcome by confronting boldly or bravely; (b) the surface front of the head.	The surface or superficial reading or meaning of something such as a document that does not take into account other information.
Frivolous	Inappropriately silly; trivial.	Lacking in any arguable basis or merit in either law or facts of the case.
Infra	Inferior to, below, or beneath.	Used in books, articles, and cases to direct the reader to later pages, sections, or footnotes, thus, *below*.
Injury	A particular form of hurt, damage or loss.	An act that wrongs or harms another; a violation of a legally protected interest for which the law allows an action for relief.
Invoke	To call on (a higher power) for assistance, support or inspiration.	To appeal to as furnishing authority or motive, such as invoking the Fifth Amendment.
Naked	To be bare.	To be incomplete without force; unjustified.
Of course	An idiom meaning in the customary or expected order; naturally.	As a matter of right. These are actions that a person may take in a lawsuit, either without asking the judge's permission or by asking and getting automatic approval.

Term	Common Usage	Legal Usage
Performance	The act or style of performing a work or role before an audience.	Carrying out a contract, promise, or obligation according to the terms of that contract so that it comes to a conclusion.
Pray	To address a divinity.	To ask of the court.
Supra	Meaning to be greater than, above, or over.	Used in books, articles, and cases to direct the reader to the previous pages, sections, or footnotes, thus, *above*.
Ultra	An extremist. Or immoderately adhering to a belief.	Beyond, as in outside the scope of powers.
Umbrella	A device for protection from the weather.	Covering or applying simultaneously to a number of similar items, elements, or groups before the court.
Unconscionable	Not restrained by conscience; unscrupulous; beyond prudence or reason; excessive.	Unreasonably unfair to one party; unacceptably offensive to public policy.
Warrant	Justification for an action or a belief.	A commission or document giving authority to do something.
Wrong	Not in keeping with fact or truth; an error.	To violate the rights of another.

The following subsections provide guidance on other terminology essential to the understanding of law, particularly case law. Knowing the meaning of these key legal terms will help the reader grasp the points of law under dispute, the courts' scrutiny, and what action is taken.

Legal terminology providing direction in case law. The following table is a small compilation of legal terminology that tells the reader something about the nature or function of a case. It should not be construed as a substitute for more substantive works such as *Black's Law Dictionary*.

Table 2
Key Legal Terms Providing Direction in Case Law

Term	Definition
Affirmed	The case in question agrees with and supports the cited case that is on appeal or rehearing.
Connected case	The case in question cites a related case that involves similar or the same subject matter or parties.
Criticized	The case in question provides an opinion that disagrees with the reasoning or resulting decision of a cited case and yet, may not affect the current case as a precedent.
Dismissed	The case in question dismisses an appeal from the cited case.
Distinguished	The case in question differs from a case in law cited by either parties or facts presented by either party for reasons that are provided.
Explained	The case in question interprets or clarifies a cited case in a significant manner.
Followed	The case in question relies on a cited case or law as the controlling or persuasive authority on the matter before the court.
Harmonized	The case in question differs from a cited case but reconciles whatever differences exist in reaching an opinion.
Dissenting opinion	The case in question cites a dissenting opinion from a cited case.
Limited	The case in question notes the restriction of application of a cited case to specific circumstances.
Modified	The case in question modifies the case on appeal.
Overruled	The case in question overturns or disapproves of all or part of the cited case on appeal.
Parallel	The case in question is significantly similar or the same with the cited case in statements of law or fact.
Questioned	The case in question raises matters of whether the cited case has precedential value due to intervening circumstances or actions taken.

The court's terminology provides direction for the parties but also for the reader. It is known from the above terms whether or not the case has been won, lost, modified, or the parties have been directed to act in some manner. Judges, through the use of these terms, will lead the parties toward determined understandings as well as the limits placed upon a case by virtue of the particular circumstances of the case itself.

Federal rules of civil procedure. Cases that come before the federal courts, beginning with the United States District Court in one's locality, are bound by rules of procedure. The language here, too, is a mix of ancient and modern terms. Jarvis, Baker and McClurg (2003) poked fun at the terminology while putting together the chapter on "New (Legal) Devil's Dictionary" in *Amicus Humoriae: An Anthology of Legal Humor*. As an example, they defined a criminal lawyer as a "grammatical redundancy." They further defined code as "encrypted language which must be decoded before it can be understood. Some codes, such as the United States Code, have never been decoded or understood" (p. 86). Noted below are key terms that are found in civil procedure.

Table 3
Key Terms in Federal Rules of Civil Procedure

Term	Definition
Capacity	This is the qualification or authority of parties. The court may inquire into the capacity of somebody to make an arrest or might question the qualifications of somebody to enter into a contract.
Demurrer	An objection. This is a method of objecting that admits the facts of the opponent's arguments but denies that they sustain the pleading based upon them.
Interrogatory	A written question required by law to be answered under the direction of a court.
Ipso facto	From the Latin meaning "by the fact itself." In court, it means "by that very fact or act as an inevitable result."
Joinder	This is the formal act of accepting or joining a case. It might be the joining of similar or same causes of action against a defendant or it could be the joining of parties in defense of a lawsuit.
Motion	When either party of the case in question makes application to the court for an order or a formal ruling.

Term	Definition
Pleading	Advocacy of causes in court. This is a formal statement, generally in writing, that either supports a cause of action or the defense in a case.
Pray	To ask of the court. The plaintiff may pray judgment against the defendant for damages or relief.
Relief	Redress that has been awarded by the court.
Redress	To set right, that which is wrong. The case in question may call upon one party to make amends for injury.
Section 1983	The section of title 42 of the U.S. Code that makes a person liable for depriving another of any rights, privileges or immunities secured by the Constitution of the United States and laws while acting under color of any statute, ordinance, regulation, custom or usage of a state.
Seriatim	From the Latin to meaning "a succession of persons or things."
Venue	The local area where a case may be tried.

Other terms of interest. In 1803, the Supreme Court decided *Marbury v. Madison* and in doing so invalidated for the first time a law of the Congress of the United States. President Jefferson ordered his Secretary of State, James Madison, to refuse to hand over some judicial commissions to Jefferson's political opponents. William Marbury, one of those designated judges, applied to the Supreme Court for the writ of *mandamus*, and the process of judicial review was forged. The traditions of the highest court of the land also provide opportunity to examine terms that readers of case law encounter. Noted below are some of these and other terms that are found in educational case law.

Table 4
Other Terms of Interest

Term	Definition
Abjure	From the Latin meaning "to swear." It is more usually found when an individual disclaims formally or renounces an oath.
Accede	To become a party to an agreement through one's associations with others.

Term	Definition
Amicus Curiae	From the Latin to mean "friend of the court." Oftentimes individuals or organizations or States may file a legal brief sharing an opinion with the court even though the person or entity is not a party to the actual lawsuit.
Animo	From the Latin meaning "with intention".
Bona fide	From the Latin meaning "in good faith." It is the characterization of good faith and lack or fraud or deceit.
Capricious	Term to denote that something is not based on fact, reason or law.
Cause in fact	A cause without which the result would not have occurred.
Certification	Certification of an interlocutory decision by a lower court allows an appellate court to review the decision and to answer a controlling question of law.
Delictum	From the Latin meaning "a crime, tort or wrong."
De novo	From the Latin meaning "to hear a case anew, a second time."
Id	From the Latin, this is an abbreviation of "idem". This refers the reader to something that has been previously mentioned.
In facie curiae	From the Latin meaning "to be before or in the presence of the court."
In loco parentis	From the Latin meaning "to stand in the place of a parent."
In pari delicto	From the Latin meaning "in equal fault or wrong." This is a doctrine that bars a plaintiff who has participated in a wrongdoing from recovering damages for loss resulting from the wrongdoing.
In rem	From the Latin meaning "against or with respect to a thing" without reference to the persons involved.
Inter alia	From the Latin meaning "among other things."
Mala fide	From the Latin meaning "bad faith."
Nolo contendere	From the Latin meaning "I will not contest it". This is a defendant's plea of no contest. The defendant submits him or herself to the court for sentencing without admitting guilt.
Nonage	A minor; somebody not of legal age.

Term	Definition
Parens patriae	From the Latin meaning "the right of the government to take responsibility for minors or other individuals who can not legally care for themselves."
Prima facie	From the Latin meaning "at first sight;" on the face of it. Something considered to be true unless proven otherwise.
Quid pro quo	From the Latin meaning "something for something; this for that."
Rebut	To dispute, and take away the effect of facts or arguments presented.
Redaction	An editing; a deletion or revision.
Scire facias	From the Latin meaning "a judge's command to a public official to come to court and explain why a record in that person's possession should not be destroyed, disclosed or some other charge."
Stare decisis	A Latin phrase that literally means "to stand on the decisions." It expresses the common law doctrine that court decisions should be guided by precedent.
Tort	A civil wrong other than breach of contract. To be a tort, there must be a legal duty owed by one person to another, a violation of that duty by breach of the duty, evidence of proximate cause, and injury.
Vacatur	From the Latin, "to be made null and void."
Writ of Certiorari	A Latin phrase that means "you wish to be informed." This is issued by a higher court to a lower court. It is one of the two ways in which a case from the U.S. Court of Appeals can be reviewed by the U.S. Supreme Court.
Writ of Error Coram Nobis	This is a writ that brings to the attention of the court facts that, in spite of reasonable diligence, were not shared before a judgment was made and might have resulted in a different ruling.
Writ of Habeas corpus	A Latin phrase that literally means "you should have the body." This can be one of several writs originating in common law that are issued to bring a party before the court.
Writ of Mandamus	An extraordinary writ commanding an official to perform a ministerial act that the law recognizes as an absolute duty and not a matter for the official's discretion. This is only used when other judicial remedies fail.

Abbreviations. Thoroughness requires some reference to the many and varied abbreviations that students of the law need to know in order to read decisions from the courts. Sometimes a single letter appears in such a place within the text that the meaning is fairly obvious. An example would be the common usage of *J* to signify a single "judge". To the untrained reader, the letter *K* would cause hours of wonderment until it is realized that this single letter means, "contract. " The use of *MD* in legal writings and research refers to Middle District, rather than the credentials of a physician. It is easy to see how one can become easily confused. The table below offers some key abbreviations that should become part of each student's working knowledge of case law and should help in understanding legal writing and research.

Table 5
Legal Abbreviations

Abbreviation	Significance
ADR	Alternative Dispute Resolution
AG	Attorney General
BF	Bona fide
CA	Court of Appeals
CL	Civil Law
D	Defendant
DC	District court
DJ	District Judge
F	Federal Reporter
FOIA	Freedom of Information Act
F. Supp	Federal Supplement
ILP	Index of Legal Periodicals
J	Judge
JJ	Judges
K	Contract
LJ	Law Journal
LR	Law Reports
MD	Middle District

Abbreviation	Significance
ND	Northern District
NLRB	National Labor Relations Board
P	Pacific Reporter
PJ	Presiding Judge
PS	Public statute
QB	Queen's Bench
RS	Revised statutes
S	Statute
SC	Supreme Court
SD	Southern District
SW	South Western Reporter
US	United States Reports
USC	United States Code
USCA	(a) United States Code Annotated, (b) United States Court of Appeals
USDC	United States District Court
V	Versus; against
WD	Western District

As amply illustrated in this section, legal writing can not be taken casually. One can not substitute familiar words and phrases easily for terms that carry legal implications. Comprehending the meaning of legal terms and making precise word choices are essential components to clear articulation of legal analyses.

Not to be ignored in this exploration of precision and meaning in legal language is the ability of the language of law to convey, to convince, and to direct. The following subsection speaks to this power and provides examples taken from case law and other law-related sources.

The Power of Language

Brennan's majority opinion in *Plyer* (1982), quoted in the previous section, illustrates another feature of good legal writing—illustration and persuasion. As the reader may recall, Brennan maintained that the purpose of the Equal Protection Clause of the Fourteenth Amendment was to protect individuals from "caste-based and invidious class-based legislation" (p. 2391). His phraseology evokes an emotional, perhaps scornful, reaction at the thought of government enacting law that discriminates against or withholds government protection from certain groups of people. Well-crafted imagery or phrases that have come to represent particular ideas or concepts sometimes can illustrate a point better than several paragraphs of explanation.

Thomas Jefferson provided numerous examples of such writing. All are familiar with Jefferson's signature phrase, "wall of separation between church and state" (*Reynolds v. United States*, 1879, p. 164). This phrase denotes the constitutional argument that government should neither establish nor interfere with the free exercise of religion. Albeit reflective of the style of composition of his day and strongly worded to press his ideas, the following passage from Jefferson's *An Act for Establishing Religious Freedom* illustrates the power of words in advancing a concept.

> That the impious presumptions of legislators and rulers, civil as well as ecclesiastical, who, being themselves but fallible and uninspired men, have assumed dominion over the faith of others, setting up their own opinions and modes of thinking as the one true and infallible, and as such endeavoring to impose them on others; ... That to compel a man to furnish contributions of money for the propagation of opinions which he disbelieves is sinful and tyrannical; ... Be it therefore enacted by the General Assembly, That no man shall be compelled to frequent or support any religious worship, place or ministry, whatsoever, nor shall be enforced, restrained, molested, or burthened in his body or goods, nor shall otherwise suffer on account of his religious opinions or belief (as cited in Alexander & Alexander, 2005, p. 155).

U. S. Supreme Court decisions are replete in descriptive phrases and explanations that encapsulate legal arguments and principles. Consider the Court's ruling in the student-on-student sexual harassment case, *Davis v. Monroe County Board of Education* (1999). The point of law under analysis was whether Title IX of the Education Amendments of 1972 provided individuals the right to sue a school district for monetary damages and injunctive relief in the event of peer sexual harassment. In concluding that the statute did, indeed, provide for a private cause of action in such cases, the Court applied an existing legal standard in Title IX harassment, deliberate indifference, to determine school district liability. This test had been articulated in a U.S. Supreme Court decision, *Geber v. Lago Vista Independent School District* (1998), in which a student had been sexually harassed by a teacher. The Court took the opportunity in *Davis* to explain under what circumstances school districts might face liability in the context of peer-to-peer harassment.

> The statute makes clear that … students must not be denied access to educational benefits and opportunities on the basis of gender. We thus conclude that funding recipients are properly held liable in damages only where they are *deliberately indifferent* to sexual harassment, of which they have *actual knowledge*, that is *so severe, pervasive, and objectively offensive* that it can be said to deprive the victims of access to the educational opportunities or benefits provided by the school.… The district's knowing refusal to take any action in response to such behavior would fly in the face of Title IX's core principles, and such deliberate indifference may appropriately be subject to claims for monetary damages.… [A] plaintiff must establish sexual harassment of students that is so severe, pervasive, and objectively offensive, and that so undermines and detracts from the victims' educational experience, that the victim-students are effectively denied equal access to an institution's resources and opportunities. [emphasis added] (p. 1675).

A few more among the many distinctive examples of language that carry specific meaning in the context of education law are "students or teachers [do not] shed their constitutional rights to freedom of speech or expression at the schoolhouse gate" (*Tinker v. Des Moines Independent School District*, 1969, p. 736), pall of orthodoxy (*Keyishian v. Board of Regents*, 1967, p. 683), marketplace of ideas (*Abrams v. United States*, as cited in *Pico v. Board of Education, Island Trees Union Free School Dist. No. 26*, 1980, p. 435), reasonable suspicion (*New Jersey v. T.L.O.,* 1985, p. 735) and separate but equal (*Plessy v. Ferguson*, 1896, p. 1144). Good legal writing will reflect judicious use of these phrases and will demonstrate a clear understanding of their intent.

Well-argued law papers also depend upon the proper sequencing of the points of law under scrutiny by the courts. The following section speaks to the importance of presenting points of law and the legal tests applied to them in the sequence that is essential to the courts' conclusions or to the writer's thesis.

Sequencing and Analyzing Points of Law

Practiced readers of case law know that a court systematically reviews the legal issues before it. The sequence in which each question of law is addressed, if there is more than one, may be dictated by issues such as procedural rules or the hierarchy of the statutes under review. Otherwise, the analysis for each question is determined by applying the appropriate legal standard or test. Each standard or test may comprise several prongs that, depending on the response to each prong, may bring to an end the analysis at a given point. This sequencing guides the reasoning of the court and leads to the court's conclusion for each legal question. It is imperative that students follow this progression and understand its implications at arriving at the court's decision and at their own attempts in comparing and contrasting case law they have selected for a particular educational issue.

There is one particularly good example for students who are learning how to read case law and how to apply judicial tests to a legal question a point of law paper. The Ninth Circuit Court of Appeals adjudicated an appeal of a First Amendment case in which two students alleged that school administrators unlawfully suppressed their right to speak out on a matter of public concern. In this instance, the plaintiffs had protested the hiring of replacement teachers for those on strike by wearing buttons with slogans referring to replacement teachers as scabs (*Chandler v. McMinnville School District*, 1992).

In arriving at their decision, the justices evaluated the facts of the case against the three existing legal tests that govern student speech in schools—the *Tinker* standard (Tinker, 1969), the *Fraser* (*Bethel*) standard (*Bethel School District No. 403 v. Fraser*, 1986), and the *Hazelwood* standard (*Hazelwood School District v. Kuhlmeier*, 1988).

The plaintiffs in *Chandler* argued that the federal district court had incorrectly applied the *Fraser* standard, which affords school officials the latitude to control student speech if it is lewd or offensive in nature. The lower court concluded that the slogans on the protest buttons the students wore were "offensive" and "inherently disruptive" (*Chandler*, 1992, p. 526).

The plaintiffs asserted that *Tinker* was the appropriate standard and, for that reason, appealed the lower court's dismissal of their case. The *Tinker* standard issued from a case in which students were disciplined for wearing anti-war paraphernalia to protest against the Vietnam War. The Court noted that wearing the armbands was a form of pure speech, a "silent, passive expression of opinion" that was "unaccompanied by any disorder or disturbance" (p. 737).

The third test, the *Hazelwood* standard, governs school-sponsored speech. This arose from a case in which students believed their First Amendment rights were infringed when the school principal censored two pages of student-authored articles in the school newspaper. The Supreme Court opined that school officials had "authority over school-sponsored publications, theatrical productions, and other expressive activities that students, parents, and members of the public might reasonably perceive to bear the imprimatur of the school" (*Hazelwood*, 1988, p. 570).

The Ninth Circuit first articulated what U.S. Supreme Court law had established as the constitutional basis for reviewing student First Amendment claims and for a school district's right to discipline students whose actions interfere with the proper functioning of the school. This provides an excellent example to students on how think about and introduce the foundation for discussing a legal question.

> Students in public schools do not "shed their constitutional rights to freedom of speech or expression at the schoolhouse gate." *Tinker v. Des Moines Indep. Community School Dist.* 393 U.S. 503, 506, 89 S.Ct. 733, 736.... "They cannot be punished merely for expressing their personal views on the school premises ... unless school authorities have reason to believe that such expression will 'substantially interfere with the work of the school or impinge upon the rights of other students.'" *Hazelwood School Dist. v. Kuhlmeier*, 484 U.S. 260, 266, 108 S.Ct. 562, 567.... The schoolroom prepares children for citizenship, and the proper exercise of the First Amendment is a hallmark of citizenship in our country. Nevertheless, this educational

> experience has its limitations. The First Amendment rights of public school students "are not automatically coextensive with the rights of adults in other settings." *Bethel School Dist. No. 403 v. Fraser*, 478 U.S. 674, 682, 106 S.Ct. 3159, 3163-64.... Student preparation for adult experiences does not necessarily ensure adult experiences on the school campus. For example, schools need not tolerate student speech that is inconsistent with the school's "basic educational mission." *Id.* at 685, 106 S.Ct. at 3165; Hazelwood, 484 U.S. at 266, 108 S.Ct. at 567. Despite the fact that the suppression of speech has obvious First Amendment implications, courts are not necessarily in the best position to decide whether speech restrictions are appropriate. "The determination of what manner of speech in the classroom or in school assembly is inappropriate properly rests with the school board," and not with the federal courts. *See Fraser*, 478 U.S. at 683, 685, 106 S.Ct. at 3164, 3165; *Hazelwood*, 484 U.S. at 267, 108 S.Ct. at 567 (p. 527).

The Ninth Circuit then identified the three standards that governed student speech and summarized their essential components.

> We have discerned three distinct areas of student speech from the Supreme Court's school precedents: (1) vulgar, lewd, obscene, and plainly offensive speech, (2) school-sponsored speech, and (3) speech that falls into neither of these categories. We conclude, as discussed below, that the standard for reviewing the suppression of vulgar, lewd, obscene, and plainly offensive speech is governed by *Fraser,* ... school-sponsored speech by *Hazelwood*, ... and all other speech by *Tinker.*...
>
> We first address the question of whether school officials may suppress vulgar, lewd, obscene, and plainly offensive speech, even when it is expressed outside the context of an official school program or event. *Hazelwood* focused on two factors that distinguish *Fraser* from *Tinker:* (1) the speech was " 'vulgar,' 'lewd,' and 'plainly offensive,' " and (2) it was given at an

> official school assembly.... Whereas both of these factors were present in *Fraser,* we believe the deferential *Fraser* standard applies when the first factor alone is present. "Surely it is a highly appropriate function of a public school education to prohibit the use of vulgar and offensive terms in public discourse....
>
> We turn next to the second category involving speech or speech-related activities that "students, parents, and members of the public might reasonably perceive to bear the imprimatur of the school." In such cases, school officials are entitled to "greater control" over student expression.... According to *Hazelwood,* federal courts are to defer to a school's decision to suppress or punish vulgar, lewd, or plainly offensive speech, and to "disassociate itself" from speech that a reasonable person would view as bearing the imprimatur of the school, when the decision is "reasonably related to legitimate pedagogical concerns." ...
>
> The third category involves speech that is neither vulgar, lewd, obscene, or plainly offensive, nor bears the imprimatur of the school. To suppress speech in this category, school officials must justify their decision by showing "facts which might reasonably have led school authorities to forecast substantial disruption of or material interference with school activities." ... However, the "First Amendment does not require school officials to wait until disruption actually occurs.... In fact, they have a duty to prevent the occurrence of disturbances" (p. 529).

The justices followed with a methodical analysis of the facts in *Chandler*, distinguishing the events from those in the Supreme Court cases. First, they concluded that the word scab could not be characterized as patently offensive.

> No effort was made by the school officials to suppress the buttons containing the statements "Students united for fair settlement" or "We want our real teachers back." Rather, the suppression only involved statements containing the word "scab." The word "scab," in the context most applicable to this case, is defined as "a worker who accepts employment or replaces

> a union worker during a strike." Webster's Third New Int'l Dictionary 2022 (unabridged ed.) (1986). Although a dictionary definition may not be determinative in all cases, it is helpful here. "To be sure, the word is most often used as an insult or epithet." ... However, the word is also "common parlance in labor disputes and has specifically been held to be entitled to the protection of § 7 of the NLRA." Given the requirement to construe the complaint in a light most favorable to Chandler and Depweg, we are satisfied that these buttons cannot be considered per se vulgar, lewd, obscene, or plainly offensive within the meaning of *Fraser* (p. 530).

The court then moved to the second part of their analysis, once again evaluating the facts in *Chandler* to the issue of school-sponsored speech in *Hazelwood*.

> There is nothing in the complaint alleging that Chandler and Depweg's buttons reasonably could have been viewed as bearing the imprimatur of the school. The buttons expressed the personal opinion of the students wearing them, and they were displayed in a manner commonly used to convey silently an idea, message, or political opinion to the community.... In addition, they expressed a position on a local political issue that was diametrically opposed to the school district's decision to hire replacement teachers. Therefore, the complaint does not show that a reasonable person could have viewed the buttons as bearing the imprimatur of the school (p. 530).

Ultimately, the court agreed with the students that *Tinker* did govern their complaint, noting that the buttons were protected speech and that no substantial or material disruption had occurred. For these reasons, the Ninth Circuit reversed and remanded the lower court's decision for further proceedings.

> We turn, therefore, to the third category of school speech and its standard: whether the "scab" buttons were properly suppressed because the school officials reasonably forecasted that they would substantially disrupt, or materially interfere with, school activities.... The district court held that the "scab" buttons

> were inherently disruptive, but nothing in the complaint or the analysis of the district court substantiates this conclusion. We conclude that the district court erred in holding, without more, that the "scab" buttons were inherently disruptive (p. 530).

This decision provides students with a model by which to construct their arguments when analyzing a legal question. It illustrates how to present the issue, what is known based on established precedent, and what judicial standard or test is required for a proper analysis. It demonstrates how to compare and contrast systematically the facts of a particular controversy with those that gave precedent to the existing test. This procedure ultimately aids students in arriving at a logical conclusion based on the evolution of their arguments and judicial evidence.

As substantiated in this section, there are a plethora of sources and examples from which students can learn how to understand and write about law, particularly case law. There are yet other strategies that students can employ in order to improve their understanding of and writing about the law. The next section offers some suggestions that students may find useful.

Strategies for Good Legal Writing

Of course, knowing the basics of good grammar, sentence and paragraph structure, and punctuation are essential elements, but there are additional means by which students can develop stronger writing skills.

Students of all ages are often advised they can improve their writing by reading good writing. The same holds true for students studying law. Understanding the language of law and how to use it can be greatly enhanced by reading court decisions, especially those authored by justices in the state and federal courts of last resort, law reviews by preeminent legal scholars, and law books by both. This will aid students in interpreting the precise meaning of law and legal reasoning and in developing well-conceived arguments in their own papers. It also will aid them in comprehending how the state and federal courts develop legal principles and how they order and cite these principles in underpinning their decisions.

Students are sometimes confused by the dual court system and, as a result, try to generalize court decisions to regions outside their jurisdiction. In the state court system, the supreme or superior court in one state has no bearing on the decisions taken in another state or region. Likewise, in the federal court system, district and appellate court decisions in one circuit court of appeal do not bind federal courts in other circuits, although other circuits are free to consider its reasoning. It is vital that care is taken when comparing and contrasting decisions across courts. Note which court has issued the decision and over what jurisdiction it is binding.

Students should provide the reader with a succinct overview of the paper in the introduction that includes the thesis of the paper and how the paper is organized. Features such as headings, citations, and footnotes that adhere to an established academic format will aid the reader in following the organization of the paper and in understanding the arguments presented.

There is no avoiding *Black's Law Dictionary* or other similar legal sources when construing the meaning of legal terminology. It is better to confirm the definition or the proper application of a legal term than to presume to know what it means and misuse it.

In a similar vein, it is important to have the most current edition of *Chicago Manual of Style* (2003) or the *Publication Manual of the American Psychological Association* (2001). Academic or publication formats serve important functions. They assist the author in organizing the material to be written, they alert the reader to how the document is organized, and they provide standardized configurations for in text citations and reference lists. These publication formats exponentially increase the readability of a document.

Perhaps one of the most under-used devises in any scholarly writing is proper citation of facts and sources of direct quotes. All statements of fact must be supported by reliable sources, preferably scholarly sources. As amply illustrated in the previous section, judicial tests, common legal principles, and other related concepts have origins, and these origins must be documented. Proper citations and references provide the reader with the necessary information to find primary sources and to read the material firsthand.

Lastly, it is often helpful to have a colleague or other qualified individual read and provide feedback on what one has written prior to submitting the paper for review by an instructor or a journal editor. Ask the reader to answer the following questions. Is the thesis clear in the introduction? Are the supporting arguments well documented and presented in a logic sequence? Are terms and concepts adequately explained or illustrated? Is there sufficient and accurate documentation of facts and quotes? Does the evidence lead to the conclusion reached? Garnering feedback and making the necessary changes prior to submission of a paper frees the instructor or publisher to concentrate on the important issues of content and relevance.

Conclusion

This chapter attempted to accomplish four important goals in instructing students in how to read and write about the law. First, it familiarized readers with key words, phrases, and abbreviations that mark what some people like to call "legalese." This also includes taking students along paths of understanding the rich history of the legal language in the United States and using language to convey ideas or legal principles. Next, explained why it is important to attend to the sequencing of points of law or legal principles, as exemplified in case law and, then, how to build arguments to support one's thesis. Lastly, it offered suggestions about improving one's writing.

According to Carp and Stidham, by 1750 "there was a competent, professional bar, dominated by brilliant and successful lawyers … in all major communities" (1998, p. 105). The College of William and Mary was the first to have an established chair in law, but that was not until the end of the eighteenth century. To learn the law, colonists sent their sons to England to study at the Inns of Court in London. This culture of law at the Inns of Court has preserved a tradition that reaches beyond Great Britain to ancient Greece and Rome.

Today, law is taught in a variety of venues from undergraduate business law, to education law, to philosophy of law and jurisprudence. The study of law has found its way into general education curriculum of America's colleges and universities. It insures that the next generation will carry understandings of concepts that begin with the intended meanings of words. Certainly, being educated about the law, even if that education is limited by rudimentary preparation and practice, advances the Founding Fathers' notion that an educated citizenry protects against a corrupt or tyrannical government…it really does help explain "who's on first"!

References

Abbott and Costello. Who's on first? *Baseball almanac*. Retrieved May 5, 2005, from http://www.baseball-almanac.com

Alexander, K., & Alexander, M. D. (2005). *American public school law* (6th ed.). Belmont, CA: West/Thomson Learning.

American Psychological Association (Ed.) (2001). *Publication manual of the American Psychological Association* (5th ed.). Washington, DC: Author.

Bethel School District No. 403 v. Fraser, 478 U.S. 675, 106 S.Ct. 3159 (1986).

Black, H. C. et al. (1991). *Black's law dictionary* (Abridged 6th ed.). St. Paul, MN: Thomson West Publishing Co.

Board of Education of Hendrick Hudson Central School District v. Rowley, 458 U.S. 176, 102 S. Ct. 3034 (1982).

Carp, R. A., & Stidham, R. (1998). *Judicial process in America*. Washington, DC: CQ Press.

Chandler v. McMinnville School District, 978 F.2d 524 (9th Cir. 1992).

University of Chicago (Ed.) (2003). *Chicago manual of style: The essential guide for writers, editors, and publishers* (15th ed.). Chicago: The University of Chicago Press.

Cicero, M. T. (2004). De Legibus, Book I (C. W. Keyes, Trans., 1928) In D. Kmiec, S. Presser, J. C. Eastman, & R. B. Marcin (Eds.) *The American constitutional order: History, cases and philosophy* (inclusive pp. of entire translation). Newark, NJ: Lexis/Nexis. (Original work published date)

Davis v. Monroe County Board of Education, 526 U.S. 629, 119 S.Ct. 1662 (1999).

Hazelwood School District v. Kuhlmeier, 484 U.S. 260, 108 S.Ct. 562 (1988).

Hudgins, H. C., & Vacca, R. S. (1999). *Law and education: Contemporary issues and court decisions*. New York: Lexis/Nexis.

Jarvis, R., Baker, T., & McClurg, A. (2003). *Amicus humoriae: An anthology of legal humor*. Durham, NC: Carolina Academic Press.

Keyishian v. Board of Regents, 385 U.S. 589, 87 S.Ct. 675 (1967).

New Jersey v. T.L.O., 469 U.S. 325, 105 S.Ct. 733 (1985).

Oran, D. (2004). *Law dictionary for nonlawyers* (4th ed.) , Albany, NY: West Legal Studies/Thomson.

Pico v. Board of Education, Island Trees Union Free School Dist. No. 26, 638 F.2d 404 (2nd Cir. 1980).

Plessy v. Ferguson, 163 U.S. 537, 16 S.Ct. 1138 (1896).

Plyler v. Doe, 457 U.S. 202, 102 S.Ct. 2382 (1982).

The Merriam-Webster collegiate dictionary. (2003). (11th ed.) Springfield, Mass: Merriam-Webster, Inc.

Redlich, N., Attanasio, J., & Goldstein, J. (2005). *Understanding constitutional law*. New York: Lexis/Nexis.

Reynolds v. United States, 98 U.S. (Otto) 145 (1879).

Stern, G. (June, 2003). Writing in plain language. *From Officialese to plain English*. City: Center for Continuing Education, The Australian National University

The Five Knights' Case. (2004). 3 How. S.T. 1 (K. B. 1627). The Stuart Constitution 106-109; In D. Kmiec, S. Presser, J. C. Eastman, & R. B. Marcin (Eds.) *The American constitutional order: History, cases and philosophy* (p. 34). Newark, NJ: Lexis/Nexis, Matthew Bender & Company. (Original work published 1627).

Tinker v. Des Moines Independent School District, 393 U.S. 503, 89 S. Ct. 733 (1969).

EDUCATION LAW ASSOCIATION

DAYTON, OHIO